ONTOLOGY OF PRODUCTION

ASIA-PACIFIC
CULTURE, POLITICS, AND SOCIETY

Editors
Rey Chow, Michael Dutton,
H. D. Harootunian, and Rosalind C. Morris

ONTOLOGY OF PRODUCTION

3 ESSAYS

Nishida Kitarō

Translated and with
an Introduction by
William Haver

DUKE UNIVERSITY PRESS
DURHAM AND LONDON
2012

© 2012 Duke University Press
All rights reserved
Printed in the United States of America
on acid-free paper ∞
Designed by Nicole Hayward
Typeset in Adobe Garamond Pro by
Tseng Information Systems, Inc.
Library of Congress Cataloging-in-
Publication Data appear on the
last printed page of this book.

CONTENTS

INTRODUCTION

This volume offers translations of three essays by Nishida Kitarō: "Expressive Activity" ("Hyōgen sayō," 1925), "The Standpoint of Active Intuition" ("Kōiteki chokkan no tachiba," 1935), and "Human Being" ("Ningenteki sonzai," 1938).[1] Nishida Kitarō was born in 1870 and died, of natural causes, in 1945. His first major work, *Zen no kenkyū* (An inquiry into the good), appeared in 1911 and was enthusiastically received by a large reading public.[2] It remains Nishida's most widely known work, although Nishida himself was to reject the "psychologism" of its focus on William James's concept of "pure experience." The work was not well received, however, by the Japanese academic philosophical establishment, dominated as it was in the late nineteenth century and early twentieth by philosophers working in the German idealist tradition. It is with that tradition, most particularly its neo-Kantian strains, that Nishida critically engaged for the next two decades; in that engagement, of which "Expressive Activity" is exemplary, Nishida's own thinking became increasingly rigorous and forceful. Between 1935 and 1945 he published some twenty-five major essays (known collectively as the *Tetsugaku ronbunshū* [Philosophical essays]), which were intended to be in the first instance a systematic exposition of the principal concepts of what had come to be called "Nishida-philosophy" (a group of essays to which "The Standpoint of Active Intuition" and "Human Being" belong), and then to take up discrete questions—the philosophical bases of physics, mathematics, or biology, for example, or the question of *Staatsräson*, or questions of the philosophy of religion, and similar topics.[3] These essays are thematically heterogeneous and certainly do not constitute a philosophical system, the closure that would be a "theory of everything," which could only be the object of a reflection after the end of the world. Yet neither do these essays collectively constitute a mere chrestomathy of philosophical curiosities. Rather, the essays form a coherent body of work insofar as, in spite of their thematic heterogeneity, they engage their disparate objects at that limit—which is also the possibility—of their respective concepts. What is it that makes it possible for us to think the *concept* of the logical (or the mathematical, the biological, the social, etc.) *as such*? For Nishida we can only take up such questions from that place, that contradiction, which is at once the possibility and limit of thinking itself. Here, there is a sustained practice of philosophy as a radically anarchic force. Whatever the statements or assertions Nishida makes about the world, statements and assertions many readers find problematic, the experience of reading these essays invariably brings that reading to the experience of philosophy as anarchic force. Conversely, reading cannot bring us to that experience of philosophy without making statements and assertions about the world. In this respect I think it absolutely necessary to keep in mind that one of the contexts of this work—Japan between 1935 and 1945—made serious intellectual work and discourse exceedingly difficult but never more necessary.[4] I will return to these questions.

I first translated these essays to be used in graduate seminars where the purpose, of course, was not to come to the certitude of a conclusion but to pursue what we thought might be productive lines of questioning. We were, and are, not looking for answers but for ways to formulate problems and questions. It is in that spirit that the essays are offered here. None of the participants in the seminars (myself excepted, of course) had any prior interest in or knowledge of someone named Nishida Kitarō or of twentieth-century Japanese intellectual history. It was never the purpose of the seminar, nor is it the purpose of this volume, to provide either an adequate introduction to or a synoptic view of Nishida's work; therefore, neither is it in the interest of the seminars or of this volume to achieve any kind of hermeneutic hegemony among students of Nishida's work. Nor were the seminars much interested in that work as symptoms of the intellectual and cultural histories within which, indisputably, they were produced. Certainly, these essays are necessarily susceptible of contextualized readings, readings from which we must learn a great deal if we are really to come to grips with the essays themselves.

We can learn much from contextualized readings on condition that we understand that "Japan" is not the context. This is not to deny that this work was produced within the geopolitical entity called Japan (which Nishida, in fact, never left), nor, of course, is it to deny that Nishida wrote in Japanese. It is, however, to say that there is no consequential question regarding Nishida's work to which "Japan" is the answer. Neither Nishida nor any other Japanese philosopher of the twentieth century would restrict the intellectual ambition of his or her work to "Japan," construed as the ultimate horizon of the context. The context of this work is nothing less than the most expansive conception of global modernity. It is not merely that Nishida implicates himself in the concepts, problematics, and themes of what counts as modern Western philosophy in his critical engagements with, for example, Descartes, Kant, and others on subjectivity; with Hegel on dialectics; with Leibniz and Herder on singularity; with Dilthey and Rickert on the "historical world"; with Marx on poiesis and production; with Kant, Schelling, James, and Whitehead on intuition; or with Bergson on temporality. It is furthermore the case that for Nishida, in these various engagements, the essential philosophical and political question of modernity, the question that defines modernity as such, is constituted in the problematics of the making and unmaking of sense.

What conditions and determinations constitute the possibility of making sense? Conversely, how can we conceive the limit at which sense is unmade, the limit at which what had been conceived to be a universal possibility disintegrates in the emergence of a hitherto incomprehensible, unimaginable sense? These and related questions proliferate beyond the compass of any synthetic treatment, because in that virtually infinite proliferation the questions of sense exceed any possible concept of sense. We can only ever have a *sense* of sense in its possibility and at its limit. But this does not mean that the problematics of the making and unmaking of sense belong to the putatively "eternal problems of philosophy." This problematics, which is the context of the entirety of Nishida's work from *An Inquiry into the Good* of 1911 to the very last fragment, "On My Logic," of 1945, however extensive it may in fact be, is nevertheless historically and politically specific: the term *modernity* names that specificity. The problematics of sense, a problematics that defines philosophy at least since the seventeenth century in Europe, takes on a particularly political urgency in the twentieth century. It is central, for example, to all of Husserl's work, from the *Logical Investigations* (1900–1901) to the *Crisis of the European Sciences* (unfinished at his death in 1938). The *Crisis* is contemporaneous with Freud's *Moses and Monotheism* (1939), with Heidegger's lectures on Leibniz in *The Metaphysics of Logic* (1928) and *The Principle of Reason* (1955–56), with Carl Schmitt's *Nomos of the Earth* (1950), and, of course, with much else besides, ad virtually infinitum.

The anonymous author(s) of *Introduction to Civil War* are only the most recent to argue that the stakes of this problematics are nothing less than the possibility of any being-in-common.[5] The common neither precedes nor survives the radical contingency of the making-of-sense that, in fact, is immediately the constitution of the common altogether. After all, it is precisely as an articulation of the stakes of this problematics that Marx developed his concepts of a "mode of production," of real subsumption, and of class—indeed, of "economy" altogether. The same may be said of the quite different development of concepts of culture, ethnos, and nation in much eighteenth-century and nineteenth-century thought, from the anthropologies of Montesquieu, Kant, and Hegel, through Herder and the whole of nineteenth-century philology, to the common sense of much of the human and social sciences in the twentieth century. It is precisely the stakes of this problematics that become explicit, for example, in Lyotard on the *différend*, in Rancière on "disagreement," and in Stiegler on the technological determinations of the possibility of sense.

All of this (and much else, of course) would constitute the "context" of Nishida's work. This context—that is, this questioning, this problematics of the sense of sense—is necessarily prior to any question of cultural difference, because the concept of culture, any concept of culture, necessarily assumes that the concept of culture already (in fact, a priori) itself makes sense. The very concept of culture as such occludes the problematic of its own possibility and limit as concept. Conversely, this is also true of any presumption of the priority of any liberal ethical cosmopolitanism. It is therefore the case that the context that would help us make sense of Nishida's work is, strictly speaking, *philosophical* and thereby *immediately* political. Here, to "do" philosophy is to take up that place (neither no place nor every place but the determinate as such) where the very possibilities of thinking, language, our most fundamental existential comportments, and the very possibility of a "form-of-life" are most seriously in question; it is to occupy that place which Descartes abandoned in the formulation of the cogito.

So these essays have been selected and translated in the hope (which of course I was able to pose as a demand in the seminars) that they will receive a specifically philosophical reading. Such a philosophical reading is not to attempt a decontextualized, ahistorical, "immanent" reading. Rather, a philosophical reading is determined not by the context of what is called the past but by the exigent problematics of the present situation. A philosophical reading is a political presentist reading, experimental in the strong sense of the term, oriented toward a futurity conceived as essential difference from the present. These essays are offered neither as exhibits nor as symptoms but as experimental tools, even as weapons. The point is not to provide yet one more interpretation, however heterodox, of Nishida, Marx, or the world; the point of these readings is to put what counts for us as sense at risk, to break the essential complicity of academic philosophy with state and capital, to resist the concomitant militarization of the globe.[6] The heterodoxy of these readings is entirely and unapologetically partisan.

These translations are offered as contributions to discussions and debates concerning the vicissitudes, pertinence, and possibilities of Marx's concept of production, in an attempt to take up once again the *sense* of the concept; these essays are offered in an attempt to *make* sense of the concept, to participate in the making-of-sense that the concept, as such, *is*. Concepts, of course, if they are to be vital forces in our thinking, are necessarily imperfect, incomplete; a perfect concept would no longer be experimental, no longer philosophical, because it would no longer be oriented toward the emergence of a future sense that must be posited as, in principle, incomprehensible to the present. An adequate concept, perfectly consistent within itself and with the conceptual system of which it would be an essential part, could only ever be an object of a terminal contemplation, never a provocation of philosophy, a point of departure for thinking. A philosophically vital concept, then, is always a work-in-progress. Concepts do not explain the world but belong to that by means of which we attempt to make sense of and articulate the imperative questions posed to us by, and as, a current situation. It is therefore not a question of deciding which concept of production is a better explanation of what we would think about under the aegis of the concept, as if we were merely shopping for the most stylish, the coolest concept at some philosophical mall. Rather, ours is the work of complication, development, exploration, and experimentation, in the interest of bringing into being a sense other than that which sustains the present order of things.

If we turn to Marx and his concept of production, and to Nishida's reading of Marx's concept of production, it is neither as an act of fidelity to any Marxist orthodoxy nor as an act of hermeneutic piety. Rather, Marx's concept of production is the essential reference for us simply because it is ultimately a historical concept of the possibility of historical becoming, because Marx's concept of production is essentially a concept of the possibility of a praxis oriented toward whatever would be something other than an extension of the present. But clearly, there is widespread acknowledgment, sometimes explicit but always implicit, that the concept of production needs to be revisited; a large and growing body of work undertakes precisely such a reconsideration. In general (and to oversimplify, certainly), two congruent aspects of present-day global capital have provoked these reconsiderations and have lent such investigations a sense of urgency.

First, it has frequently been noted, most often with considerable apprehension, that the global economy is increasingly driven not by production but by the machinations of financial markets, in particular by credit-driven finance capital. Historically, this apparent rupture between speculative markets and "the real economy" of production has probably been true of every speculative bubble; what might differentiate the current state of affairs from previous speculative fiascos is that there is a sense that in certain national economies—the US economy, for example—there is no longer a "real economy" of industrial production that would be the basis for the recovery of "the" economy. Markets seem to be no longer reflections of real economies of industrial production but appear to be entirely autonomous. Christian Marazzi has gone so far as to argue that it no longer makes sense simply to oppose the "real" economy of industrial commodity production to the hocus-pocus of financial markets; the economy of global capital is now driven as much by finance capital as by commodity production. In a not entirely dissimilar vein, Bernard Stiegler has recently followed speculations of Jeremy Rifkin, Michel Rocard, and Dominique Méda on "the end of work," arguing that labor, in the Marxist sense, is disappearing and that the concept of production is therefore no longer central to economic thought.[7] Certainly, there is much in both Marazzi's and Stiegler's analyses that is more than merely pertinent to any consideration of the present situation, and it is no less certain that the phenomena to which they point cannot merely be recuperated for analysis under traditional Marxist categories. One cannot, for example, simply conceive all kinds of financial instruments to be commodities just because they look like "commodities" in the marketplace precisely because such instruments are all variations on the theme of money—which has itself not been what Marx called money (a commodity possessed of use-value as universal equivalent) for nearly forty years (i.e., money now only expresses price but can no longer express value). Nor can we ignore what Stiegler emphasizes as the proletarianization of immaterial labor and the consequences thereof. But Marazzi and Stiegler alike (as well as a number of others, of course) treat certain aspects of the economy, certain aspects of production, as the hegemonic or "leading" sectors of the economy, *as if* certain tendencies are therefore synecdoches of an emerging political economy in which the very concept of production will be all but entirely irrelevant. The problem here, however, is the implicit assumption that "the" economy is in fact a totality, that credit-driven financial markets or hypertechnological postlabor production express the essence of "the" economy qua (at least potentially) a coherent and integrated totality. But, in fact, we can no longer speak of "the economy" as an at least ideally integrated totality. Indeed, we are forced to acknowledge that there are only plural economies—the economy of the banksters, plural economies of production, service economies, and in principle innumerable informal economies, paraeconomies as it were, which are the only possibilities for survival of a growing number of people—not all of which are sustained by industrial production. This is not to say that capitalism does not enjoy global hegemony; but it is also to say that capitalism's paraeconomies collectively constitute a limit of capitalism. If the sense of production is reduced merely to that of industrial-commodity production (which, nevertheless, has certainly not simply disappeared), then the status of production would be no longer ontological, and it would be beside the point to conceive capitalism to be essentially a question of the expropriation of labor power; the wager of these translations is that production and its concept as ontology are nevertheless essential to any consideration of the heterogeneous multiplicity of contemporary economies: finance capital divorced from production has, unaccountably, not done away with the expropriation of labor power.

Second, and concomitantly, putatively clear-cut distinctions between manual and intellectual labor (or material and immaterial labor) are no longer persuasive, if ever they were. Marx himself seems to have been of two minds regarding this distinction. On the one hand, Marx seems to be in full accord with much subsequent Marxist thought in accepting this distinction between the manual and the intellectual, the material and the immaterial, and thus materiality and ideality in general as not only unproblematic but determinative. In the early pages of the *Grundrisse*, for example, Marx summarily dismisses all intellectual workers as "lackeys and lickspittles" — servants — of the bourgeoisie, and he does so because immaterial or intellectual work is construed to be unproductive, mere service.[8] Only manual and material labor is considered productive and, therefore, "labor." Yet in the fragments scattered throughout the remainder of the *Grundrisse*, and referred to collectively as the "fragment on machines," Marx develops the concept of the "general intellect" as that which is at once the condition and effect of communication among workers in the "automated system" of the machine that the modern industrial factory had become; as such, the general intellect is indispensible to all machinic production. It is as such, as Marx demonstrates in chapter 15 of volume 1 of *Capital*, "Machinery and Large Scale Industry," that the general intellect is both the possibility and effect of real subsumption, conceived as the global hegemony of the *logic* of capitalist production.[9] The machine, the automated system that is the industrial factory, is necessarily the transduction of manual and intellectual, material and immaterial labor, the transduction of materiality and ideality.

That is, material labor necessarily presupposes intellectual labor as its own a priori condition; intellectual labor in turn necessarily presupposes material labor as its own a priori condition: here there is the original co-implication (or "complication") of materiality and ideality, which would seem necessarily to imply that materiality and ideality do not constitute a mutually exclusive binary opposition. Ideality is no longer merely immaterial, still less merely a reflection of materiality; conversely, materiality is no longer merely insensate determination. Indeed, in Marx's account the worker becomes nothing more nor less than organic consciousness in the service of that "real abstraction" (or virtuality) that is the machine: this constitutes what Deleuze and Guattari called "machinic enslavement."

In chapter 15 Marx presents this machinic enslavement as the dialectical inversion of the Aristotelian poiesis that had grounded his discussion of the labor process in chapter 7: it is the machine rather than man that has become the master and subject of production; man is merely a tool (organic consciousness) of the machine. But it is important to note that Marx was never an entirely faithful Aristotelian. Certainly, in Aristotelian poiesis, man is master of production insofar as he is the embodiment of that ideality that will be actualized in poiesis: man is *homo faber* as *homo sapiens*, *homo sapiens* as *homo faber*, and it is thus that man becomes subject, everything else mere object. But for Marx, as perhaps for Hegel before him, the relation between subject and object is rather more complicated insofar as the relation between man and nature is one Marx nicknamed "metabolism," *Stoffwechsel*, a relation of transduction in which subject and object are originally codeterminative. The object—dead, objectified labor—determines the subject, and the subject, thus determined, determines the object: whatever else production produces, it produces subjects and objects; neither subject nor object exists as such before the metabolic process of production, nor, indeed, do they survive production. It is precisely this ontological possibility—that is, the coming-into-being of subjects in production—from which the worker is alienated in the machinic enslavement that articulates the capitalist expropriation of labor power, because the worker is alienated from the (transductive, metabolic, in fact "dialectical") appropriation that is the constitution of the human altogether.

There are always two senses of the concept of production in Marx's thought, because there are always two senses of appropriation, the constitutive metabolic relation between "man" and "nature." These two senses of appropriation and the correlative two senses of production are not necessarily mutually exclusive, in spite of—or perhaps because of—the fact that they are in many respects, respects that are perhaps essential, contradictory. There is the sense of appropriation as the "exchange of stuff"—*Stoffwechsel*, metabolism—between man and nature, which is a concept of production as the process that constitutes the worker's *Eigentum* as the power-to-be, his *potentia*; and there is a sense of appropriation as mere expropriation (the master's mere consumption, in Hegel's terms), which is, ontologically speaking, completely unproductive because it is an appropriation that results only in the philosophically absurd concept of "private property," itself a concept that reduces the common to being merely the object of division and distribution (I will return to these questions).

This double sense of appropriation and the correlative double sense of production, perhaps rather obviously, have immediate effects for Marx's anthropology. On the one hand, there is considerable explicit evidence throughout Marx's texts (and not merely in the "early Marx") to support the contention that Marx subscribed to the modern humanism of the European Enlightenment. Yet to locate the being of man in production, and the expropriation of human being in machinic enslavement (which is an index of the essential technicity of human being), is to complicate that anthropology in essential ways. If production is necessarily ontologically constitutive for man, if in fact we exist not merely *because* we make things but only *in* the making of things (poiesis), then what Marx called a "mode of production" is a materialist nickname for ontology. The concepts of production and of modes of production are therefore concepts of the radical historicity of human being, concepts of being as becoming, concepts of the human as an orientation in production toward a futurity radically other than the present: for Marx, the essence of man is to be without essence. It is thus that poiesis is the condition of political praxis, as some of Marx's most astute readers have noticed (I think here of Balibar and of Nishida, of course and for example).[10]

These few observations on some of the complexities and complications of Marx's concept of production in the current conjuncture are offered as indications that they belong to what is yet vital in Marx's thought, indications that in the very incompletion of the concept of production, there is something that has not been exhausted, something that remains indispensible. We are not done with Marx's concept of production (and related concepts); on the contrary, the concept in itself is a provocation; in itself it constitutes a demand for an other thinking, a thinking otherwise. These translations are offered in the hope that they might help us exploit the radicality of Marx's concept of production; the texts translated here take up the concept, develop it, transform it, and maintain the concept in a state far from equilibrium.

If it is, in fact, useful to consult certain of Nishida's late essays in order to pursue a renewed sense of Marx's concept of production, it is not because Nishida offers a concept of production that would somehow, miraculously, be adequate to the understanding and explanation of the vagaries and contradictions of the present conjuncture. Rather, it is because he rigorously and forcefully articulates what is conceptually at stake in Marx's concept of production, which is still conceptually and politically at stake for us in our present. Nishida's most explicit engagement with Marx's texts is found in "Human Being." Although he could not name Marx, it is quite clear from internal evidence that he was reading, at the very least, volume I of *Capital*, the "Economic and Philosophic Manuscripts" of 1844 (first published in 1932), and the "Theses on Feuerbach." The engagement with Marx is not limited to "Human Being," however, but extends throughout Nishida's work from the early 1930s until his death in 1945. This is not to argue that somehow, secretly, Nishida was a closet Marxist. It is, however, to argue that in Nishida's later work there is a sustained and rigorous engagement with Marx's problematic and that there are profound agreements with the Marx who never abandoned philosophy, least of all in *Capital*. Nishida's most profound agreement with Marx is the insight, as radical in our present as it was in 1938 or 1844, that ontology is production, and production is ontology. But if this insight is to be something more than a mere assertion, if it is to exert vital force in our thinking, if, in fact, the proposition is to make sense, it must be sustained by a patient and rigorous exposition of the concepts according to which it would make sense, as well as of its philosophical—political—effects.

Those who conceive Marx's intellectual trajectory as a movement from the essentially philosophical indiscretions of his Hegelian youth to the clear light of the science of economics (without even the inconvenience of a road trip to Damascus), those who would have the mature Marx be nothing but a social scientist, may well find Nishida's reading of Marx to be merely recidivist heresy. The accusation from these quarters is that Nishida fundamentally recuperates Marx for a (neo-)Hegelianism. I think this view is wrong for two reasons. First, it is not a question of whether either Marx or Nishida was an idealist or a materialist. Nishida's argument (quite explicit in note 1 to "Human Being," below) is that in the concept of production—including language and consciousness itself—ideality and materiality are not a mutually exclusive binary opposition. Rather, the relation is one of coimmanence in which each is the necessary presupposition of the other, and neither is the sublation of the other. It is never possible to escape philosophy.

Second, and of even greater importance in this context, there is in Marx and Nishida alike a concept of production as the radical historicity of autotelic becoming. For both philosophers production is the necessary simultaneity of negativity as remainderless destruction with a creativity in which the unforeseeable emerges: being is not the goal of becoming. In this sense, of course, ontology becomes becoming; production takes the place of ontology, and thus catachrestically becomes "ontological." Nishida reads in Marx's concept of production the concept of the radical historicity of becoming. After all, this is why Marx insists time and again that it is the proletariat rather than the bourgeoisie that is possessed of historical (and therefore potentially revolutionary) consciousness; this is why Marx can say that capitalism is merely one historical "mode of production," *merely* hegemonic, *merely* dominant. What Nishida, in fact, does in these texts is read Marx beyond those forms of Marxism that would domesticate the most radical possibilities in Marx.

Nishida's engagement with Marx's concept of production can be conceived under three extraordinarily expansive rubrics: the transcendental, the appropriative, and the anthropological. "The transcendental" here, as in the Kantian formulation, indicates that sense which is the a priori possibility of making sense; it is that according to which sense is possible, but that itself is the object of immediate intuition, a kind of "knowing" that precedes all knowledge. There have been all kinds of nicknames for what is at stake in the concept of the transcendental: Marx's "real subsumption" and the real abstraction of the "machine"; Althusser's "problématique"; Foucault's "historical a priori," just for example. Of course, there are major differences among these and other thinkers with respect to what is at stake in the transcendental. For Kant "the transcendental" is abstract and ideal—indeed, it is the very possibility of abstraction and ideality, a possibility that is necessarily universal and ahistorical, without empirical determination. Although Nishida rejected the presuppositions and consequences of the idealist formulation, he would remain concerned throughout his life with what was at stake in the Kantian transcendental. Critical he most certainly was of Kant's idealist humanism, but he was not so philosophically (or politically) naïve as to give up on the universal altogether; concomitantly, he refused to situate the possibility of sense (or reason) in a necessarily ideal essence of the human but sought it in the *logos*, conceived as the original immanent transduction of ideality and materiality.

Nishida's considerations of the universal almost invariably took the form of a meditation on the relation between the unity of the One and the innumerable differentiated Many. Attentive though he was to Platonic, Neoplatonic, and Hegelian formulations of the relation, his own thinking was clearly closer to Spinoza and, most particularly, Leibniz; but his conception is undoubtedly most indebted to Buddhist thought. In any case, the formal assertoric exposition is relatively straightforward. The One, in and *as* its unity, is neither prior to nor does it survive its differential articulation in and as the innumerable Many; conversely, the Many in and *as* the infinite proliferation of the constitutive differences of multiplicity, is only ever the Many *of* the One. The One is nothing apart from its immanence *in* the Many; conversely, the Many is nothing apart from its immanence *as* the One. Multiplicity and difference are therefore not the dispersion of a prior unity, nor are they destined to be overcome in any eschatological redemption as the reunion of the One with itself. Nishida specifies the relation as the "absolute contradictory self-identity" (*zettai mujunteki jiko dōitsu*) of the One and the Many.[11] Or, in a terse formulation inherited from Buddhist philosophy, he will refer to "One *soku* Many, Many *soku* One" (*ichi soku ta, ta soku ichi*). Here, *soku* could be read as "qua" (which is the term for which I have opted throughout these translations), as "or" or "as," or even as "is." In fact, Nishida's reader is presented with exactly the same difficulty as confronts the reader of Spinoza's use of *sive* in the formulation "*Deus sive Natura.*" What is at stake in both Nishida and Spinoza is the contradictory coimmanence of the One and the Many, identity and difference, ideality and materiality. But the coimmanence of the One and the Many, which implies that totality is present in all singularity precisely as exception to totality, is not merely an assertion in Nishida but an argument.

It is an argument to which Nishida returned almost obsessively (as he himself acknowledged in a 1939 preface to the third volume of his *Philosophical Essays*), and is constituted in a consideration of singularity (*kobutsu*).[12] Nishida's concept of singularity is necessarily constructed as a contradiction. On the one hand, singularity is a concept of a radical empiricism for which all that is are singularities. A singularity is first of all that which resists predication absolutely (singularity is neither a predicate, quality, or characteristic of anything else, nor is it possible to predicate anything of a singularity save its singularity); a singularity is never a symptom or example of a universal; singularities are not divisions of the universal; singularities are not particulars subject to subsumption within the universal. Neither can singularities be deduced from universals, nor can universals be inferred from singularities. It makes no more sense to ask what causes singularities than to ask what came before the big bang or what is inside a black hole; like Spinoza's God, singularities are *causa sui*, causes or determinations of themselves, autonomous in the strongest sense of the term. Singularities are not *what* they are; they are *that* they are. On the other hand—and this is what constitutes the contradiction, of course—singularities can only be conceived in terms of what they are *not*; they can only be conceived in the crossing out of predicates, in negating their determination by universals. Singularities can only be conceived as nothing but exceptions, as the very movement of separation. So singularities are that they are, and cannot be conceived in terms of what they are not, but they can only be conceived in terms of not being what they are not. It is as exception or separation that singularities are the differential articulation of the universal; the universal is nothing but its presence in and as singular exception to universality. (In this sense, of course, the universal is nothing but exception to itself or separation from itself.) This means, to cut a very long story very short, that the transcendental universal is only ever immanent in what is. That is, Nishida does not seek the possibility of sense anywhere other than in what he called the "historical world."[13]

To situate sense and its possibility in the historical world *and nowhere else*—Nishida's historical world is not the narrative of Reason alienated from itself in Nature and destined to a reunion with itself at the end of History—means both that what makes sense for us is merely relative and that the sense that we make and its possibility are necessary and absolute. Aristotle did not merely believe the earth is two hundred miles from the sun; he knew it as fact. Descartes did not merely believe the earth to be at least thirty earth diameters from the sun; he knew it as irrefutable fact. And for us it is not a matter of faith or superstition that the earth is ninety-three million miles (more or less) from the sun; we know it. And this is because it is not by mere fiat (divine, mechanistic, whatever) that sense, knowing, and their possibility vary from epoch to epoch but because sense is *made*. The possibility of sense is "given," to be sure, but it is given as the *made*. This much currently counts as common sense for significant sectors of the social sciences and humanities. What we sometimes do not acknowledge, however, and was of correlative importance for Nishida when it was a question of the historical determinations of sense and its possibility, is that *for us* the sense that we make and its possibility are also both necessary and absolute. We make our own sense, but we do not make it just as we please. We can recognize that for Aristotle the fact that the earth is two hundred miles from the sun made sense, and we can even to a certain extent grasp the (historical) transcendental universal possibility of sense according to which the statement made sense for Aristotle. But it does not thereby make sense for us that the sun is two hundred miles from the earth. For us, the fact that the earth is ninety-three million miles, more or less, from the sun, and everything that sustains the truth of that fact, is *absolute* and *necessary*. Ultimately, nothing, absolutely nothing, can bridge the historical distance between Aristotle and ourselves; there are no round trips, Nishida was wont to say, in history. We cannot imagine how far the earth will be from the sun a hundred or a thousand years from now.

Thus, the possibility of sense is not merely *logos*, the necessary conjunction of speech and reason, but *nomos*, the way (or "law") of the world, the way the world is taken *to be*. We cannot simply "choose" to think otherwise, which is to say that the *nomos* is determinative. This is not to assume, however, that that determination, which is economic (the *nomos* of the *oikos*) in the contemporaneity of the last instance, is mechanistic, impervious to human praxis. We make sense, and *in* the making of sense, we create the possibility itself of making sense. Possibility is situated nowhere above, behind, below, outside of, or prior to its actualization. Sense, in its essential possibility, is utterly anarchic; as Nishida repeatedly insisted, the ground of rationality is the irrational. The possibility of sense is in the historical world but only because that possibility itself is something made.

"Expressive Activity" I translated in the first instance because the concept of expressive activity is central to the arguments of the later essays, and I thought it best to provide access to Nishida's argument in extenso, rather than requiring readers to make do with any summary account I might offer. But it is also important in its own right because it is a relatively early attempt to think through a concept of the material historical determination of the possibility of sense, a concept of nontranscendent transcendentals. Nishida's nickname for the material historical conditions of sense was "logos" (*rogosu*). The question of the logos as possibility of sense, as that according to which we make sense, was to be one of Nishida's constant preoccupations in a number of major essays for the next twenty years; this essay is far from his last word. Let us, for present purposes—an investigation of the concept of production—limit our reading of Nishida on the logos to a few questions. What makes what Marx called the "general intellect" or the real abstraction of the "machine" possible? How is it that the general intellect or the machine is necessarily constituted as such *in and as* the circulation of sense? Furthermore, how is it that real subsumption—the hegemonic extension of the *logic* of capitalist production not only to all of production but to the social altogether—possible? In fact, these questions come from the empiricist's astonishment that sense is possible at all. This, again, is the question of the transcendental as such. But the problem has become: how can we conceive the logos, *as* the possibility of sense, in the specificity of its historicity? In "Expressive Activity" the answer is "language." Three aspects of Nishida's reflections on language bear emphasis.

First, language belongs to that without which our species could not be; it is "essential." In this sense language belongs to the technical prostheses — tools — that are indispensible to the survival of the species. For Nishida language can be said to be instrumental, on condition that instrumentality is irreducible to merely a means to an end; language is not merely the means, transparent or opaque as you will, for the communication of meaning: it is the material support of sense — but only on condition that sense can never be divorced from its support.

Second, then, "language" belongs to — *is* — the coimmanence of ideality and materiality. Ideality and materiality are mutually transductive in language. That is, there is no sense that does not presuppose material expressivity as its possibility, and there is no materiality innocent of sense. "Ideality" and "materiality" are inextricably bound each to the other; each is the determination or possibility of the other. Sense is, in fact, this coimmanence, this transductive relation of mutual determination. Materiality and ideality do not constitute a mutually exclusive opposition, such that materiality would be the mere actualization of ideality, or that ideality would be the mere reflection of materiality. It is on the basis of this argument that Nishida is able to argue in later essays that what has been made, *tsukurareta mono*, is of the logos.

Third, consequently, sense and the logos that is the possibility of sense are constituted in a radical exteriority; for Nishida there is no more private sense than there is private language. Sense is sense only by virtue of its exteriority. Indeed, Nishida holds to the radical position that consciousness itself is in no case a subjective phenomenon, because it has no existence apart from its material supports, its materiality. There can be, on Nishida's account, no phenomenology of language, sense, or consciousness. Nishida rejects phenomenology — with considerable impatience — ultimately because it does nothing to disturb the presuppositions of the Kantian transcendental. Language and sense circulate, and they are language and sense because they circulate; language is an inexhaustible resource that "belongs" to anyone because it belongs to no one, and in that sense is "something public" (*ōyake no mono*). "Expressive activity," then, is not something that we happen to do, either by inclination or necessity. It is that activity, that doing, *as* which what is exists. It is not that I engage in expressive activity but that expressive activity is the very power to be, that differential articulation that now and again produces effects that sometimes, according to various historical *logoi*, are nicknamed "I." Not all machines are capitalist.

Clearly, in all this Nishida took extraordinary pains to distance himself from Kant, Hegel, and their epigoni, and this with respect to four principal points. First, the complications of the relation of "the Many and the One," and which Nishida was at great pains to think, as I have just attempted to sketch, in terms of "absolute contradictory self-identity," is resolved in Kant and Hegel alike into the essential coherence of a unified, closed totality of universals and merely exemplary particulars; no longer is there cause for thought in the idealist formulation; it is the occlusion of all singularity, ultimately the foreclosure of any possibility of heterodox sense.

Second, for Nishida the possibility of sense is radically *para*subjective; possibility lies in that which lies outside and alongside the subject, in the technical instrumentality of tool and language. For Nishida consciousness itself is not a subjective phenomenon; subjectivity happens but only as an effect, never as cause. For Kant and Hegel, of course, reason (as the possibility of sense) is a faculty of the subject that, in fact, constitutes the subject as such.

Third, those particular versions of appropriation we call perception, apperception, and cognition are not for Nishida merely inscriptions on an essentially passive epistemological or phenomenological subject but modes of an active, aggressive, appropriation, driven by a daemonic *potentia*, the power to be. Here there is an implicit return to the early Greek sense of *aisthēsis* as *both* the sensuousness of the senses *and* the sense of sense. In *aisthēsis* both senses of sense bespeak the inescapable embodiment of sense. (This is the burden of "The Standpoint of Active Intuition," to which I will turn momentarily.)

Fourth, and consequently, there is here a rejection of idealist cosmopolitanism and of the pretension of global citizenship (which is also—and immediately—the "freedom" of the worker to contract to alienate his capacity for labor in the abstract universality of "labor power," you will recall). It is important in this regard to emphasize that Nishida insists that his dialectic is essentially Heraclitean rather than Hegelian; for Nishida there is no sublation that would subsume negation within the positivity of a teleology. Negation is absolute, not simply a ruse of Being. The past has passed, and there is nothing to be salvaged. Again, I will return to these points, but here let me emphasize that if Nishida is concerned to distance himself from the idealist traditions of Kant and Hegel, he also thereby distances himself from much of the common sense of global modernity (without thereby giving in to the dangerous comforts of nostalgia).

It will occasion small wonder, then, that Nishida increasingly found seventeenth-century European thought to be a relevant reference for the articulation of his own thinking. Questions that were presumptively resolved in Kant and Hegel—questions of universal and particular, of the possibility of sense, of *aisthēsis*, and of cosmopolitanism and political agency—were entirely problematic sites of questioning and contestation for seventeenth-century philosophy. It is not that Nishida simply "agreed" (whatever that might mean) with Descartes, Spinoza, or Leibniz, for example, but that he found their questioning provocative in articulating his own formulations. If, for example, in 1938 Nishida opens an essay on "singularity in the historical world" with a reading of Leibniz's *Monadology*, it is not because singularities in Nishida's thought *are* monads, because they are not (for one thing, as substance, monads are metaphysical singularities without beginning or end, and are therefore not "historical" at all), but because a concept of singularity irreducible to that of particularity is at stake in both the monad and the *kobutsu*.[14] It is at the level of the problem—always a question of the possibility of making sense in its formulation—that certain of Nishida's most important formulations rhyme with the "seventeenth century." I will simply mention four of these rhymes. The first is a thought of the coimmanence and coimplication of the many and the one in Nishida, Spinoza, and Leibniz, with the consequence that difference is never overcome in the one and that the one is never anything other than its articulation in difference from itself. The second concerns the doubt that precedes the formulation of the Cartesian cogito, which, Nishida frequently argued, did not take reflection far enough. Pursue that reflection to its limit and one is faced with the radical impossibility of proving the existence of the self (as Nishida argued in 1936).[15] The third is therefore a question of Spinozist *potentia* as the power to be, the anarchic force of being and the *conatus* (which in Nishida figures as the daemonic, or as desire) that drives all *aisthēsis* and knowing. Finally, there is a common questioning of the transcendental, the possibility of making sense, which for Nishida is situated otherwise than for Spinoza and Leibniz, and most clearly otherwise than for Descartes.

Turning to the problematic of the "seventeenth century" does not merely expose possibilities that what came to call itself "modern" European philosophy was concerned to foreclose; it is not merely a transition in the history of Western philosophy that is at stake but a transition in economic and political forms that was also under way; all that came to call itself "modern" foreclosed economic and political possibilities, as well as philosophical ones, and that in no uncertain terms. In this sense Nishida's attention to the seventeenth-century problematic anticipates more recent attention on the part of thinkers such as Deleuze, Balibar, Negri, and others.[16] And this is why the thinkers of seventeenth-century Europe, rationalists and empiricists alike, remain for us an essential reference.

The second of the rubrics under which we might consider Nishida's engagement with Marx's concept of production is that of "appropriation." This constitutes the core of Nishida's own conceptualization of production and, thereby, the argument that sustains the assertion of the identity of production and ontology. Indeed, what distinguishes Nishida's concept of active intuition is the fact that it is appropriation. Allow me to venture a preliminary, certainly inadequate, definition. Active intuition is a mutual appropriation between that which will have been said to be perceived and that which will have been said to be what perceives. It is *logically* prior to—without being merely a primitive developmental stage of—the constitution, in reflection, of the subject who perceives. Active intuition is a sensuous relationality (that relationality or metabolism, *Stoffwechsel*, that is sensuousness as such) that is prior to and constitutive of its relata (subjects and objects) and that does not thereby simply disappear into the relata. That is, concepts of subject and object are essentially inadequate accounts of what is at stake in active intuition. Active intuition is therefore irreducible to the mutually exclusive binary opposition of passive and active but is nevertheless the possibility for that opposition. Active intuition is appropriation as a relationality of forces, and it is as appropriation that it is the condition and possibility of production.

It is not merely that active intuition is "a kind of" appropriation but that active intuition is at work in all appropriation; active intuition is the condition and possibility of all appropriation and production. What is at once the effect and object of appropriation is called "property." Here it is necessary to recall that there are, very generally, (at least) two senses of the concept of "property" (*das Eigentum*) as the object of appropriation within production in Marx. The first, developed in philosophic terms in the "Economic and Philosophical Manuscripts" of 1844, and in historical terms in the long section on "precapitalist economic formations" in the *Grundrisse*, is essentially a concept of the inalienable (and therefore the indivisible) as such. Recall, if you will, Marx's famous discussion "Estranged Labour" in the 1844 manuscripts.[17] In the pages devoted to a consideration of man in his species being, his *Gattungswesen*, Marx gives a clear, albeit uncharacteristically succinct, exposition of the relation between man in his species being and nature, a relation that in *Capital* he would refer to simply as "metabolism":

> The universality of man manifests itself in practice in that universality which makes the whole of nature his *inorganic* body, (1) as a direct means of life and (2) as the matter, the object and the tool of his life activity. Nature is man's *inorganic body*, that is to say nature in so far as it is not the human body. Man *lives* from nature, i.e. nature is his *body*, and he must maintain a continuing dialogue with it if he is not to die. To say that man's physical and mental life is linked to nature simply means that nature is linked to itself, for man is a part of nature.[18]

And that metabolic relation is in the first instance essentially productive—ontological—outside of which, for man, there is nothing: "Productive life is species-life. It is life-producing life. The whole character of a species, its species-character, resides in the nature of its life activity, and free conscious activity constitutes the species-character of man. Life itself appears only as a *means of life*."[19]

Some thirteen years later, in the extended section of the *Grundrisse* devoted to "precapitalist economic formations," it is first of all a question of a relation to the land and of its uses and the ways in which it is appropriated by the community. For the nomad, according to Marx, the relation to the land is a relation to the land's "elemental limitlessness": "They relate to it as their property, although they never stabilize this property."[20] In the Asiatic mode of production, land becomes a stabilized territory—property—which is nevertheless the property of the entire community and only of the community in its *Gemeinschaftlichkeit*, the community as such. The relation of the individual to the community is the strongest form of "dependence": identity. The Asiatic peasant, as is also the case with the slave and the serf, belongs to the land; the land does not belong to peasant, serf, or slave. It is that relation of identity designated in the term *autochthony*; in the Asiatic mode of production it is the community itself that is autochthonous. In the ancient Roman and German feudal modes of production, property is a question of the division and distribution of the common. The Roman citizen is entitled to the appropriation and use of land only insofar as he is, in fact, a Roman citizen; it is his belonging to the community of citizens that entitles him to a share of the land. Furthermore, it is precisely because land is subject to distribution at all that the distinction between public and "private" land appears. Still, community is prior because the citizen is entitled to a share in the distribution of land only because he is *of* the community; the so-called private is thus only an articulation of the common. To that extent, even the richest of Roman citizens is absolutely dependent on the community. In Germanic feudalism, however, the priority is apparently reversed. It is the individual holding (consisting of extended family, retainers, and serfs) that is essential and the coming-together, the *Vereinigung* or *Zusammenkommen*, that constitutes the common. The relation to the land is double. On the one hand, land subject to agricultural appropriation is held individually; but land for hunting, grazing, and timber belongs to the populace and in large part constitutes the community as such. What bears emphasis is that in all precapitalist economic formations, land as such is, first, *inalienable*; and, second, it is precisely that inalienability that defines *property* as dependency. Thus, the precapitalist sense of "property," Marx claimed, is logically (and etymologically, for all that) original:

> *Property* thus originally means no more than a human being's relation to his natural conditions of production as belonging to him as his, as *presupposed* along with *his own being*; relations to them as *natural presuppositions* of his self, which only form, so to speak, his extended body. . . . *Property* therefore means *belonging to a clan* (community) (having subjective-objective existence in it); and, by means of the relation of this community to the land and soil, [relating] to the earth as the individual's inorganic body; his relation to land and soil, to the external primary condition of production—since the earth is raw material, instrument and fruit all in one—as to a presupposition belonging to his individuality, as modes of his presence.[21]

Production is that appropriation by which the worker comes to be who he is and to possess himself as such, inalienably. "Property" names this inalienability. It is precisely the expropriation of the worker's labor power, the power-to-be, and therefore the possession of his own being, that constitutes the alienation of the worker under capitalism. In the logic of capital there is nothing that is inalienable. What the liberal apologists of the bourgeoisie call "private property" is only the nickname for the essential alienability of everything as ontological principle. Sooner or later (and more often sooner rather than later), all private property is for sale. (It is also the case, of course, that liberal apologetics, including the law, depend on the conflation of these two senses of *property*.) Early and late, Marx insists on this distinction. The chapter in the first volume of *Capital* titled "The Historical Tendency of Capitalist Accumulation" opens, in fact, with a rehearsal of this distinction: "Private property which is personally earned, i.e. which is based, as it were, on the fusing together of the isolated, independent working individual with the conditions of his labour, is supplanted by capitalist private property, which rests on the exploitation of alien, but formally free labour."[22] Strictly speaking, capitalist production is never appropriation, merely expropriation—theft.

Nishida's engagement with questions of appropriation focuses exclusively on the first sense, particularly as articulated in the 1844 Manuscripts (which had been published in 1932), and in the first of the "Theses on Feuerbach." In "The Standpoint of Active Intuition" and "Human Being," Nishida reads the first of the "Theses on Feuerbach" ("The chief defect of all hitherto existing materialism [that of Feuerbach included] is that the thing, reality, sensuousness, is conceived only in the form of the *object or of contemplation*, but not as *sensuous human activity, practice*, not subjectively.") against both the Aristotelian figure of *homo faber* as man the rational subject who stands over and apart from the inert objects of passive nature in a masterful poiesis, and the Kantian figure of *homo sapiens* for whom all perception is reduced to contemplation in the passive intuition of the transcendental a priori of time and space. The Aristotelian subject of poiesis is never implicated in nor complicated with the nature of the object; the Kantian subject of reason is constituted in the distance from the object of perception and is never complicated with the empirical. For Nishida, Marx's subject of "sensuous human activity, practice" is essentially complicated with its objects in a constitutive original transduction, a mutual appropriation (or "metabolism"). The Marxist subject of praxis emerges from sensuous activity and practice as *shutai*; the Kantian subject of intuition is nothing but an abstraction from the empirical, caught in the disinterested observation of transcendental time and space, the *shukan*.

Active intuition is "intuition" insofar as it is an immediate apprehension logically prior to any distinction between apprehending subject and apprehended object; the apprehension of active intuition has a certain essential resemblance to Whitehead's "prehension" (hence Nishida's continued interest in Whitehead's work): there is a seeing, for example, that is neither the exercise of a subject's faculty nor, therefore, the perception of an object.[23] Active intuition is the transcendental condition of possibility for subjects and objects altogether, but it exceeds at all points that relation and therefore does not simply disappear into any subject-object relation. But active intuition, or prehension, does complicate the subject-object relation, which itself does not simply disappear in some supra-epistemological ecstasy. Active intuition necessarily implies the original transductivity from which what will be called subjects and objects emerge. This prehension or intuition is precisely the sensuousness of the dialectical metabolism of "man" and "nature." (Central to Nishida's conception of the dialectical world is precisely this priority of relation over relata.)

For Marx this sensuousness, this metabolism, is entirely bound up with material practices and praxis. For Nishida, as well, this intuition is always "active" (*kōiteki*). The acting that makes this intuition active is, as the Japanese word *kōi* suggests, intentional. Active intuition is always "interested," nonneutral, even partisan. Nishida referred to this intentionality of active intuition in "Expressive Activity" as "transcendental will"; ten years later, he rejected that formulation because the "will" is an abstraction. Increasingly, in later years, he would refer to "desire" and to the "daemonic." As such, transcendental will is a force of which I am neither the cause nor origin; what is at stake here is a physics rather than a psychology. Before there is that which moves, there is movement (what else could it mean to speak of singularities such as the big bang or black holes? What else could it mean to speak of creation ex nihilo?). More elemental than Bergsonian élan vital, it is perhaps closest to Spinoza's "affectivity," the capacity to affect and to be affected. Ultimately, the "transcendental will," or desire, or the daemonic in Nishida is nothing other than the *potentia*, the will-to-be of the nonneutrality and therefore the nontranscendence, of singularities. Whatever his terminology, it is of first importance to recognize that this intentionality, this passionate intuition, is not that of an already-existing subject: there can be no phenomenology of the intentionality of active intuition, for this is an intentionality unaccompanied by any reflection. A subject will emerge from active intuition to be sure, but it will bear no essential resemblance to the epistemological and phenomenological subjects of modernity; reflection there will be, but it will be reflection implicated in the affirmation of negation, the affirmation of nontranscendence, the affirmation of becoming (which we will see in his brief but important reflections on Nietzsche and Dostoevsky at the end of "Human Being"; he was to return to these themes in his reading of Kierkegaard's *The Sickness unto Death* in 1940 in "Prolegomenon to a Philosophy of Praxis").[24]

Clearly, time and space are not the transcendental objects of active intuition. But if they are not given a priori, then neither are their concepts apodictic. So, how do we know that there is time and space? How is it possible to have a *sense* of time? Logically, the concept of time can only be presented as a contradiction. On the one hand, there must be a pure duration of an array of singular instants; but if time were nothing but that pure duration, it would be impossible to think that there is "time." Time cannot be conceived as mere discontinuity. So time must be conceived as the continuity of discontinuities, and the array of singularities must be conceived as a succession. It is only on that basis, logically, that there can be a concept of time. But yet again, to conceive time simply as a succession of singularities, merely as the continuity of discontinuities, is not yet to have a sense of the radical rupture according to which the differentiation of past, present, and future is conceivable. The instant, as singularity—and if it is to be truly singular rather than merely particular, not merely a part *of* the universal called "time"—must not only be an extreme point of the determination of the universal, but it must also be that which *surpasses* the universal. The concept of the singular instant as the absolute rupture that gives a sense of the radical difference of past, present, and future is at once the possibility and limit of time. As limit, it is, in fact, spatial. The concept of time necessarily assumes this spatiality as possibility and limit; the concept of space necessarily assumes this temporality in turn as its possibility and limit.

As the singularity, as the absolute rupture that exceeds universal determination, as that which is both "of" time and exceeds the temporal, the instant is spatial, which is to say it is the simultaneity of the mutual affectivity of things, that is, of force. It is this force and movement that is the material determination of the temporal-spatial altogether. Movement and force do not happen within a priori temporal and spatial coordinates; rather, it is movement and force that in fact create material time and space (hence Nishida's interest in contemporary physics).[25] Furthermore, that a thing affects another thing, that force and movement happen, determines temporality-spatiality as an original orientation toward the radical discontinuity of futurity; it is this material, active anticipation, rather than passive recollection, that is the possibility of the concept of time. Active intuition is precisely the always original appropriation that constitutes actual time and space. In this respect, then, our concepts of time, space, and their necessarily transductive (or dialectical) opposition are in fact concepts of force, movement, and resistance. In short, our

concepts of time and space are the most rigorous conceptualizations of
what is called materiality.

It is on precisely this point that there is the most profound congruence
between Nishida and Marx, a congruence at the heart of their insistence
on the identity of production and ontology. One can, of course, insist on
a naïve concept of materiality in Marx, a concept of materiality as merely
self-evident, a concept that therefore does not really call for thought. Yet
many commentaries on Marx, and many works that take their inspiration
from Marx, have, often implicitly, given the lie to the assumption of such
naiveté in Marx. Indeed, the entire analysis of capital essentially depends
on this conception of materiality qua the transductive relation of time
and space. Not only is it that concepts such as exchange, money, and
credit are concepts of temporality; and not only is it that capital is what
it is only in the alienation of money in production; nor yet is it merely
that the concept of productivity articulates in the analyses of coopera-
tion and the machine the capitalist desire to overcome time and space—
materiality—in the impossible instantaneity of an absolute productivity
and valorization that would transcend all production; nor, finally, is it
merely that capital enforces the abstractions of clock time in the disci-
plines of the factory, in Fordism and Taylorism. It is also the case that it
is *in and as* the abstraction of the capacity for labor (*Arbeitsvermögen*) or
labor power (*Arbeitskraft*) from the empirical instances of labor that time
and space become merely ideal. From this perspective Nishida and Marx
would agree with Kant that time and space are the transcendental objects of a priori intuition, but they would diverge from Kant because for
Kant time and space are pure idealities. For Nishida and for Marx time-
and-space—materiality—is the transcendental object of a priori active
intuition or appropriation, irreducible to any phenomenology. The logic
of capitalism is, as it were, the reductio ad absurdum of all idealism.

The third rubric under which we might consider Nishida's engagement with Marx is that of production "proper." This is the explicit theme
of "Human Being," which opens with the assertion of the identity of
production and ontology. This is therefore, as the essay's title promises,
to take up the question that has animated every anthropology: What is
man in his essence? Nishida does not fail to respond to the question, but
his response is no less provocative and unsettling than was Marx's. For

all of its complexities and complications, Nishida's concept of production here is apparently one of a straightforward common sense; it is also very much Marx's concept of "living labor." Encapsulated in the phrase "from the made to the making" (*tsukurareta mono kara tsukuru mono e*), which recurs incessantly in the Nishida of this period, production is the movement from the already-worked-on (Marx's objectified or dead labor), which is the very materiality of the historical logos (as the possibility of sense), to the creation of something new, that is, the creation of something that is neither merely the reproduction of what has been made (as the "given") nor the realization of a plan, which would be merely the extension of the present into a determinable future, Aristotelian poiesis. This is a difference that will make all the difference.

What is first of all at stake in the movement from the made to the making is a process of the differential articulation of singularities as such; it is the process by which a singularity comes to possess itself in its identity to itself. It is that movement by which the singular would appropriate itself as such; it is always a movement of separation by which the singular would exceed all subsumption *within* the universal One but that, in fact, is the coimmanence of the One and the Many. This is a process Nishida called "idiosyncratic constitution" (*koseiteki kōsei*). Of course, if idiosyncratic constitution is truly idiosyncratic, truly original, truly singular, it must be radically anarchic. To the extent that production is creative, rather than merely reproductive, it is necessarily mediated by a radical transcendental negativity, by the "absolutely absolute" as futurity in its essential indetermination. All production, all creation, necessarily transpires in the transduction between the logos, what has been made as the material possibility of sense, and the radical singularity of the new. This process of idiosyncratic constitution or differential articulation is necessarily imperfect (in the scholastic sense, where "perfection" is the completion of production); production is, then, a vector, the nonaccomplishment of singularity; production is in this sense a tendency toward singularity, always a becoming (recall that for Marx, too, the "labor-process" is *Unruhe*).

In the becoming of production, in the transductive metabolism between worker, tool, and "nature," there is formed a subject (*shutai*) that is neither the Aristotelian master of time and nature nor the Kantian subject (*shukan*) of essentially passive perception, knowledge, and judgment. The *shutai*, subject of production in and as creativity, is constituted in the anticipation of the new; more, the *shutai*, in the material engendering of the new, affirms a futurity that is the negation of the present in its entirety. This affirmation is, in fact, the affirmation of the negation of an essential reflection that emerges in production. The *shutai*—"man"—is thus itself necessarily a vector, a tendency, as part of a radical historicity, a becoming. For Nishida, "man" in his species being is in fact man only insofar as he exceeds the possibility of essence. The essence of man is to be without essence. "Man," then, is nothing more and nothing less than an anticipation or orientation qua production toward the transcendental negativity of the "absolutely absolute," toward futurity. The subject that emerges in production is a subject that is defined as such not insofar as the subject *interprets* the world but because he *changes* it. Poiesis is the condition of possibility for all praxis. As Nishida was to argue at length in his essays of 1940, the relation between poiesis and praxis is transductive; that is, each is the necessary presupposition of the other. There is no praxis that is not also, and essentially, poiesis; there is no poiesis that is not also, and essentially, praxis. This, of course, sabotages a tradition of political philosophy, from Plato and Aristotle through the present, that has been concerned to present poiesis and praxis, labor and political agency, as mutually exclusive, and the further mutual exclusion of both praxis and poiesis from *thēoria*, construed as a more or less passive contemplation— and all this in the interest of political order altogether. To argue, then, that poiesis and praxis are, in their very possibility, each contaminated by the other is also to acknowledge that the mutually exclusive opposition between the active and the contemplative, the "active" and the "passive," is also contaminated by their essential coimplication or complication of one with the other. But to maintain that praxis and poiesis, and the active and passive, as well, are from the very beginning essentially implicated each in the other is to divorce praxis from its presumptive teleological determinations (such as the Good, in the *Nicomachean Ethics*). Praxis-poiesis becomes not a means to an end but an end in itself, as the articulation of the power-to-be of singularities. This is the force of Nishida's readings of Nietzsche, Dostoevsky, and Kierkegaard (especially his concept of "despair"): to be without hope—to act without the presumption of any continuity between the present and the future—is precisely to affirm the radical negativity of an inappropriable futurity, the affirmation of singularity in its nontranscendence. But this is to orient praxis-poiesis not toward what should be (the Good) but toward what we want, a more profoundly disturbing question than that of the Good; no wonder that political philosophy has for so long avoided the possibility that we may not want what is said to be the Good. And although Nishida declined to say anything substantive about this "new humanism," this is undoubtedly why the proletariat is possessed of historical consciousness and thereby is the subject that bears within itself the potential of a revolutionary praxis.

But Nishida never said that the proletariat is possessed of historical consciousness and thereby becomes the subject that bears within itself the potential of a revolutionary praxis. Nishida was to maintain repeatedly that the subject of praxis and agency, formed in the poiesis of production, itself conceived as an essential orientation to the absolute negativity of futurity (futurity's radical difference from the present), was nothing other than the *minzoku*. *Minzoku* can be translated as "people," "race," "nation," or "ethnos"; at the time of Nishida's writing it would undoubtedly have been read as the identity of people, race, nation, and ethnos. For Nishida the *minzoku* was within and was the self-formative, autotelic agent of *Gemeinschaft* (after *Tönnies*, "community," characterized as a fundamental agreement or social will, formed in and by custom). As we will see (in sec. 4 et seq. of "The Standpoint of Active Intuition"), a *Gemeinschaft* for Nishida is both a singularity and the human cultural equivalent of the biological concept of species. With these formulations, of course, immediate problems and questions proliferate. Logically, how is it that a *Gemeinschaft* or a *minzoku*, which is nothing if not a nearly infinite concatenation of predicates, be construed as a singularity, of which one can predicate nothing save its tautological singularity? My question is not rhetorical, because in any more nearly adequate consideration of the question we would have to entertain the possibility that *Gemeinschaft* or *minzoku* is not simply a logical and grammatical subject, of which one might predicate this or that property, but singularities as infinite concatenations of predicates, the effect of which is *Gemeinschaft* or *minzoku*; that is, the concatenation of predicates is prior to and constitutes the being of community or race rather than conceiving community or race as being without properties. Perhaps. But it would still be not at all cer-tain that *Gemeinschaft* or *minzoku* are exemplary singularities (again, how can there be "examples" of singularity; does that not reduce singularity to particularity?). And why race/nation/people/ethnos rather than class? And what of class within race/nation/people/ethnos? All of these ques-tions are questions of the logic of the argument. The political questioning would begin in asking whether this concept of *Gemeinschaft* is not simply a familiar romantic nostalgia for what Marx (following Montesquieu and Hegel) called precapitalist modes of production (for which Marx himself entertained no nostalgia whatever), or more generally for the "premod-ern."[26] We would also ask, given the historical appropriations of such nostalgia for fascist apologetics, what is at stake in such romantic nostal-gia such that it is entangled with the desire of many of those who have no sympathy for the political forms that affirmation of *Gemeinschaft* has taken in both the twentieth century and the twenty-first.

The point of such a double questioning—at once logical and political and their essential complication with each other—would be not to come to judgment on Nishida, Nishida-philosophy, or even fascist apologet-ics, for that matter, but to confront ourselves with certain embarrassing questions. Not: what is the Good, and how do we deduce a praxis from the concept of the Good (a morality), but: what do we want, and how do we constitute the "we" that is said to want, and *how* do we orient our-selves within that desire? "We neither strive for, nor will, neither want, nor desire anything because we judge it to be good; on the contrary, we judge something to be good because we strive for it, will it, want it, and desire it."[27] How do we act on our inescapable transcendental partisan-ship? And a further embarrassing question, at once philosophical and political: how do we orient ourselves, bereft of the security of a faith that there is a Good, that we might know it, and that such knowledge could be a guide for praxis? This question is specifically historical, and it is as such that it is as embarrassing here and now in the United States of the twenty-first century as it was in Japan in the early twentieth—and in ways that, perhaps surprisingly, may not be all that dissimilar.

So, why should we read Nishida? Or rather, and only slightly more modestly, why read these three essays? Because in the concept of active intuition, Nishida gives us perhaps the most rigorous philosophical exposition of the first of the "Theses on Feuerbach" and because he offers thereby a no less rigorous exposition of the concept of "metabolism" as the relation between "man" and "nature," a concept that Marx left largely undeveloped. Because, therefore, we are required to conceive production, once again, as historical ontology, what Marx called a mode of production; because, concomitantly, we cannot but think Marx's concept of economy as the "form of life" that determines the *nomos* as such; and that therefore it is at the level of the technological (the material technical determinations of whatever passes these days for culture and daily life) that the most serious interventions are possible.

It would be indeed naïve, not to say beside the point, to claim that these essays, severally or collectively, constitute a political manifesto, revolutionary or otherwise. Neither do they constitute policy guidelines or even the philosophical ground or justification for any political form of governance, organization, or concerted actions. It is not necessarily the case that there are immediate applications for this work. Even in 1925, and all the more in 1935 or 1938, interventions at that level were simply impossible—and Nishida does not seem to have imagined himself a parrhesiast in any case. But philosophy comes into its own when politics is occluded in its very possibility. Philosophy comes into its own precisely when it is the political as such—the very possibility for the negotiation of power—that is disappearing into routine performance, the impossibility of crisis, and the culture of political despair, and when that disappearance is a matter of no widespread concern. Then, philosophy "comes into its own" not as consolation but as the frankly speculative—experimental—production of concepts ("production," for example, or "communism"). This is a *political* practice of philosophy because it opens upon the necessity, not yet a possibility, of making sense according to protocols entirely other than those that, here and now, constitute what counts for us as the logos. It is in the interest of *that* politics of philosophy that I have undertaken these translations.

THERE IS PERHAPS one aspect of the translation itself that requires comment. Lexical issues are relatively straightforward; I treat such difficulties as require explanation in the glossary and notes. Nor does Nishida's style—throughout its trajectory from the earliest published text in a style readily identifiable as belonging to the end of the Meiji period (1868–1912), through an academic style that seemed to echo that of contemporary German academic writing, to the relatively lean and even muscular style of the period from 1939 to 1945—offer insuperable difficulties. But there are in the texts translated here, as in others of the period, certain rhetorical constructions that are constantly repeated, and that can be equally clumsy in Japanese and English: "it might be thought that . . ."; "it is necessarily that . . ."; or "it cannot but be thought that . . ."; for example. One is tempted to dismiss such phrases as rhetorical tics that could have been omitted in the interest of greater fluency in the translation. Clumsy, even annoying, such constructions may be, but I do not think they are merely rhetorical. Invariably, such constructions are stagings of an assertion or argument, stagings that, as such, objectify assertions and arguments. What is being staged is therefore invariably either the *possibility* or the *necessity* of a given assertion or argument. What is it possible to say? And what necessarily follows from a given assertion or argument? It is always sense, in its essential possibilities and historical determinations, that is at stake. I have therefore in every case chosen to sacrifice fluency and grace to what I take to be the philosophical sense of Nishida's rhetorical and syntactic strategies.

EXPRESSIVE ACTIVITY

("HYŌGEN SAYŌ," 1925)

1

It might be thought that when we speak of expressive activity, we are thinking first of all of something like the movement of the external manifestation of emotion or sentiment. But expression expresses some content. What is expressed in something like external manifestation is the subjective emotion or sentiment of a certain individual, but what is expressed in something like the activity of verbal expression is the content of objective thought that can be understood by anyone. Even though it be something like artistic expressive activity, what is expressed therein is not simply the content of subjective emotion or sentiment; it must possess objective significance. It can be thought that all expressive activity is constituted of three elements; that is, the content of some sort that is expressed, the expressive activity, and the expression itself. One can claim that in something like the movement of external manifestation these three elements become one, but in something like language each is differentiated from the others.

What sort of thing is the content that is expressed? The content of all mental activity must in some sense point to or indicate an Object [*taishō*]. Be it something like meaning itself or a proposition itself, an objective Object [*kyakkanteki taishō*] is being thought.[1] It is thought that in something like the exposure of a merely momentary feeling, the content of the activity and the object are one, but it is probable that what exceeds the activity can be differentiated from the activity itself. It is the case both that the expressed content is thought to be objective and that it must necessarily be thought that even what bears the expression belongs to objective actuality, or at least to objective fact. Things like language or artistic works, as objective actuality, all possess the significance of being; and even though they are something like external manifestation, it is movement of the flesh that appears in exteriority. Thereby, even the content that is expressed and expression itself can be said to be objective, in the sense that both transcend our psychological activity. The expressed content belongs to the world of meaning; expression itself belongs to the world of being. Thus, subjective activity becomes what unifies these two. Still, in the case that the activity expresses the content of the self within the self, in something like the movement of external manifestation the three elements can be thought to become one.

2

What sort of thing is activity? What merely changes is not yet what is acting. When we see something changing before our eyes, we cannot immediately assume it is acting. What acts must be what can change of itself. When a certain phenomenon invariably follows a certain other phenomenon, it is thought that the prior phenomenon acts. But cause is not something independent of effect; cause and effect must be interrelated. It is not that red becomes blue but that what was formerly red subsequently becomes what is blue. First of all, we must think that behind two phenomena there is a unity between the phenomena themselves, independent of the [perceiving] self. Here, we first of all think that a thing possesses various qualities, but to say that a thing possesses qualities is not to say that a thing acts. To say that a thing acts is necessarily to say that of itself the thing is continually changing its own qualities. It is said that, there being a thing apart, for the sake of which a certain thing changes its characteristics, the former is cause and the latter effect. Were both absolutely independent, however, it could not even be said that one acts upon the other. Both must exist in a single unity. Thus, if it is posited that the latter is absolutely passive with respect to the former, that is nothing other than to think the latter is subsumed within the former, but what is acted upon must also be that which acts. Thus, to the extent that two things mutually interact, both together lose their independence and are unified by a single force. The concept of the thing is dissolved within the concept of force. More than thinking that a thing acts, it can be thought that a thing is caused to move. To say that a certain phenomenon arises within a certain other phenomenon is to say that force is changing from one state to another. That a thing or phenomenon itself is changing itself is force. And without a certain force being brought to move by another force, we might not even be able to speak of the fact of changing. There must, however, exist an unchanging force that is continually acting. Thus, to the extent that forces mutually interact, they must be unified as a single force.

We must admit the logical contradiction that, at the ground of acting, the one gives birth to the many, and the many constitute the one. Were there not the unity of the one and the many, of course, our very thinking itself could not come into being. That the universal itself determines itself is the fact of our thinking. We might even think that in something like mathematics, a single principle constitutes illimitable truths. In extremely formal knowledges, such as the three laws of thought, activity and the content of activity possess an indivisible relation; but when it comes to something like mathematics, the unity of principle and the activity of thinking can clearly be separated. Activity is a temporal event; principle necessarily transcends time. Even the content of time might be said to consist of the fact that, being multiple, it is one. But the unity of truth and the unity of actuality cannot but be thought to differ in the significance of "unity." What sort of thing is the unity of time? Kant considered time as a form of intuition. The content of our experience is given according to the form of time. It is the fact that the content of our thinking is unified with the content of sense perception according to the form of time that constitutes the actually existing world. But if what we mean by the "content of sense perception" is merely something like the representation in itself, then it must, like the content of thinking, transcend time. Knowledge of what actually exists is not born of the unity of the nonexistent and the nonexistent. We both know things and, knowing knowing, we know the thinking behind our thinking. These two knowledges have fundamentally different standpoints. One might well say that to know knowing is also knowledge; to think the fact of thinking is itself thinking. But these two knowledges must utterly differ in their secondary aspects. If to think the thing and to think thinking are of the same order, then something like the self-consciousness of our thinking necessarily disappears. Even in thinking the thing there must be a principle of unity, on the basis of which a certain thing is distinguished from everything else. But to know such a unity is not this unity itself; it is in the unity of such a unity that for the first time we can know this. Even in something like formal logic, which cannot differentiate the content of activity from the cognitive epistemological object, both aspects must already be differentiated. Time is the form of unity from the standpoint of knowing this kind of knowing. All that is given to us must be given from this standpoint. That even the experiences of sense perception are given to us as the actually existing world must be given from this standpoint. The content of the experience that constitutes the actually existing world is given on the basis of the fact that I see, I hear. We can say that even the fact that we speak of the content of thinking as given is given from this standpoint. It is from this standpoint that thinking and sense perception are unified.

In order to say that a thing changes, there must be at its ground the knowing of knowing. It is from this standpoint that the linear succession of such a "time" that cannot return comes into being, and it is within the category of such a "time" that we see change. Were that not the case, then we would see nothing but different things. However much a certain schema may be independent within itself, and however infinitely inexhaustible its content may be, it is not what changes. When we speak of knowing the fact of knowing, we can say we know something above or beyond the mere cognitive epistemological object; that is, activity knows activity itself and, in contradistinction to knowledge [that belongs to the faculty of] judgment, intuitive knowledge comes into being. From this standpoint, the self, transcending the thinking self, sees a unity unattainable by thinking, and even the contents of sense perception enter into the unity of the self. Sense perception [in itself] is completely irrational. But if sense perception entered into no unity whatever, then even the consciousness of sense perception could not come into being. In fact sense perception is sense perception because sense perceptions relate to each other on the basis of memory (in the broad sense). So memory is possible from the perspective of the self knowing the self. Here, thinking is united with immediate awareness, and we can speak of conceiving that of which we are immediately aware. The constitutive categories of thought come into being in self-awareness.

There is a supraconscious unity at the ground of our self-awareness. Our unity of consciousness is established on this basis. Notwithstanding the fact that it can be thought that between the consciousness of the I of yesterday and the consciousness of the I of today there is a rupture, they are immediately unified. This unity cannot be explained by anything else; it is the condition of possibility for the constitution of knowledge. What we call our "intuitive unity" is the unity of this standpoint. From this standpoint, our intuition moves from the one to the many. Because this standpoint transcends the consciousness at work in judgment, from this standpoint, in contradistinction to the consciousness at work in judgment, the infinitely irreversible, unrepeatable linear succession of "time" comes into being. Time is the footprint of the transcendental self. From this standpoint, not only do one and another mutually differ, but one can see a changing from one to another. Were we, however, to take such change to be merely change within the orbit of our unity of consciousness, no matter how often it might recur, it could not act. What acts is not a unity within time but must be what stands in a standpoint that transcends time; it must be the ground of our self-awareness, that upon the basis of which our self-awareness comes into being. Force is what has transcended time; force is time that possesses positive content.

3

There are various senses of "acting." We call the case where a certain phenomenon necessarily accompanies another phenomenon, with absolutely no end or telos whatsoever, mechanical activity. Such are things like physical phenomena. Although it be the same natural scientific phenomenon [as in physics], when it comes to something like biological phenomena, although each of its processes can be seen as mechanical activity, the totality is thought to be unified on the basis of a single end or telos; that is to say, the totality constitutes teleological activity. Even our psychological phenomena are thought to possess a single unity within the totality, but because that unity is immanent within the phenomenon itself, it differs essentially from natural phenomena. What does it mean to render unity immanent? In biological phenomena that unity is given from without. It is from without that thus we see; I do not know if an organism's unity is also contingent, but we cannot even know the end or telos of the biological activity of the self. Contrariwise, in psychological phenomena, process and unity are in an inseparable relation; we can say that the unity is prior to its elements. Even if it is a matter of simply one sense perception, it makes no sense without the premise of its relation to other sense perceptions. Consciousness cannot come into being without such a unity.

In all mental phenomena the unity must be immanent; that is, someone must be conscious of a mental phenomenon. But in mental phenomena we are capable of differentiating between what is teleological and what is not. Something like sense perception, it might almost go without saying, is involuntary, even in something like the association of ideas. The greater parts of our mental phenomena are involuntary; any teleological unity is never rendered conscious. It is only in the activities of thinking or in willing or in the activity termed *apperception* that for the first time the teleological unity is rendered conscious, and our mental activity is considered to be free. Even our mental phenomena belong to the world of second nature in opposition to the self; it is in this objective world that we continually actualize the end or telos of the self. Situated therein, only the activity that follows the desire of the self can be considered teleological. It may be that we can consider all mental phenomena to be teleological in the sense that biological phenomena are teleological. In mental phenomena in which the unity is considered already immanent, however, what is teleological is that the unity must return to the unity itself; the unity is necessarily the becoming-objective of the self itself. Both thinking and willing are considered to be active apperception, but we might well say that, in the strict sense, only in willing does the activity make of activity itself the end or telos. We can conceive, moreover, that in thinking, the end or telos is outside the activity, but in willing, the end or telos is truly within the activity itself.

It is thought that in mental phenomena the unity is internal: I must attempt to think about this point. As Aristotle said, in order to say that a thing changes, there must be that which changes. Voice does not become black or white; it is necessarily color that becomes black or white.

If the question "What is color?" is taken to be merely a universal idea, we do not expect the universal idea to become either black or white. If so, and one were to try to think, as do physicists, that behind [a phenomenon] there is mechanical activity, I would ask, with Plotinus, how it is that pushing and pulling gives birth to such varied hues of color. Aristotle claims that what changes changes into its opposite; but the more two qualities are opposed, the more must there be an identity that grounds them both. In short, even all the discriminations of color must be based on this. That can be thought as the thing in itself that becomes the logical subject with respect to judgment but does not become predicate: our mental phenomena are no more than the development of such a unity. Even to posit the cognitive epistemological object as immanent in mental phenomena likely expresses no other sense than this. What is differentiated is immediately that which differentiates; and it is necessarily the case that between the two no sort of mediation is either authorized or required. It is for this reason that the more sensuous qualities are in opposition, the greater the clarity of sensuous consciousness, and thought becomes more rigorous, based on the law of contradiction.

There are, as I said above, various senses of the term *activity*, but although one can speak of mechanistic nature, it is not that there is no unity but simply that there is no teleological unity. Just in the way that Kant thought that the natural world was constituted by the bringing together and unification of pure apperception, the natural world must be one unified world. The natural world progresses in the one single direction in which it must move according to the iron laws of causality. What acts both appears within time and is that which is subsumed within time; it is necessarily that which makes of time the expression of the self, and it is according to this that the objectivity of nature must necessarily be constituted. Be it mechanistic causality or be it teleological causality, temporally both progress in a single direction; but it is thought that in mechanistic causality it is on the basis of the condition given at the beginning that what subsequently appears is determined; in teleological causality it is on the basis of what subsequently appears that what has appeared since the beginning is determined, what has appeared from the beginning is conceived in terms of stages. But to say that what appears subsequently has determined what appears from the beginning, one must think that what appears subsequently was there from the beginning; one must think it had been acting from the beginning. And to say that everything is determined from the beginning is to say that the determination is determined on the basis of appearing in the effect. As I said before, cause and effect must be two aspects of a single thing. In any instance whatever, the unity itself does not appear within time on the same order as the process; in this sense it can be said to transcend time. In all causal relations, beginning and end must be conjoined in one. There must be such a unity even in mechanistic causality. It may be that in the case of mechanistic causality one can say that there is no sense whatever in the unity. All natural scientific causalities can be decomposed into their constitutive elements; their conjunction is entirely contingent. If one posits that from the conjoining of A and B a certain determined effect comes about, then an identical effect must come about in whatever conjunction these relations enter, and it is on this basis that natural law can be considered universal. But to establish this kind of causal relation, one must conceive that behind the relation there is allotropic substance; substance follows the internal qualities of the substance itself, in accordance, as it were, with its end or telos. Just as the parts of the body form an organic unity on the basis of its particular formation, so, too, material, substantial nature constitutes a mechanistic unity on the basis of each element's being allotropic. This is regarded as ateleological merely because it is seen from the perspective of organic unities. We may well consider substantial conjunctions to be contingent, and we may very well be able to regard actuality as differing and various conjunctions; but the nature that is conceived is not the nature of given actuality.

All that acts, acts within time; indeed, it is possible to conceive time itself, said to be a priori without content, to be a kind of acting. We say that time passes, but behind time there must be that which does not pass. When everything of the single world of cognitive epistemological objects is subsumed within that which does not pass and unified at a higher level, an infinite linear succession is established; when the world of cognitive epistemological objects of idealist cognition is unified in the higher world of intuition, the linear succession of a time that is unrepeatable with neither beginning nor end is established. The standpoint of a higher intuition is at once the origin and the end of the linear succession of time.

Even though one speaks of the mechanistic world of nature conceived as the eternal present in contradistinction to time, to the extent that it is the objective world based on intuition, such as that of which Kant spoke, it must nevertheless bear this sense. If, the things and forces that constitute the universe being finite, merely identical things and forces could be repeated, then what is it that does the repeating? If it is time that does the repeating, then time must be force; what is merely repeated is not what acts. As DuBois-Reymond said, the origin of movement is incomprehensible.[2] But it is precisely the incomprehensible, as nature, that is the cause of what acts. Still, when it is thought that the content given in the beginning and the content that is to appear in the end are the same, then although time is conceived as an infinite linear succession, time itself is thought to be without content. The positive content of the higher standpoint that unified beginning and end does not itself appear, and it can be thought to be ateleological. But to lose all relation to that absolutely higher standpoint is nothing other than to be left with the world of cognitive epistemological objects of thought, utterly divorced from time.

Even though we can speak of the world of mechanistic nature as ateleological, insofar as it is an acting world, it is based on an intuition that transcends judgment's consciousness, and it must be conceived to progress in a fixed direction within infinite time. Pure apperception, which Kant thought to be based on the natural world, as the conjunction of thinking and intuition, necessarily subsumes time within itself. But pure apperception must be based on the consciousness of the self knowing the self. To say that the self knows the self is to say the self knows the content of the self as a cognitive epistemological object; it is to say that activity knows activity itself. Therein, the positive content of time appears, and the world of so-called teleological causality comes into being. In teleological causality it is thought that, because the content of the higher standpoint on which time itself depends becomes clear [as the concept of teleological causality], what has appeared earlier is conditioned by what comes to appear subsequently, and therefore one can think that time can progress in the opposite direction. All that comes to appear possesses an inalterable relation within the unity of the totality; each part is necessarily heterogeneous. In the world of things everything is thought to be unified in a single center, but in the world of time based on our self-awareness it can be thought that each single point becomes the center of unity. When it is thought that pure apperception subsumes schematic time, then already it subsumes the orientation of the particularization of the self itself. The self that is the self of no person is no self; the merely universal self is no self. The self must to the greatest extent be particularized. In self-awareness taken to its furthest extreme, the unity itself of formal time is lost. In the innermost recesses of the particularizations of nature is hidden the self of praxis. Pure apperception proceeds, through the intensification of the self-awareness of the self itself, from the unity of formal time to the teleological way of seeing nature according to the power of reflective judgment and, on the basis of proceeding in this direction, can see various organic unities. What we call organic unity is nothing other than the content of a will we should designate as concrete time. According to this way of thinking, we are able to think of organic unity as even the end or telos of nature, and its progression within time can be conceived as stages in the development of living beings.

Certainly one can think in this way, but it likely also becomes clear that in the natural world teleologicality is no more than a subjectivist way of seeing. In the natural world constituted on the basis of pure apperception, teleologicality is a merely reflective category and cannot be a constitutive category. The "category" of teleologicality is necessarily a category that appears for the first time when pure apperception, as cognitive activity, takes the form of will. It is not the category of nature itself but is necessarily a category of nature given to be understood as a cognitive epistemological object of study. The nature that is the world of objects of reflective judgment should probably also be said to be nature given to be understood. Contrariwise, in the so-called world of conscious phenomena, teleologicality is already not a reflective category but is necessarily a constitutive category. The entire world of conscious phenomena is necessarily a world of cognitive epistemological objects that can be seen on the basis of the fact that pure apperception is a looking back into the self itself. To say that pure apperception is a looking back into the self itself is to say that pure apperception becomes that which acts; it is to say that it takes the form of will. In pure apperception's world of objects it cannot see the will, whatever its form; the self-awareness of the will appears on the basis of pure apperception looking back into the self itself. Albeit something like sense perception, to the extent that it is a phenomenon of consciousness that belongs to the unity of consciousness of a certain person, at its ground there must be something we should call the self-awareness of pure apperception. To say that in mental phenomena the unity is immanent must mean that the logical subject of judgment becomes the substrate of the activity itself of judgment.[3] When the consciousness involved in judgment makes of mental phenomena a cognitive epistemological object, the consciousness itself involved in judgment looks back upon the self itself.

4

All that acts acts within time; time comes into being on the basis of self-awareness; the will resides at the heart of self-awareness. The linear succession of a time without beginning and without end appears where the world of cognitive epistemological objects for thinking and the standpoint of what thinking can never reach are unified. Although we speak of mechanistic causality and teleological causality [as if they were heteronymous], fundamentally they do not differ in essence; both are self-aware forms of will, and proceeding in the direction of teleological causality, the will can be thought to return to the ground of the self itself. If we think of acting in this way, then contrariwise, what sort of thing might be the world of cognitive epistemological objects of thought divorced completely from time? In what relation do the acting world and the non-acting world stand?

I want first of all to try to think about what are called the eternal laws of nature. To the extent that nature is in itself a single independent actuality, it must stand above unrepeatable determinate time. It may very well be that we are not given the means to know something like Newton's absolute time. But where a sole unique temporality is not acknowledged, the concept of nature as an acting actuality cannot come into being. Even an infinite accumulation of hypothetical universal laws such as "if there is A, then there is B" does not bring actually existing nature into being. In order to say that a single thing acting upon another thing gives birth to a certain event in actuality, whatever the time, there must be subsumed therein a relation to the totality. Even in saying that gunpowder explodes when fire is brought near it, taking account of all of the surrounding circumstances must be an acknowledgment of a relation to the totality. In this sense, even when a single incident occurs, it stands in relation to the entire world. So in this case what bears the relation to the totality must be a singular instant of time. To the extent that what belongs to the so-called laws of nature is the law of acting actuality, it is not something divorced from time but must be unified with time in a single point of continually moving actuality; that is, it must be unified with the totality. What is called universal law is not that which is abstracted from the concrete totality; it is what, with respect to unique particular mathematical coordinates, constitutes a so-called invariant set; at the heart of universal law, at any time whatever, there must be anticipated the unity of the totality. That the laws of nature are thought to be abstracted from actually existing nature is because it is conceived from the standpoint of a concrete actuality above natural phenomena.

If one can conceive universal law as above, in nature conceived as continual movement within time, then might not we conceive what is thought as the universal content of thinking as a kind of invariant set within the world of the activity of thinking? In personal time the content of all thinking mutually acts together; that is, each stands in a relation to the totality. One can say that any content of thinking whatever potentially possesses personal time. What does "personal time" mean? As I said before, time comes into being on the basis of self-awareness; behind time there is self-awareness, and behind self-awareness there is will. When the will returns to the self-awareness of the will itself, time that is content — that is, personal time — comes into being: that is, the world of the unity of will comes into being. Seen from this perspective, the world of nature that is above a time without content becomes a world that has been thought and, thus, being the content of thought, enters into relations of mutual activity with other contents of thought. What was formerly unchanging activity within the world of nature now becomes universally applicable universal law. What is regarded as an invariant set in the world of objects of and for the will? In the world of objects of and for the will, which might even be called Kant's "kingdom of ends," will is ever and absolutely moving in the direction of particularization. What, with respect to the direction of this kind of particularization—personalist coordinates, as it were—constitutes an invariant set, must be the universally applicable content of thought; it must be, that is, the law of what should be with respect to each person.[4] One can also think that the universally applicable contents of thinking are the force that constitutes our mental life activity. This force is always potentially acting within our internal perception that is the actually existing present of personal time. Just as in the temporality of physics the totality of relations is thought to be acting, and infinitely repeatable universal laws are undisturbed by the situation or the context, then when in the internal perception we should call the actually existing present of personal time the infinite content of thinking is thought to act temporally undisturbed by infinite other relations, what is universally applicable becomes visible. We might even be able to think that the apodictic evidence of internal perception in the world of the contents of thinking possesses the same significance as does the experiment in physics. Necessarily, all the contents of thinking are acting in something like what is called God's thinking. Just as it is thought that all physical force is acting simultaneously in the entire universe, all thinking is necessarily present in God. The activity of our thinking must be the manifestation of God's thinking. Unrepeatable time manifests the unity of an unattainably high standpoint. To the extent that it can be thought that behind our consciousness there is that which transcends the individual person, it can also and therefore be thought that the content of thinking is acting in personal time. But in the instance that we consider something like temporality in physics, what is called eternal truth is nothing other than that which is completely unrelated to time.[5]

5

Time comes into being on the basis of self-aware unity; what acts, acts within time; although there are various senses of "acting," in acting self-awareness returns to the self-awareness of the will that is the ground of the self; in accordance with the fact that time brings to fulfillment the content of the self itself, "time" can be considered in various forms. Even what is considered eternal truth that is without acting might be thought, as I said before, to be within the same fundamental form. Now, to discuss what sort of thing expressive activity is, and to clarify the relations of various forms of activity, it is necessary to attempt to think by returning to the profound ground of self-aware unity.

What does "self-aware unity" mean? Although it is not the self-awareness that is the self's consciousness, consciousness must be thought to possess a unity in itself. Without this internal unity there is no consciousness; even something like sense perception must be within this unity. This kind of unity can doubtless be called present consciousness, and it can moreover be thought that such a single unity persists from morning to night. But according to what sort of unity are yesterday's consciousness and today's consciousness, interrupted as they are by sleep, immediately unified? It cannot be thought that between the two there is a continuity in the sense that what is subsequent appears within a past that never ends. When we speak of today's consciousness, yesterday's consciousness has clearly disappeared. Where does the consciousness that has disappeared exist such that it acts in present consciousness? Perhaps we may speak in terms of traces being left in the cortex of the brain, but to do so is to put the cart before the horse. In order to speak of a single consciousness as the immediate unification of the consciousness of yesterday and the consciousness of today, what has already become nothing must be thought to be acting. It is not merely that the consciousness of yesterday cannot be thought to exist within material substance but that what, not being consciousness, has in self-contradiction been rendered consciousness. The unity of consciousness must be thought to be the unity of that which is absolutely divorced from time; it is sense that acts within consciousness. Of course, in any instance whatever, a relation itself is not within an element of the relation; even in the case of physical force we cannot say that there is force in the same sense that we say there is material substance. But it must be thought that something like what is called physical force exists at any time whatever. Regardless of what has or has not been made conscious to us, physical force, as physical force, must exist and can be said to be acting somewhere. Yet in conscious phenomena what, having once been rendered conscious, has lost the sense of being a conscious phenomenon cannot be said to be conscious anywhere; at the least, it cannot be said to possess the same quality of actuality. Perhaps one can conceive of it as potential or latent consciousness, but potential or latent consciousness and actually existing consciousness necessarily differ in status; potential or latent consciousness is not potential or latent in the same sense as the potentiality or latency of physical force.

For reasons such as I have offered above, we can say that what does not become consciousness or what is, as consciousness, nothing—in the sense that in consciousness we are conscious of something—acts. It is likely on this basis that it can be thought that mental activity is considered creative and that the temporal flow of the self is singular and irreversible. To render rational this contradiction that consciousness includes within consciousness itself, we conceive of an external world of material substance. But this world of material substance does not exist divorced from the unity of this consciousness that, being nothing, becomes being; it is no more than the shadow of being cast in the direction of nothing. In this sense we can discover profound sense in the fact that in the ancient period Plato conceived of matter as that which suffers actuality, and Plotinus conceived of it as a mirror that reflects actuality. For the world of material substance to come into being, there must exist the illumination itself that throws the shadow of the self; what is called the natural world must be the image that the transcendental self projects of the self within the self itself. What I call the "direction of nothing" is not divorced from the unity of consciousness. It is because this direction of nothing is included within the self that the unity of consciousness is in fact the unity of consciousness. Just as Plotinus said that our mind makes a circular movement, the unity of consciousness must be both the beginning and the ending; it must be both cause and effect. When this circle is merely a circle and does no more than make the same circular movement, however many times it does so, then we only see the natural world; but when this circular movement itself becomes a spiral and possesses positive significance, then we can see the world of the unity of consciousness. At the ground of consciousness there must be something like what Scotus Erigena called the fourth standpoint, uncreating and uncreated. When such a standpoint becomes immediately the standpoint of the first creation, we see the true unity of consciousness. In the unity of consciousness, unity is immanent; that it is thought that each point includes the significance of the totality has no other meaning than this. The unity of consciousness must in one aspect be nothing; it must be the negation of the self itself; at this point the self is indifferent with respect to all the contents of the self. We can also say, however, that because both cause and effect exist at every point, the self acts at every point.

Heretofore in instances when what is called the unity of consciousness has been considered, it has been conceived as something like a certain center and has further been considered as something like a continuous single creative activity. However, something like such activity is no more than a seen shadow. For such creative activity to come into being, there must be that which is neither created nor creates; there must, that is, be that which is the substrate of creative activity. We can say that form is the shadow of that which is without form; infinite forms are established in a space without shadow. At the ground of our selves, thought as the infinite activity of the self growing and developing of itself, there must be that which, being born, is unborn, and moving, unmoving, on the basis of which our unity of consciousness comes into being. We might well call this the "nothing," but it is not nonbeing in mutually exclusive opposition to being but the nothing that includes being. And we might think this to be potential, but it is not an actuality that has merely not yet appeared but is necessarily that which infinitely transcends that which must appear; it must be that which includes infinite potential. Augustine, in awe at the greatness of memory that comprehended the whole of both what is with form and what is without form, said that even forgetting is within memory. Fichte said that the self and the not-self are opposed within the absolute self but that at the ground of this absolute self there must be that which absolutely transcends the self. As Plotinus said, self-awareness is not a being; for one to see what is personal, there must be a suprapersonal standpoint; there must be a standpoint that, negating the self, establishes this self-awareness within the self. Even something like [Kant's] "kingdom of ends" is in truth established from this standpoint; it is only in the standpoint that infinitely transcends the personal that the infinite personal can be reflected. We can say both that this standpoint is in one aspect without direction and without self-awareness and that what I have previously called the standpoint of absolute will signifies a standpoint such as this.

It is thought that in the *Phaidon* Plato put in place the immovable basis of idealism when he said that we have not seen our own bodies as equal but that we know equality because in seeing equal things we share in the idea of equality. Although the ground of judgment is given on the basis of this sharing, however, the activity of knowing cannot emerge from this sharing. To clarify that the idea sees the idea itself, we must turn to Fichte's concept of *Tathandlung*.[6] According to Fichte's conception, we can never arrive at the profound internal unity of acting and knowing. In self-awareness we can say that truly to act is to know, and to know is to act. For such self-aware activity to come into being, however, there must be a standpoint that transcends self-awareness. From the standpoint that unifies the personal and the suprapersonal, the self and the not-self, we can make a cognitive epistemological object of the content of the person. We should even say that it is precisely such a standpoint that is the standpoint of true intuition. When we say that the knower and the known are one, the "one" is no more than a cognitive epistemological objectified "one." Even though we speak of an infinitely productive activity that is without ground, this is an activity that has been rendered a cognitive epistemological object. The true "One" necessarily transcends even this sense of the unity of activity; it must be that which has gone yet a step further. And we might even be able to conceive of something that, as the infinite unity of self-awareness, is the self-awareness of a transcendental person, the self-awareness of God, that is to say. But even such a unity is not the a priori of truly free self-awareness. Such a God is merely relative, a God made cognitive epistemological object. It is for this reason that in the notion of such a God, the freedom of each human is lost, and the origin of evil cannot be explained. Something like the self-awareness of God developing in world history is nothing more than something like a merely conceptual empty time at the heart of nature, as it were. The true God is not a creative God but must be something like the so-called *Gottheit* of the mystics. When a thing acts, what acts and what is acted upon are opposed; what is active and what is passive are opposed. When we say that knowing is the known, that what acts is that which is acted upon, the pure activity of the unity of subject and object comes into being; once this is transcended, what acts is subsumed within what does not act. Thus, what does not act is not merely passive. Even were we to speak of the so-called a priori of cognition, in order to say that cognition gives the objective world, it must be that it is not merely the cognitive epistemological subject but must be that which includes the objective; it is necessarily not mere form but that which includes content. Kant's transcendental object is not the same as the transcendental subject; it can rather be conceived as that which subsumes the transcendental subject. All that is seen as the objective world vis-à-vis subjective consciousness subsumes within itself the activity of our consciousness and is necessarily that which causes our consciousness to come into being. And so, what in this sense subsumes all within itself, and what causes all to come into being, is necessarily something like what Plotinus called the One. As I said before, the negation of consciousness must be included within consciousness; consciousness comes into being because consciousness includes within itself the negation of the self itself.

6

If the ground of the unity of self-awareness is something such as I have articulated above, then we can probably say that the "time" that shows the conjunction with an infinitely higher standpoint necessarily comes into being on the basis of the One. As Plato said in the *Timaeus*, in order that this world resemble the original form of the Idea, "time" can be thought to be something made or created. If we can think that, from mechanistic activity to teleological activity, from teleological activity to the activity of consciousness, the unity of self-awareness returns to its ground, thus rendering perfect and complete the content of time, then perhaps we can also say that expressive activity is activity that appears in the profound depths of the self-awareness that negates even self-awareness itself; herein, time loses the form of time itself and enters into an aspect of eternity.

Unless one is a solipsist, one cannot but believe that when I speak, it is by means of language that I immediately transmit my thought to another person, and another person transmits his thought to me. How is this reciprocal exchange of thought possible? In terms of physics language is thought to be no more than a vibration of the air, in terms of psychology no more than a phenomenon of the sense of hearing. There is no way that language so considered can transmit thought. We cannot but think that there is something the same in our minds and that there is a mutual recognition of this same by virtue of the signs called language. Because expression itself, being impersonal, is this reciprocal transmission, and is its mediation, it becomes possible that two minds know each other. Thus considered, even expression can be conceived to be contingent, senseless signs in our thinking. Just as Plato said that thinking is a wordless conversation between the mind and itself, we can ask if it is at all possible to think without verbal expression in some sense. For my previous mind and my subsequent mind to meet and understand each other, there must in some sense be verbal expression; there must be a whispering between my mind and my mind. Our thinking is rendered objective by verbal expression; on the basis of this becoming objective, thinking comes into being. Even in cases where we think we do not depend on linguistic representations, there must be some representation that stands in as proxy for language. Although when we think of the idea of red, we recall the representation of red, the representation of red and the idea of red are not the same thing. For thought to become, in fact, thought, it must be brought out into a public place at least once; although it is not the same place as that of another person, it must at least be brought out into the public place of the mind of the self itself.[7] This is verbal expression; we might even say that verbal expression is not the effect of thought but its condition of possibility. Our thinking possesses its possibility on the basis of verbal expression, and on the basis of verbal expression our thinking escapes its subjectivity and becomes objective. The ground of our thinking is the world of verbal expression. It is likely for this reason that Bolzano and others undertook to ground logic on the basis of something like the [ausgesprochener] Satz an sich.[8] The activity of thinking is no more than the development of such content. Pure thought must be something like the Satz an sich expressed in language; our thinking begins here and ends here. Fiedler said that language is not the external sign of thought but the endpoint of the development of thought, but it is not just its endpoint; it must also be its point of departure.[9] Pure thought is not subsumed within the activity of our thinking; it resides, rather, in the world of language; language is something like the body of thought. Of course, just as a body without mind is no more than material substance, language that does not harbor meaning or sense is no more than mere sound. Our lives, however, begin with the birth of flesh, the result of which moreover is preserved in the world of things. As Hegel said, there must be objective spirit behind objective being; the unity of objective spirit resides in exteriority. As Plotinus said, beautiful form chiseled into the marble is not within the marble but is prior thereto. We might say that form is within the head of the artist. But the artist does not possess form because he has eyes and hands; rather, he possesses form because he shares in the idea of art. There exists within art itself a distant and exalted beauty, which, although it resides within the self itself and does not enter into the marble, gives birth to form inferior to the self. Just as we can say that all that is mental copies the self within the self, so, too, we can even think that objective mind reflects the self within the self by means of language. That one and another of our minds understand each other becomes possible at any time whatever from the standpoint of such objective mind. By means of language we live within objective mind and understand each other. To submerge the subjectivity of the self and live within the objective, we must depend on objective expression; that is, it is on the basis of verbal expression that we take up the standpoint of objective thought. Thought that is clearly thought must possess clear verbal expression; moreover, thought that cannot be expressed clearly is not clearly thought. We must depend on language even when we construct the concept of the thing; that from the representation of red we construct the concept of red depends, as well, on the power of language. It is on the basis of the activity of denotation that we transcend the activity of representation and enter the world of sense and meaning. We might even say that something like the conjunction of thinking and perception depends on the activity of verbal expression. For perception to become the content of thinking, it must first of all be rendered sensible or meaningful by the activity of verbal expression. When one verbally expresses to oneself that red is red, one acquires citizenship in the world of experience.

We can say that it is on the basis of language that we transcend subjective mind and take up the standpoint of objective mind. It is because objective phenomena such as language carry subjective content that objective mind expresses the self itself. We can say, therefore, that thought transcends our activity of judgment. In expressive activity the center of consciousness moves from the conscious self to the supraconscious self, and the so-called activity of consciousness, contrariwise, is a shadowy image cast upon the body. If we can think of language in the above manner, then perhaps art should be called expression in the strongest sense of the term. It is thought that in language there is no internal unity between sense or meaning and language, that language is mere sign. When we say that a thing expresses sense or meaning, it is perhaps thought that there is an activity that unites the sense that is expressed and the thing that expresses. Even something like language, being already the comportment of objective mind, cannot be said to be merely the intentional action of the conscious self; but although the conjunction of sense and language is not immediately apparent, one cannot but think that nonetheless there is an activity that conjoins sense and language.[10] Contrariwise, we can say that the activity is subsumed within the content itself that is expressed in art; we can say that sense itself acts, that sense subsumes the actual. Painting and sculpture are immediate expressions of a sense itself that differs from language. Of course, we can probably say that that is the intentional action of the artist. As I previously cited from Plotinus, however, the artist does not create because he possesses eyes and hands but because he shares in the concept. Because the artist submerges the subjectivity of the self within the objective, he intentionally acts. In the activity of artistic production there is necessarily something equal to nature's creations. Moreover, the fact that we see art is that we see from this standpoint. In order for us to make anything from anything, there must be the activity that conjoins form and raw material. It is thought that form is immediately that which acts, but the mental image of a house in the head of an architect is not that which immediately acts. But the house that is conceived and the house that is built, however much they may correspond at each point, are not one and the same actuality. It is not the image in the head of the sculptor that is beautiful; it is the image expressed in marble that is beautiful. When Plato said that it is because we partake of the Idea of equality itself that we say that equal things are equal, equality itself is not in our heads but—it might almost go without saying—an Idea that grounds truth. However, even if it is the ground of truth, it is not an Idea of actuality, and consequently we can say it is without relation within our activity. Contrariwise, the Idea of art must be an Idea of actuality in the sense of being above nature; it is the content of actuality seen through the activity itself; it is necessarily the content seen on the basis of acting. We can say that the artist's production is the creative activity of the Idea itself.

In expressive activity, what is thought to be "actual" is enveloped within the nonactual, within something like sense, that is to say; and what is actual becomes the raw material of the manifestation of sense. We might even say that in something like teleological activity it becomes the means to an end. We cannot say, however, that in teleological activity the ideal ever conceals the actual; the actuality of sense is sustained by the actuality of activity. When it comes to expressive activity, if we pursue this line of thought, then the ideal sustains the self itself; what is actual necessarily becomes the means of its free expression. We can say that the artistic ideal in Plotinus remains within itself and gives birth to inferior form. In teleological activity time sustains sense, but in expressive activity time is the shadow of the eternal. This is because in language the conjunction of sense and language is contingent and, being expressive activity, is thought to be incomplete or imperfect; but contrariwise, we can in one aspect see the transcendental nature of sense itself. It is the fact that we can see the free nature of thinking. In art, on the contrary, because the conjunction of sense and expression is internal, the subject is submerged within the objective and is even thought to be conditioned by the objective. But the Idea in art must absolutely transcend so-called objective actuality; it must be that which possesses its ground above the natural world and occupy the standpoint of freedom vis-à-vis nature. Therein is the difference between the activity of artistic production and the teleological activity of nature. Where, acting, there is no acting, we can see the unity of subject and object.[11] In this sense we can say that art is all the more perfect or complete as expression than is language. We can say that, like language, nature is an incomplete or imperfect expression of the Idea.

As I have said, the thing that is made is made from something, and it is made into something; there must be a maker in making; form is within the maker; material substance is external. Even in the case where the form is thought to be external to the one who makes, it is according to the form that the one who makes in fact makes, and therefore form, as well, can be thought to be what acts. We can thus consider there to be form, material substance, and the one who is active; but also, in order to say that a thing changes, we must conceive of that which should be called "place."[12] Even to say that a thing acts, we must conceive that it moves from a certain place to a certain place; we must conceive, that is, that it changes its situation or location. Even in instances where we think that a thing changes its form in the same place, the thing must change the location or situation of its part within space. Yet if we posit that a thing does not change its form and merely changes its color, we must conceive that it changes its color within time. Even when a thing changes in time, we cannot but conceive that thing as "being-at-a-place."[13] Even in linear time, to pass from the prior instant to the subsequent instant requires a certain singularity that, subsuming both the prior and the subsequent, interrupts the linear passage from the prior to the subsequent. Behind the ever-moving present there must absolutely be the interrupted present. When we posit that time passes instant by instant, there must be that which sustains its result. It is on this basis that its result is unified, that one-dimensional time is rendered a cognitive epistemological object. It is only in a productive activity that merely passes from one instant to the next that we cannot unify its result; in order that activity see activity itself, there must be a standpoint divorced from activity.

I wonder if perhaps we cannot conceive the difference between, on the one hand, the fact that a certain thing changes, that a certain thing acts, and, on the other hand, that a certain thing expresses sense and is the expression of sense, in the relation between acting and place. An acting without substrate is no more than merely something like mental activity. What truly transcends activity and makes of actuality the expression of the self must be that which provokes activity within the self and, moreover, comes to a standstill within the self itself; it must be that which, within the self itself, sees the activity of the self, without being affected by activity. For example, when an architect builds a house, material substance is conceived as objective actuality, exterior to form. Even when we speak of the teleological activity of living beings, what is called teleological activity is our subjective way of seeing, and what is conceived as substance is what changes its form, which we can think of as moving from material substance to material substance; yet when it comes to the activity of consciousness, we can say that form is giving form to the self itself qua material substance; in the activity of consciousness, there must be form, albeit latent. But when it is thought that the activity of consciousness is changing the self itself qua material substance, there must be something like the place where it is changing; there must be the place of form itself changing. With regard to mental activity, as well, we can likely conceive of something called latency or potentiality. But that is necessarily subsumed within the activity itself and is necessarily undeveloped form. What does the "moving place of form" mean? It is thought that what possesses material substance is simply advancing toward the future but that what is mental, as already thought to be the case in teleological activity, can be thought to be advancing toward the past, that it can be thought to be returning to its origin, to advance time in the opposite direction. When it is thought that in such mental activity beginning and end are conjoined, then what is mental can be conceived as giving form to the self within the whole self; it is probably in the self-awareness that reflects the self within the self that we can most clearly see this kind of essence. Thus conceived, in what is mental not only are what acts and what is acted upon one, but we can think the place of acting to be one with what acts and what is acted upon. We can even say that what is mental, being eternal, is what does not move. But we can differentiate between knowing and willing with respect to the activity of consciousness. We can think that in the activity of knowing, the universal is continually actualizing the self within the self, but in the will we destroy the ambit of the self's consciousness and are conjoined with what lies behind consciousness. As Plotinus said, the mind is what strains to intuit the One and can be thought to be continually moving in the direction of the One. If we think of the world of objects for our consciousness as the place where the self reflects the self, then the contents of the will must be the inexhaustible content of this place; it must be, as it were, that which envelops our consciousness from without. We might even consider the substance that is the ground of what is mental, the substance of wisdom or intelligence, to be the content of the will. We can think that, taking this kind of substance as substrate, what is mental is continually moving. Plotinus, deepening our concept of substance, said that the material body is not substance, that even various sensible characteristics such as the form or size of a thing belong to form, that true substance must necessarily be something like the place that receives form or a mirror that reflects it. When this nonbeing becomes being, the actuality of wisdom or intelligence comes into being, and that which causes what is wise or intelligent to come into being must be the One. Plotinus said that what is wise or intelligent is enveloped within the One, but the One is the space of what is wise or intelligent. Just as a line in physical space is conceived as a vector, so, too, a line from the point of view of the One is pure mental activity. To the extent that what is intelligent or wise is conceptualized as perpetually moving in the One, it is will. Seen from the standpoint of the One that, transcending even the will itself, establishes pure mental activity within itself, everything is expression suffused with sense. If pure substance is the mirror that reflects the Light, the One might even be called the eye that sees the Light itself.[14] When what moves is seen from the standpoint of place itself, what acts becomes expression.

Plotinus said that the essence of things that create is in the incessant movement toward what is wise or intelligent; take away the future from things that create, and they forfeit their existence; conversely, add a future to what is eternal, and it forfeits its existence; but what creates within time must be what is called the actual world; not only can the activity of the development of living things or the activity of consciousness not be divorced from temporal direction, but even the activity of the will cannot be divorced from temporal direction. Yet when the will, negating the will itself, returns to its origin, it becomes eternal actuality, wherein time becomes the shadow of the eternal; and intentional action can be thought as incomplete or imperfect expression. The case of building a house can likely be thought to be one kind of actualization of the will. The built house is within us, a house that is neither wood nor stone. But in this case the content of the will is the desire to live. The desire to live is the desire that would sustain our existence in this spatiotemporal world; it arises from the fact that the will follows upon nature; it is not the content of a will that envelops the actual world but the content of a will enveloped within the actual world. If the natural world is constituted on the basis of what Kant called the syntheses of the pure ego, such constitutive activity would not consist in making a certain thing from certain other things but necessarily the fact that explains the content of the self itself. In this case to constitute is to predicate something concerning the self itself; to predicate something concerning the self itself is to predicate. The contents of the independent will in this way must be seen behind the cognitive self. From this standpoint the actual world is conceived as the place of the actualization of the will, and what with respect to the knowing self was the place of reflection becomes, with respect to the will, the place of actuality: that is, this world becomes the point of intersection between knowledge and the will. From the standpoint that transcends this kind of antithetical intersection and includes the will itself within itself, that is, from the standpoint of intuition, this world becomes the world of expression. Language is incomplete or imperfect expression, but although we speak of a "world of language," it may well be thought to belong to *this* actually existing world. The world of sense expressed by language, apart from time and man, is in itself an eternal world and can, as the intellectualists believe, render sensible the entire actual world, and the entire actual world can be thought to be within the world of sense. Albeit in a sense opposite to that of the fact that the content of practical will such as building a house cannot envelop the actual world, the mere world of sense cannot envelop the actual world. The content of thinking is transcendental but possesses no substance of expression within the self itself; it must express itself by means of the other; it must see activity outside the self. Contrariwise, when it comes to artistic content as the unity of subject and object, the activity itself becomes immediately expression, and we can see the face of the eternal actuality that subsumes within itself time itself. But even artistic content does not yet negate all will; it does not render expressive actuality itself, because artistic content is conceived of as a temporary aspect. I should like to try to consider something like Kant's wise character as the actuality of intelligence or wisdom. Perhaps we could consider our bodies to be a kind of expression that harbors wise character. In the body that should be called the point of an antithetical intersection between the entirety of the ideal and the whole of the actual, the content of expression, activity, and the expression itself are one. It is on the basis of rendering the body itself expression that all of actuality can be rendered expression. All expressive activity is possible through the movement of the flesh. Moral intentional action must be the process of rendering all actuality into expression, on the basis of rendering our bodies expression. From a religious standpoint, all actuality is seen as a kind of expression.

7

Let me summarize what I have argued above. We can think that what acts acts within time; time is the form of self-awareness; various activities come into being because the self returns to the self: from mechanistic activity to teleological activity, from teleological activity to the activity of consciousness, it is according to the self-awareness of the will that constitutes the ground of the self that there is movement from abstract activity to concrete activity. We might also say that because time acquires the content of time itself, various activities come into being. But there must be a standpoint in the most profound depths of self-awareness that negates self-awareness itself; that is, there is a standpoint of the negation of the will, and it is from this standpoint that we can render even the self itself a cognitive epistemological object. This standpoint is that of intuition. It is from this very standpoint that time itself is extinguished and everything becomes expression. It might almost go without saying that the case of what is seen is much greater than that of what sees, and even in the case that the seeing and the seen are thought to be one, we are still not speaking of true intuition; it is when the seeing envelops the seen that for the first time there is true intuition. The standpoint of this kind of intuition might well be said to be the standpoint of religion. True actuality, existing on the basis of the self itself and understood on the basis of the self itself is necessarily what expresses the self itself. I ask if we cannot, taking as our point of departure that intuition we should think of as the final limit of all activity, contrariwise conceive of all that is called activity as imperfect or incomplete intuition.

The content of the experience of the color or sound that are the objects of our sense perception, seen as direct or unmediated experience, more than being something like the vibration of the ether, is a fundamental fact; it is to see the content of the experience of our sense perception as nothing other than the spontaneous presentation of the experience itself of color, the experience itself of sound.[15] When we speak of "spontaneous presentation," a sense of "activity" is already implied, but in this case it is that only color sees color itself, that only sound hears sound itself; if we borrow the term *logical predicate*, the predicate concerns only itself. Such self- or autoclarification is called the activity of sense perception, from the standpoint of the self. But when we speak in that way, there is not yet the conscious self; such a standpoint is the standpoint of expression. Of course, the content of expression, the activity, and the expression itself are not yet divided, but we would do well to say that, in the broad sense, it is the standpoint where the self negates the self and the self sees the self within the self. Therefore, the content of sense perception immediately enters the world of sense and even becomes the content of the activity of verbal expression. Even at the ground of the so-called world of experience constituted on the basis of the unity of pure apperception, there must be the active subject [*shutai*] of self-clarification or autoclarification.[16] If we posit that pure apperception is not a merely logical subject but the synthetic unity of form and content, then such a subject must explicate itself. To say that we cognize objective actuality is, conversely, that objective actuality predicates something or other concerning the self itself. In the experience of sense perception the content of expression and the activity itself are hidden behind the one who expresses; but when it comes to the world of constitutive thinking, that which constitutes and that which is constituted, form and content, are set in opposition, yet because the content of the activity itself is not manifest, the significance of the expression is not yet clear; and the content of the expression is extinguished by the words *time*, as the form of a self-awareness without content, and *activity*, as the form of a will without content. When it comes to the teleological world of nature, however, the content of expression being independent of mere activity, we can say that the activity is subsumed within the self; activity becomes a means to an end, and the world of objects for the will (in the broad sense) comes into being. Of course, it is not that we should see the content of teleological nature and the content of expression as precisely the same, but what becomes the content of art is necessarily the content of pure life; and to the extent that the content of life is objective, it is necessarily situated, just as with the objects of art, at a point that transcends knowledge.[17] In the teleological activity of mere nature the content of expression cannot yet transcend activity; we cannot say that life itself is situated within the self itself: it is life sustained on the basis of the thing. When, in the activity of giving-form, material substance subsumes form, it does not touch upon the activity of teleological nature; when it comes to the mental activity that we should call "activity without substrate," everything becomes form. At the ground of the continuity of an infinite activity, there must be a certain unchanging something that has transcended the activity; there must be what we should even call internal substance. When such internal substance subsumes form, the activity of giving-form becomes expressive activity. What brings about the transposition from the world of nature to the world of expression is pure apperception. When we go beyond the standpoint of pure apperception, we transcend the world of nature and enter the world of the actuality of intelligence and wisdom; therein even nature itself becomes a single Idea. Therefore, reason is even thought to be the basis of true art and morality. In this world all actuality subsumes activity within itself; each must be free personhood, and activity becomes its means, becomes incomplete or imperfect expression. Each self, in being self-aware, because it includes time within itself, can be conceived as the actuality of eternity that transcends time. A world in which value sustains value itself is not a world without time but rather a world that subsumes time within itself. Like Aristotle's Prime Mover, thinking thinks thinking itself, and thereby becomes the actuality of eternity. If we posit that the natural world is established as the axis of abstract time, then the world of intelligence and wisdom comes into being on the basis of concrete time. Because concrete time progresses in the direction of differentiation and individuation, it is what sustains the self itself. As I said in section 4, what is called the concrete universal constitutes an unchanging set with respect to this kind of direction.

THE STANDPOINT OF ACTIVE INTUITION

("KŌITEKI CHOKKAN NO TACHIBA," 1935)

1

What is called "time" is usually thought of as a straight line; the instant, conceived as an infinite linear progression stretching from past to future in which it is impossible to return to a previous instant, is thought to be ungraspable. Of course, one aspect of what is called time must possess such characteristics; were that not the case, it would be impossible to speak of "time." But if time were nothing more than that, then we could not conceive of "time." The before and after of time must in some sense be linked. If it merely continuously passes instant by instant, what is called "time" could not come into being. Time must, in one aspect, be circular. But to say that time is circular, linking past and future, is to negate time.

On what grounds and how is the unity of time constituted? I think that time is constituted on the basis of the fact that the actually existing present determines the present itself. To think that time, continuously moving from past to future, possesses a certain direction is ultimately to conceive time as simply something like an infinite line. To think otherwise would be to fall into contradiction.

Although it is thought that time continuously flows from past to future, in order to establish the unity of time, it must be that in some sense the past, although already passed, has not yet passed and that the future, although not yet come, has already appeared. Thereby we can think various forms of time on the basis of how one sees the present. If one regards the present as instantaneous, then the form of time will be linear; yet it is also possible to conceive a form of time that possesses no instant.[1] In our ordinary experience we consider the present to possess breadth such that we can never reach the instant. To think of time as circular, however, must necessarily be to negate time. If, for example, one thinks time as an infinitely large circle, then it cannot be called time. The past and future of time must be absolutely unlinked. There can be no round trips in time. For this reason I think time comes into being as determination without that which determines, or as the determination of the universal of radical negativity. We can say both that the fact that the present determines the present itself is the fact that the part determines the whole and that a linear time is thinkable because the instant determines the instant itself. But even if one conceives time to be something like a curved line in which each point possesses its own direction, and that each point is productive, it is impossible to conceive something like time. The instant of time must be thought not only simply as the extreme point of the determination of the universal but also as that which surpasses it. Time must therefore be thought as the continuity of discontinuity. That is a contradiction. To conceive the instant of time as the extreme limit point of determination is necessarily to spatialize time.

Time is thought as the form of internal experience; internal experience is thought to come into being on the basis of the unity of time. It is even thought that the self is time, that time is the self. The self is not thought to be spatial. External time can be thought on the basis of internal time. What sort of thing is the unity of consciousness? The unity of consciousness is thought to be linear, but the unity of consciousness should not be thought to be merely linear. It must be circular; it must be that which possesses a form something like the field of consciousness. And this is because the self is thought as dialectical being. There is neither the past without a future nor a future without the past. We cannot conceive of the self without recollection, but neither is there any recollection without anticipation of the future. The self is conceivable as the circular unity of a present in which what has passed has not yet passed and what has not yet come has already appeared. Because the fact that one says the self is a circular unity is not simply to say the self is circular but is also to say it possesses the characteristics of the dialectical universal; because, that is to say, it is linear-qua-circular, and circular-qua-linear, the self can be thought to be both linear and circular.[2] In the instance of decision the self can be thought to be instantaneous. And so, like the time that can make no round trips, the self is thought to be linear. Contrariwise, in the instance of representation-consciousness the self is thought to be circular; therein, we even lose the sense of time altogether. Thereby we can think the circular determination that would be the ground of time, the temporal universal, tentatively as the self. If we consider something like the "unity of consciousness," then we can think, according to what I have written above, that in respect of its linearity it is something like the unity of the will; in respect of its circularity it is something like the unity of representation. Or again, if one considers the concrete self, then in respect of its linearity it is something like pure duration; in its circularity it can be thought as something like the universality of consciousness. Of course, I do not maintain that the universality of consciousness is merely this, but I do think that there is something like the self of the universality of consciousness situated at the extreme limit of the circular determination of the self of pure duration. It is at that extreme limit that time becomes spatial.

Although one can say that past, present, and future such as I have discussed above can be thought to be within the mind, time thought from the standpoint of the self of such internal perception is nothing other than an utterly subjectivist time. And subjectivist time is necessarily not true time. Also, the self thought simply in terms of such internal perception is not the true self; the self must be intentionally active. True time must be conceived as internal perception–qua–external perception, external perception–qua–internal perception. It is where internal perception is thought qua external perception and external perception is thought qua internal perception that we think the active self. Time must be the continuity of discontinuity; the self must be the affirmation of negation. To think time merely inwardly is necessarily to negate time, to negate the self. To speak of unity is not merely to say that many things become one; it is necessarily to say the many are one, and the one is many. To speak of internal unity is to say that a singularity becomes the mediation of the singularity itself; it is to say the singularity mediates the singularity itself.[3] It is thus that internal time or the internal self is thought. The singularity is a singularity, however, on the basis of its juxtaposition or opposition to another singularity; the actually existing world must be thought as the self-determination of the mediation of the continuity of discontinuity. Were that not the case, time would be merely something like an infinite line; the self would necessarily be merely consciousness. The universal that determines true time and the true self must be a dialectical universal.

What sort of thing is space? The space that I here take to be a problem does not mean geometrical space; it is actually existing space. What is called "space" is thought to be diametrically opposed to time. Things exist simultaneously in space. Space is the relation of interchangeability of thing and thing. To say that things exist simultaneously, to say that the relation of thing and thing is one of interchangeability, is to negate time. But it is not actually existing space that has negated time; necessarily, actually existing space must subsume the temporal. Actually existing space must be thought as the place of the mutual interacting of thing and thing. Thus, things that mutually interact must together be independent; what acts must be something of singularity. Actually existing space must be the mediation that mutually relates singularity and singularity together; it must be the mediation of the continuity of discontinuity. What acts must be temporal; it must be thought to be within time. If not, then it is no different from a geometrical form. But time, as I said before, must be utterly spatial. What is thought, as the unity of time, to be circular must be something "spatial." There is no space that subsumes the instant of time. The instant of time must be that which cannot even be thought as the spatial extreme limit-point of the division of a curved line. There is no universal that subsumes singularity. Singularity cannot even be thought as the extreme limit of individuation; true singularity is something that has gone beyond the universal. The synthetic is not what is independent in itself. The further one carries an analysis, the more thing and force alike become infinitesimal; force must be thought as instantaneous. But time and space are never unified; the vertical never becomes the horizontal. Yet actually existing space must be temporal; physical space must be four-dimensional. Something like a collection of points is not actually existing space. Actually existing space must possess the characteristic of the circular unity that links the before and after of time. Time truly becomes time because it negates time itself; it is because space negates space itself that it becomes true space. Where there is interior-qua-exterior, exterior-qua-interior, subject-qua–the objective, the objective–qua-subject, there is the self-identity of time and space; there actually existing time and space come into being as the mutually opposed aspects of dialectical self-identity. The affirmation of the self-negation of time must be space; the affirmation of the self-negation of space must be time.

What we call the actually existing world must be a world of the inter-acting of thing and thing. What interacts must be things that are utterly independent of each other; they must partake of the nature of singularity. Thing and thing can be thought to be mutually interacting as the mutual relation of what are both independent things. In order to say that thing and thing relate mutually, there must be something called a mediation. Yet if that mediation is thought as continuity, there is no mutual inter-action. What is mediated is mediated to the extent that it possesses the characteristics of what mediates. It is usually thought that on the basis of the fact that thing and thing are mediated spatially, they mutually inter-act; but we can say that thing and thing mutually interact, that thing and thing are spatially mediated, to the extent that the thing possesses the characteristics of space. If one takes such a notion to its logical con-clusion, one might conclude that the thing is something like an aspect of the mediation. And the notion that thing and thing interact disappears. Is that to think that the mediation is merely nothing and that thing and thing are merely discontinuous? What is merely without relation cannot even be said to interact. Therefore, what is called the mediation of acting thing and thing must be the continuity of discontinuity; it must reside in the fact that being, as being, is nothing, and nothing, as nothing, is being. So what we call the mediation of the mutual relation of indepen-dent things must be circular; it must be a parallelism. To say that A is independent with respect to B, and that, moreover, they relate to each other, is necessarily to say that A stands in a similar relation to C, and similarly with B and C. What is called the actually existing world can be thought in the above manner as the world of the mediation of dis-continuity, as the world of the dialectical universal. It is neither to think the thing before the mediation nor to think mediation before the thing. There is neither mediation without the acting thing, nor can one speak of the acting without the mediation. To say that the mediation of the continuity of discontinuity itself determines itself is to say that thing and thing interact; to say that thing and thing interact is to say that the mediation of the continuity of discontinuity itself determines itself. This is to say that place determines place itself; it is to speak of the self-determination of the dialectical universal.

The world of things is conceived according to the forms of space and time, but in actuality the former is conceived according to the latter. In the sense in which I have spoken above, the world of things is dialectical; it is time in its singular determination, space in its universal determination. A singularity is conceived as the extreme limit of individuation, but a singularity cannot be thought as that alone; a singularity must be thought as that which itself determines itself. Moreover, a singularity cannot be thought merely as one thing in isolation; it is because a singularity is a singularity in contradistinction to another singularity that it is a singularity. Therein we must conceive the mediation of the continuity of discontinuity. The world of the mediation of the continuity of discontinuity must always be thought as the self-identity of two mutually opposed aspects. To say that a singularity determines a singularity itself is to say that the part subsumes the whole, that the thing becomes the mediation of the thing itself. The extreme limit of such a notion can be conceived as something like a point of production. The world of an internal unity, the world of continuity, can be conceived in that way. Our selves can be thought as singular determinations of such a world. The individual self is a singularity in a world so conceived; it is a point of production. In contrast, what interacts must be utterly independent; it must be utterly discontinuous. The thing must therefore be conceived as the mediation of the thing itself; conversely, the thing must be thought to be utterly mediated by the other. Mediation in this sense cannot be said to be discontinuous. It is therein that actually existing space can be thought. To think space to be continuous is to think according to geometric space. And that is no more than abstract space. The acting thing is absolutely not a geometrical point. What is called the external world appears from the world of the continuity of discontinuity in its self-determination, that is, in the negation of its internal unity. The external world is the world that utterly negates our selves, the world that utterly negates the subject. It is the world of law, the world of universals. It is the world of external mediation. Thereby, even the self must be rendered utterly objective. Just as I said that true time resides in internal perception–qua–external perception, in external perception–qua–internal perception, so too our selves actually exist because in one aspect they are of the external world; that is, because we possess bodies—if not, our selves would be nothing but empty phantasms. Therefore, when we consider the world of acting things, and the fact that we are in a world of acting things, we are already not in a merely internal world but in a world that is constituted as inside-qua-outside, outside-qua-inside, transcendence-qua-immanence, immanence-qua-transcendence. There is no merely internal world, nor is there a merely external world. Neither can one speak of an acting world without positing that a singularity utterly determines the singularity itself. There is no such thing as time divorced from space nor of space divorced from time. In the world of acting things, in the actually existing world, there must be universal determination–qua–singular determination; there must be time-qua-space, space-qua-time.

At the ground of what changes there must be that which does not change. What changes is thought to be temporal; what does not change is thought to be spatial. However, what changes and what does not change are not separate things. There is nothing unchanging without changing; neither can we speak of what changes without the unchanging. The thing must be spatiotemporal, temporospatial. What changes is thought to change first of all within its kind. Color changes color, sound changes sound: color does not change into sound. In such a case what is called color or sound can be conceived to be that which itself determines itself in the manner of a singularity. That is, the self is what mediates the self itself; the self itself unifies the self. We can therefore speak of seeing or hearing such an activity. We cannot, however, speak of that as acting; indeed, neither is it yet *to ti en enai*.[4] Acting must affirm on the basis of negating the self itself; it must be mediated by the other. It is not the intensive unity that becomes the mediation; it is necessarily the extensive unity that becomes the mediation. Even what is called movement must be the relation of thing and thing. *Phthora* is not *alloiosis*.[5] Of course, because it is a matter of time-qua-space, space-qua-time, singular determination–qua–universal determination, universal determination–qua–singular determination, intensive unity and extensive unity must be absolutely one.

The intensive and the extensive can be conceived as a dialectical univer-sal, that is, as the self-determination of the continuity of discontinuity. When intensive unity is thought extensively, we can conceive of a world of a common *telos*. Even the biological world is not a world of acting, however; it is not the true actually existing world. Moreover, for this reason, as the actually existing world, the physical world is taken to be the ground of the biological world. The actually existing world must be a world of force. What I am here calling force does not mean simply some-thing like force in physics. What I am calling force, as being entirely the self-determination of the mediation of the continuity of discontinuity, just like the distortions of physical space, can be conceived as the trans-formation of such a mediation.

In order to say that a certain effect is born of the interaction of thing and thing, there must always be conditions; there must always be a situa-tion. A thing, nevertheless, must be something independent, something fixed. But in that an independent thing is constituted in a double oppo-sition, in an infinity of oppositions, change cannot even be conceived. This is because with the disappearance of thing interacting with thing, something like force is inconceivable. Force does not merely belong to a single thing, nor is it something divorced from the thing. Merely to imagine a moving world, a simple world of force, is nothing more than to imagine the change of merely one thing, and there is no acting in that. To negate external causality is of necessity nothing other than to lapse into subjectivism or idealism. What sort of thing, then, is "condition"? It is not something called a thing as the third. To think of the thing as condition, moreover, is nothing other than to think the parallelism of an infinite number of things. The true condition, such as gives rise to a certain event that depends on its conditions, or what is called situation, is the world of things; rather, it is something called the world. The fact that a single event emerges is the fact that the world determines the world itself; the whole determines the whole itself. The thing is not mutually opposed to the situation; it is within the situation. Natural scientists ab-stract from the self-determination of such a whole and think the relation of thing and thing. In such cases they would render another condition inactive, but that is entirely a matter of degree. The acting thing is always an acting thing vis-à-vis the whole; indeed, what acts is at the same time enacted. The subject of acting is necessarily always a dialectical subject.[6] Even the most infinitesimal movement must be a historical event.

We consider our selves or our consciousness to be separated from the world. Whether as the mutual determination of subject and object, or as that which reflects consciousness, we consider self and thing to be counterposed. The philosophy of modern subjectivism takes the self, or something called consciousness, as its point of departure and tries to view the world from the self, tries to think from interiority to the transcendental; but never is the self itself, as such, problematized in any profound way. But it is what is called the self or consciousness that is thought as the singular determination of the world that itself determines itself. What is thus conceived is the temporal as the linear determination or continuity's determination of the mediation of the continuity of discontinuity. As I said earlier, time must be both linear and circular. So the circular, as the ground of objective time, must be spatial. It may seem absurd, but contradictorily, objective time or true time can be conceived starting from the fact that the instants that can never return are arrayed simultaneously. To say that instants are arrayed simultaneously is not to say that points are arrayed in a circle. That is no more than to think time spatially. To speak of time in terms of the self-determination of the mediation of the continuity of discontinuity (temporally speaking) or as the self-determination of the eternal now, each instant, instant by instant, must be thought as an infinite linear progression without regress. To say that the instant determines the instant itself is to be able to think time as an infinite linear progression; to think time as an infinite linear progression is to be able to think that the instant determines the instant itself. To the extent that it is thought there is an internal continuity between instant and instant, time is posited as subjectivist. Each temporality is an infinite linear progression, utterly independent, not bound to any other temporality. Moreover, such independent temporalities, as together the self-determination of the mediation of discontinuities, can be thought as true time. Even what we call our individual selves, dying yet unborn in this world, and existing once only, must be conceived in this way. The self is singular time, and singular time is the self. Of course, what is called time, as well as what is called the self, cannot be considered only formally in this way but must be thought from the world of acting things. In the world of acting things, time is space and space is time. The acting thing is temporospatial, spatiotemporal. Our true self is the intentionally act-ing self. In the world of historical actuality the smallest bit of singular determination is the world of things; as singular determination–qua–universal determination, universal determination–qua–singular determi-nation, what is concrete is the world of the intentionally acting self. Only the intentionally acting self is truly temporal. Thus, what we call our selves are what is thought as singularities within the dialectical unity of time-qua-space, space-qua-time, and is always thought to be centered on the "now, here"; but in one aspect it must possess the significance of the singularity that itself utterly mediates itself; the aspect of our conscious-ness must possess the characteristics of the continuity-mediation of thing and thing. One aspect of the mediation of the continuity of discontinuity must belong entirely to continuity; one aspect of the true time that is in-ternal time–qua–external time, external time–qua–internal time, must be utterly internal. What we call the aspect of our consciousness is the aspect of the circular determination of time. Furthermore, there is true time insofar as it is a matter of internal perception–qua–external percep-tion; time is, in fact, time on the basis of the fact that time negates time itself. In that time loses time itself, in that the self loses the self itself, an atemporal consciousness-aspect is conceivable. Such a consciousness-aspect can be conceived as representation-consciousness. From the per-spective of such a consciousness-aspect, the thing is conceived entirely in terms of its qualities, and the dialectical world is conceived as the world of change. In that world an objectively acting thing is unthinkable. The self-determination of such a world is, as I have already said, simply to see, to hear. From this standpoint, even though we speak of conceiving singu-larity, true singularity goes unthought; it is only to conceive singularity as the extreme limit of the individuation of the universal. Even though we speak of space from such a standpoint, space is then nothing other than a universal idea, and something that might be called objective space becomes unthinkable. I think that Greek philosophy, for the most part, occupied such a standpoint. Because the self-negation of the dialectical world is absolute, in its abstract temporal aspect, in its consciousness as-pect that is to say, a subjectivist aspect that has lost objectivity comes into being; or again, in a temporal aspect that has lost time, a consciousness aspect that has lost the self is established. Such a consciousness aspect is thought to be intentional; from the perspective of such a consciousness aspect, the world of objects is conceived as the world of meaning.

We think the thing to be immediately perceptible. The thing must be wholly immediately perceptible. Sense perception, as well, is considered the extreme limit of immediate perception. Without immediate perception there is no thing. When those who begin from the standpoint of the opposition of subject and object speak of immediate perception, they think that what is objective is given to the subject, that the thing is given to the self. Immediate perception, however, must be the identity of subject and what is objective. And this without exception, from the psychologist's "cognitive perception" to the artist's "intuition." Even the phenomena of physics are not divorced from the subject, and the work of art is not simply imagination. So all of immediate perception should be called active intuition. Immediate perception is thought to be passive, but there is no such thing as merely passive immediate perception; more, even passivity must be a kind of acting. If we speak from the standpoint of the opposition of subject and object, then immediate perception is the fact that the subject determines the object, and the object determines the subject. Even intentional action does not simply emerge from the depths of consciousness but, as a subjective-objective activity, makes things; thus, the thing that has been made is what determines the activity. We usually simply use the term *intuition*, but even intuition cannot but be intentionally active. Of course, I do not mean to consider all of this as merely undifferentiated; still, even immediate perception is not what could be thought to be merely passive.

So what sort of thing is immediate perception? I said that the temporal can be conceived to lie in the direction of the singular determination of the dialectical universal construed as time-qua-space, space-qua-time. The active self is conceived as the extreme limit of such determination. I said that the ground of time must be circular and that what is conceived to be our consciousness-aspect, when it negates the self itself, is what can be called the self that itself is negating the self. Therein, so-called immediate perception, cognitive perception of the thing, can be conceived as passive consciousness. Usually, immediate perception, as the activity of consciousness, is subsumed within the subject; the thing, as cognitive epistemological object, is subsumed within the objective. In actuality, however, they are one. The actual world is at once subjectivist and objective, both temporal and spatial; that is, it is the world as the self-determination of the dialectical universal. What is called the activity of consciousness is, as it were, the principle of individuation in that world: there is no thing without consciousness; there is no consciousness without things. Usually the objective world is conceived to be a world of things, but the thing is both temporal and spatial; it is an acting thing, which is to say it is already implicated in consciousness. And to speak in this way is not to advocate any animism. Animism construes consciousness to be in the depths of things. When one attempts to posit universality or spatiality as ground, then this world is thought as a world of things; but being dialectical, the concrete world is in one aspect utterly temporal, utterly singular. As I have already said, the world must be conceived in terms of time-qua-space, space-qua-time, which is the simultaneous existence of instants. In this way we can think of each individual's consciousness. When we conceive simultaneous instants to be both linear and circular, we can conceive of individual consciousnesses. Of course, it is not that the world of things disappears when we pursue such a line but that it is truly a dialectical world of things. It is therein that the thing is seen on the basis of active intuition and that, conversely, the thing determines our action. The thing is truly singularity. Even to say that we have cognitive perception of the spatiotemporal thing is to say that the thing is determined as the self-determination of the dialectical world, that the singular, as the self-determination of the mediation of the continuity of discontinuity, is determined. The thing is therefore implicated in cognitive perception; without cognitive perception there is no thing. Yet it is because its temporal aspect is simply circular that the thing is thought to be given. Having said that, however, the world of active intuition, as the true actually existing world, is not to be thought as the world of cognitive perception, the world of appearances. To think the world dialectically is not to think in terms of the opposition of inside and outside. The dialectic resides in thinking what is absolutely opposed as self-identity, in thinking immanence-qua-transcendence, transcendence-qua-immanence. The aspect of the contradictory self-identity in the concept of space-qua-time and time-qua-space, as the world of active intuition, is always the actually existing world; in that contradiction we can conceive the world to be constituted. It is from there that the world of the subjective and the objective is to be conceived. It is for that reason that actuality possesses depth. One can say that the so-called world of cognitive perception is a plane; the world of active intuition is a solid body. The side of singular determination in the world of active intuition can be thought abstractly as the subjectivist world. But even though we can speak of the world of cognitive perception, it must concretely in one aspect be impulsive.[7] Something like the physical world of the natural sciences is no more than something thought abstractly in the objective direction of the world of active intuition.

To say that thing and thing are reciprocally independent, to say that a thing acts, is necessarily to say that a thing changes another thing because a thing itself changes itself. But there must be "conditions" in order to say that such a thing acts upon another thing, giving rise to a certain event. When no thing whatsoever obstructs another, then A can act upon B. But to say that an other does not obstruct must be at the same time to say that the other possesses the possibility of obstructing. To the extent that A acts on B and is acted on by B, and to the extent they are each independent, they act on and are acted on by C. To act is of necessity always at the same time to be acted upon. Thus we must say that even the original possibility of A acting on B is established by the totality of relations. So in order to say that thing and thing interact, there must be a mediation; moreover, it is to the extent that the thing possesses the characteristics of the mediation that it is mediated. It is as the self-determination of the mediation of the continuity of discontinuity that the thing can be conceived to act. To the extent that the thing is conceived to be mediated—that is, to the extent that the concept of continuity-qua-discontinuity, discontinuity-qua-continuity can be thought—it is, as subjective-qua-objective, objective-qua-subjective, immediately perceptible. The true world of experience, which we think to be the ground of all knowledge, must be this kind of thing.[8] On this basis we can conceive its opposing sides as the subjective world and the objective world. Consciousness always belongs to actuality; true consciousness belongs to acting, and the self is an acting singularity. Consciousness does not begin with the individual's consciousness but is born of the self-determination of the dialectical world. The quality or characteristic of consciousness is usually conceived as an expansion of an individual's self-consciousness, but consciousness must be the aspect of circular time of the world of acting things. Even the so-called unconscious, or matter conceived as the outside of consciousness, is conceived from the standpoint of consciousness centered on the individual. The immanent world and the transcendental world are not mutually opposed; in the world of acting things, the actually existing world, the dialectical world itself, is possessed of no ultimate limit. The fact that we think the transcendental in terms of ultimate limits is because we think from a standpoint centered on the individual's consciousness. This is not to say that the actually existing world is merely a continuity with no ultimate limit. Even time possesses no ultimate limit; the universal of actually existing time is not the mathematician's closed set. Were this not the case, time would be nothing other than a straight line. Time comes into being in that the instant is conceived to touch upon the eternal, in that the ungraspable instant is thought to be grasped, in that nonbeing is conceived as being. And that is the fact of acting. Were time merely ungraspable, then there would be no such thing as actually existing time. The dialectic is neither to conceive the infinite from the finite nor to conceive the finite from the infinite; it is neither to think the universal from the particular nor to think the particular from the universal. The dialectic resides in respect of the fact that the ungraspable is grasped. The dialectical universal subsumes infinite limits within itself.

Our thinking must begin with actuality. To say that we conceive the thing is already to think within actuality. I do not say that actuality must abstractly be this sort of thing. I am not trying to constitute actuality logically. I am saying that what every person conceives as actuality is this sort of thing. Actuality must be the world of acting things. As I have said, what we call consciousness, as already the singular determination of the dialectical universal, comes into being as the dialectical process of the world that itself determines itself. Knowledge is deictic in the conjunction of discontinuity-qua-continuity, continuity-qua-discontinuity, and of subjective-qua-objective, objective-qua-subjective.[9] When we claim to know, already we are not merely inside, but we have emerged into the outside. Neither does one know merely in the outside but necessarily is situated in a standpoint that goes beyond the opposition of inside and outside. Many people consider what is called experience to be the ground of knowledge. But even the word *experience* can be conceived in various ways. To speak of experience, there must be that which experiences. Certain people conceive experience on the basis of internal cognitive perception. Contemporary phenomenology is the pure form of this standpoint. However, although space, or time, or the thing of external cognitive perception is explained from this standpoint, it is utterly subjectivist. Even hermeneutic phenomenology does not escape this standpoint. Contrariwise, were one to make the experience of external cognitive perception the basis, that would necessarily mean that what might be called the logical structure has already been assumed as premise. So the actually existing world, and what might be called the logical structure of the actually existing world, is not something that might be characterized as "scientific," as something like what I call "thinking." The subjective does not enter at all into a world conceived merely objectively. People say we should think from the finite to the infinite, that all that exists in the exposure of its appearance is particular and thereby mutually opposed. I do not argue otherwise. But is it not the case that when many people make that argument, they are thinking the relation between particular and universal according to an abstract logic? From what standpoint does one conceive the particular or the universal? The acting thing must be both singular and universal, finite and infinite. Even when one conceives what acts as something like a "point of production," what acts is not that which acts but a merely thought thing-in-the-world. When what acts is called the particular, then the instant must be the particular of the simultaneously existing universal. I do not say that because such a universal can be conceived, so can the acting thing be conceived. It is when what acts can be conceived that it can be conceived as the particular of such a universal. All that exists exists as dialectical being. And this is without exception, from the so-called thing to our selves. What I call a singularity says precisely that. A singularity is neither the particular, conceptualized according to a merely abstract logic, nor is it the universal. There is no sense whatever in which it is a matter of there being a universal behind a singularity. Moreover, I do not say that there is merely no universal but that what acts is always both temporal and spatial. It is because the thing is temporospatial that it possesses force. When it is thought that behind the thing there is something of the universal-ideal, the thing is conceived as the merely particular. People think that the instant is ungraspable, that in the world of experience the present possesses breadth. I think so too. But it is only insofar as what is called the world of experience is thought as the actually existing world that time is truly time; therein, time must be circular. Were that not the case, time would be merely subjectivist time, conceived in terms of internal cognitive perception. Many people think of "experience" as what continually moves, as change. But that is not actually existing experience. Actually existing experience must be the affirmation of absolute negation; the self, too, must be among that which is determined on that basis. And it is precisely for this reason that actually existing experience can be thought to be the ground of knowledge.

2

To speak of action is to say that a self moves a thing and a thing moves a self, that the subject determines what is objective and what is objective determines the subject. The subject and the objective are necessarily and in all respects mutually opposed; thing and consciousness differ utterly from each other. One might conceive consciousness, as that which reflects, to be something like a mirror; but what reflects and what is reflected must differ absolutely; absolute negation must be interposed between them. Although we say that the thing, being objective, negates the subject, then to say that the thing reflects the thing itself is necessarily the same impossibility as saying the eye sees the eye itself. If the thing, being dialectical, itself subsumes its negation within itself, then the thing must fundamentally in one aspect belong to consciousness; it must be subjective. To speak of something like reflection is not the same as saying that the thing objectively possesses various characteristics or possesses the capacity to act. I do not know if we can think of consciousness as something in a certain situation of the development of the world of things, but to speak of "a certain situation" must be to speak of certain conditions in the sense of which I have spoken above; it must mean the totality of relations. Moreover, self-negation, as in reflection, cannot emerge from a world thought to be merely objective. To think that way, one would have to think that the totality itself negates the totality itself. Although there are those who think this can be explained empirically, empiricism is constituted in thinking the thing as objective determination. To view even the subjective as objective constitutes scientific method. Although we can say, as in physiological psychology, that consciousness accompanies a certain physiological constitution of the living thing (i.e., the brain), in order to explain that empirically, what is then called experience must already be both internal cognition and external cognition, both external cognition and internal cognition. So if one posits experience as originary, experience must in one aspect be utterly that which possesses subjectivity. Experience is originarily subjectivist/objective; it is in its temporality that our selves are determined, and it is in its immediacy that experience can be thought to be the ground of knowledge.

When one posits that the subject determines the objective and the objective determines the subject, then consciousness too must, like the thing, in some sense be possessed of actuality. If one posits that consciousness is merely that which reflects and that conscious phenomena are like the shadows of things, the shadows cannot be thought to determine the things. To say that thing and thing codetermine each other, one must posit the existence of that which mediates. It is thought that material substance and material substance codetermine each other in space and that to the extent that the mediation is the same, thing and thing can be said to codetermine each other. For one to say that consciousness determines the thing, or that the thing determines consciousness, space must be the field of consciousness, and the field of consciousness must be space; material substance is of consciousness; consciousness is of material substance. It can be thought that it is as the self-determination of that which mediates the continuity of discontinuity that thing and thing interact. Even the thing is a dialectical thing; consciousness, too, is a dialectical thing. As I have repeatedly said, the fact that the material world conceived as the objective interaction of thing and thing is the fact that it is thought as the self-determination of the mediation of the continuity of discontinuity. In the mode of abstract speculation, the material world can be conceived as the universal determination of the dialectical world of things, and the world of consciousness as its singular determination. All that is actual is singular-universal, universal-singular. Even the "knowing" that is the point of departure for epistemology must be thought from the dialectical relation of the subjective and the objective. It is therein that the activity of cognition comes into being. To speak merely of giving form to material substance is not to speak of the activity of cognition. It is necessarily the case that form determines substance and that substance determines form. Mere substance is nothing other than what the Greeks thought as "nothing." What the epistemologists call the cognitive subject is really no more than the apotheosis of the individual's self-consciousness. And even though one speaks of that self-consciousness as an extreme limit, it does not escape the standpoint of the abstract individual self.

TO SPEAK OF THE STANDPOINT of intentional action is to say that inside is outside and outside is inside; it is to say that the temporal is spatial, and the spatial is temporal. Thus, we see things on the basis of intentional action; the thing determines the self, and the self determines the thing. And that is active intuition. Even the fact that we necessarily think experience to be the ground of knowledge is because what is called experience belongs to that kind of active intuition. What we call experience is not merely what confronts me immediately. Were that the case, there would be no difference between experience and a dream. There is no experience apart from action. We think the self acts intentionally. To say that the self acts intentionally is necessarily to say that the movement of the self is conscious; acting must come from the conscious self. Acting, however, must be the manifestation of force. Mere consciousness is not force. In this we consider force to be in the depths of the conscious self, and we think acting as what goes beyond consciousness. That "force," however, is absolutely not what moves the self from the outside. If force is conceived to be what moves the self from the outside, then what we call the self disappears. Therein, we are thinking of impulse or the unconscious. But if we conceive what is called impulse simply as the self-determination of a teleological world, something like animal instinct, then there is no self; or again, even when we consider what is unconscious, and think it to mean merely the negation of consciousness, then there is no self. The self must be absolutely that which itself determines itself. The self must be free; therein is the significance of the fact that we act consciously.[10] To think that there is something like an unconscious at the heart of the self's acting is to deny the freedom of the self. Really, our self-consciousness is constituted in a profound contradiction. We must see that in the depths of our selves there is that which utterly surpasses the self. Moreover, to the extent we think that as mere outside, what we call the self disappears. Yet our selves exist as the self-determination of the active world in which inside is outside and outside is inside.

When I speak of acting, many people think I divorce what I call the self from the world. They think I mean the self is simply a singularity that itself determines itself. It is not that there is something called the self divorced from the world; that the self is born of the world is not thought with sufficient profundity. Contrariwise, those who consider the self from an objectivist standpoint think of the self as something like a singularity construed as the determination of the universal. But from that perspective, the self is necessarily a thing, not the self. As I have repeatedly said, the fact that a thing acts must be thought as the self-determination of the mediation of the continuity of discontinuity. The acting thing is thought as the self-determination of temporal space in which instants are arrayed simultaneously. To act is necessarily to affirm by negating the self itself. And it does not lose this sense even in the case that it is thought that a thing acts. Yet it is thought that in a case such as material movement that the thing is moved from outside and that therefore, when it comes to animals, it is considered to be all the more a case of self-acting. In biological phenomena it becomes clear that we are born already dying. It is thought that in the physical world time conforms to space but that in the biological world time possesses an autonomy of its own. But even when we speak of the biological world, it does not escape the spatial. Therefore, and moreover, the living thing is not that which truly acts on its own. It is truly in affirming on the basis of negating the self itself that there is that which is necessarily conscious of the self itself. To say that the thing reflects the thing itself, that the self reflects the self itself, is necessarily to speak of the affirmation of negation. To be self-aware, or rather, to be conscious, is necessarily already the affirmation of negation. Although it is as an object of cognition that the thing is a thing, to say so is not yet to think that the thing reflects the thing itself. To speak of the affirmation of negation is not to say that the thing disappears, nor is it to say that the same thing appears twice, as if the thing appears changing time and place. And even though one thinks of something like a teleological process, neither is that to think the affirmation of negation. To say that the self reflects the self itself is to say that the self absolutely goes outside the self itself; it is to say that the self negates the self itself absolutely. Moreover, although the self is the self on the basis of seeing the self as an object of perception, the self is thereby in the other. To posit that, as the continuity of discontinuity, the thing acts, means that it is conscious. Many people without any profound consideration of what is called consciousness think the thing from the perspective of consciousness. And so they think that to be conscious and to act are separate phenomena. But it is when one posits that the thing truly acts as the continuity of discontinuity that one necessarily first of all thinks of the activity of consciousness as the affirmation of absolute negation. The self-determination of the world of the eternal now, in which instants are simultaneous, the world of space-qua-time and time-qua-space, must at its core mean reflecting the self within the self. In saying this I am not trying to think the world in terms of consciousness or subjectivity. Neither am I trying to think the spiritual as the ground of the actually existing. On the contrary, I am trying to think consciousness as a moment of the self-determination of the dialectical world. The actually existing world that itself determines itself is always thought as the actually existing present; one aspect of the actually existing present is always consciousness. Outside of this there is no such thing as consciousness. Yet, because the individual self is thought merely as singularity, and the aspect of consciousness is thought as an enlargement of such an individual self, the aspect of consciousness is considered to be completely separate from the world of acting things.

As I said before, one must always posit the existence of conditions in order to say that a thing acts. John Stuart Mill says that in the case that a certain phenomenon occurs, it must always without fail be accompanied by a certain set of conditions and that in cases where the phenomenon does not occur, those conditions do not exist as anything at all; between those conditions and the phenomenon there is a causal relation. What are called conditions are always a relation of the totality. Even when one abstractly isolates only two things and considers the relation of A and B, then what is called physical force becomes unthinkable; it is, moreover, the same even if one isolates a number of things. To think of what is called physical force, it must be thought as the self-determination of the totality; it must be thought as what I have called "local determination."[11] To speak of totality is not merely to speak of an infinite number. One might even think of things in the manner of the mutuality of independent things, one by one. But that is not to think the acting thing. The acting thing must be thought as the self-determination of the mediation of a continuity of discontinuity. The mediation of the continuity of discontinuity can be thought as the "totality." Each thing can be thought to possess the significance of the totality when things are thought to be unified while being mutually independent. And that can be thought to be so even in our field of consciousness. The "unity of consciousness" means this. But that is not yet to be able to think the acting thing. The acting thing must be that which affirms the self itself on the basis of negating the self itself. To say that certain conditions arise is to say that they arise temporally. To say that they arise temporally is to say that they are to be made conscious. Whatever: it is because what is called consciousness is conceived as the self-determination of the universal of time that this is so. The activity of actually existing consciousness cannot be thought to be an extension of individual consciousness; rather, it can be thought to be the self-determination of spatial time. To speak of things occurring temporally is to speak of becoming conscious in the manner of the individual person; it is not to say that any person whatever is conscious. It is, so to speak, a consciousness that cannot be made the consciousness of an individual person. Even to pose such a question is to think consciousness abstractly. The individual person is constituted at the extreme limit of the singular determination of the dialectical world. The world cannot be thought from the self of the individual person; the self can be thought from the depths of the world.

To say that A acts on B is to say that A acts in the conditions of the totality; the very fact that A acts is the fact that it is to act, determined by the totality; it is to be moved by another. And so, when considered in this way, what is called the totality is neither merely spatial, nor is it merely temporal, but it must be temporospatial, spatiotemporal. This is to say that the thing appears, that the thing in itself expresses itself. Even what we call the activity of our consciousness must be conceived from that standpoint. Seen only from the perspective of the temporal aspect of the world, from the so-called subjectivist world, the transcendent is thought to appear. But when the thing is considered as at once internal cognitive perception and external cognitive perception, the transcendent is already immanent. And that is to say that the thing acts. To say that the thing acts is necessarily to say that the thing negates the thing itself. But merely to negate the self itself is not to act. Negation must be affirmation; it must be a matter of coming into being in passing away. And to take it as the mediation of continuity, as if time itself were to stop, is not to be able to think the acting thing. Or one might posit that a thing acts without our consciousness of the fact, that there was a physical world even before the birth of man. But then, what is called consciousness is thought as individual consciousness, and even though one speaks of human consciousness, one is simply thinking of it as an enlarged version of individual consciousness. Consciousness is not thought from the depths of the world. To speak of being conscious is to posit that the discontinuous continues, that each independent thing is linked. To say that the thing in itself happens is to say that the outer becomes the inner, that the discontinuous becomes continuous, and that it is as the continuity of discontinuity that the thing acts.[12] What is called the world of experience comes into being in the standpoint of immediate perception that is internal cognitive perception–qua–external cognitive perception, external cognitive perception–qua–internal cognitive perception. Being the singular-qua-universal, universal-qua-singular, the actually existing world is always singular. In the world according to physics, simultaneous instants tend to be construed as an infinite number of points; that is, they tend to be construed spatially. The universal of consciousness, as the cognitive subject, is spatiotemporal; it is the sequential at the extreme limit of discontinuity. At that moment, cognitive perception is thought as sense perception. It is thought that the sequential itself is possessed of no independence and therefore merely reflects. It may be that in speaking that way my thinking may be misconstrued as something like Mach's sensationalism. But those who think so must be subjectivists who consider consciousness to be divorced from material substance and consider consciousness to be something like a mirror; they adhere to a notion of an abstract independence of consciousness. To say that a thing acts is necessarily to say that the thing itself affirms itself because the thing itself negates the thing itself; and that is necessarily to say that first of all the thing itself reflects itself. To speak of going from quantity to quality necessarily says that. This is not to say one should argue scientifically according to the example of thermodynamics. To say that what together are separated interrelate is perhaps to say that they first of all reflect in a single place. That is the most attenuated relation or connection of thing and thing. It is in that sense that our consciousness aspect is a reflecting mirror; logically, it is mere extension. Nevertheless, without continuity there is no discontinuity, no discontinuity without continuity. Without that mutual relation there is no thing; without the thing there is no consciousness. Apart from the self-determination of the dialectical world, actually existing consciousness is inconceivable. The activity of our consciousness, as well, must be thought from this world of experience that determines us. Therefore, the more concretely we conceive our consciousness, the more we conceive the self to be intentionally active, the more must we think something objective to reside in the depths of our selves. That my thinking here is thought to be difficult to understand, and is therefore something like subjectivism, is because subject and the objective are thought to be originarily opposed, that to act and to be conscious are thought to be mutually opposed, to differ absolutely from each other, and to be mutually independent. Many people think even experience subjectively from the standpoint of internal cognitive perception, like Berkeley.

I have frequently maintained that what we call self-awareness is not that the self knows the self, and that what is known and what knows are one, but that self-awareness is to see the self within the self (in *Mu no jikakuteki gentei* [The self-aware determination of radical negativity] and other works). I have said that the activity of consciousness cannot be thought simply as activity but must be thought as local determination that subsumed activity. To the extent that such a local determination, that is, mediation, is thought as the mediation of continuity in which the singular thing mediates the singular thing itself, that is, as the universal of time, it is the internal world. When, however, we think that we see the self on the basis of our action, then it is not merely a mediation of continuity but must necessarily be thought as the mediation of the continuity of discontinuity, as dialectical universal. It is from there that we can conceive our self-activity. Our actually existing selves must be thought from the perspective of internal cognitive awareness–qua–external cognitive awareness, external cognitive awareness–qua–internal cognitive awareness. Therefore, the more intentionally active our selves are, the more are they our true selves. The self that possesses no body is no more than a ghost. To speak of the seeing self without seeing means local determination. Thus it is to the extent that the self is thought to be actually existing that it is necessarily the mediation of the continuity of discontinuity. Our selves come into being from the depths of the historical world. It is to the extent that the mediation of the continuity of discontinuity is thought to be the continuation of the absolutely discontinuous (singular) that one can necessarily speak of reflection. Thus, even reflection is a variety of activity. There must be reflection or seeing in the world of the mutual determination of singularity and singularity in the world of the absolute dialectic. Yet that this is not conceived to be acting is because one is not conceiving a truly dialectical world. It is because the historical world in which subject determines the objective and the objective determines the subject is not conceived as the true actually existing world; it is conceived as a world of merely abstract thought. It would be a misstep to conceive internal cognitive awareness–qua–external cognitive awareness and external cognitive awareness–qua–internal cognitive awareness to be the thing-in-itself. It would be to contradict the problematic of Kantian philosophy's thing-in-itself. Epistemologists of this persuasion posit something like a kind of causal relation between the subjective and the objective. Were that not the case, knowing would be nothing other than giving form to mere substance. Contrariwise, materialists attempt to argue that a subjectivist-objectivist actuality is constituted from material substance considered in exteriority, and they attempt to think the concrete from the abstract. Although they speak of the dialectics of nature, and think that consciousness is born under certain conditions of the development of the physical world, there is, in fact, nothing much different from Kantian epistemology. In the self-determination of the dialectical world characterized as discontinuity-qua-continuity, continuity-qua-discontinuity, outside of its continuity there is no such thing as consciousness; outside of its discontinuity there is no such thing as material substance. And those who think that to act and to be conscious are completely different are fundamentally imprisoned in the concept of the opposition of subject and the objective. In the world of historical actuality there is no thing that is not expressive. The dialectical determination of absolute negation-qua-affirmation is both the fact of acting and the fact of being conscious. When we attempt to think that which determines the self itself in the depths of the world of actuality (and it is unfortunate that this [figure of speech] posits the actually existing as already outside, but . . .), it is neither something within us nor something outside of us. It must be that which, as absolute radical negativity, determines the self itself, in the sense that it absolutely cannot be determined. That is necessarily what creates. If one thinks of it as latent potential in any sense, then it is already not the affirmation of absolute negation. It is from there that our selves are born, and it is toward there that we die. It cannot be called spirit, nor can it be called material substance; moreover, neither can it be something like a compromise between spirit and material substance. People who think so are thinking thing and mind abstractly. What is truly objective with respect to our selves must be something like the above; it must be that which envelops us without standing over against us. What stands over against the self as cognitive epistemological object must be that which is already in the self. If not, then it is nothing at all. What stands over against me in the actually existing historical world must be that which expresses the self-itself; it must be that which stands in a dialectical relation to me. Thing and self codetermine each other on the basis of the mediation of the continuity of discontinuity. And [what stands over against me in the actually existing historical world] is therefore called the Thou. What I call the Thou does not mean simply the neighbor. That there are many who feel themselves to be, in various ways, against this notion is because they take the self to be born of the self.

We cannot but acknowledge the merit of those who have introduced what is called expression into the world of objects for philosophical thought, as well as regret that expression, up until the present day, has been considered only hermeneutically. Expression is considered nothing more than an object of understanding. But what is called expression must be an objective activity. In the actually existing historical world, thing and thing codetermine each other expressively. Even what is called the activity of our selves must be considered in that way. The activity of our selves comes into being as the self-determination of the spatiotemporal, temporospatial world. Therein are our selves. In the world of artistic intuition, for example, all things are both singularities that determine the self itself and are one; the singularity is qua the universal, the universal qua the singular. What is called the unity of artistic intuition must be this sort of thing. The various parts of an artistic artifact are not merely what is thought as the particular of the universal; neither are they merely the extreme limit of individuation. They must be the singularities that completely determine themselves. Moreover, what is called the unity of artistic intuition is the unity of such singularities. Thus there is no such thing as the singular apart from such a unity; the part must be a part of the whole. Even when we consider the physical world, various things are not merely particulars, nor are they limit-points; they must be singularities that determine the self-itself. But to posit that in artistic intuition each thing is singular must be thought in a more profound sense. In the physical world what is called a singularity is the singularity seen from the standpoint of the universal; it is singular determination rendered infinitesimal. Even the singularity in the world of artistic intuition must of course be seen in that way; the artistic artifact must be actually existing. It must possess material substantial being. But to say that the thing in the world of artistic intuition is singular does not mean that alone, each thing must be a born thing. It is, moreover, not merely that it is a born thing in the sense of a cell of a living being; it must be that each singularity itself expresses itself; it must be a thing possessed of historical facticity. The activity of artistic creation is not the activity of subjectivist consciousness. It must be established from the self-determination of the historical world. For this reason I have frequently tried to explain the self-determination of the historical world on the model of artistic intuition. This is not to see the historical world artistically. Because many people take the physical to be the actually existing world, they think something like the world of art to be merely subjectivist; they think it no more than an empty phantasm. But nothing at all comes forth from the physical world determined only in terms of external cognitive perception; it is merely eternal physical movement. But the true world of concrete actuality is not a world in which time is subsumed within space; it must be a world of space-qua-time, time-qua-space; it must be both a world of completely external cognitive perception and of completely internal cognitive perception. Even Marx's commodity is not merely physical substance but a historically factual thing that itself determines itself expressively. The creative world is what intuitively determines the self itself; it is what determines it singularly. The activity of artistic creation is thought to be subjectivist because it is the internal cognitive perception of the creative world.

All acting is the affirmation of negation; it is not the mutual relation of thing and thing conceived merely abstractly; acting is the dialectical world itself determining itself. Acting or activity, therefore, is always both subjectivist and objective, both objective and subjectivist, both internal cognitive perception and external cognitive perception, both external cognitive perception and internal cognitive perception. It is on that basis that the world of material substance for external cognitive perception is thought according to the rendering-infinitesimal of internal cognitive perception. Even what is called reflecting consciousness is conceived in that way. Reflecting consciousness is circular time subsumed within space. In the world of historical actuality space is entirely space, and time is entirely time. The true actually existing world is not a plane. Seen from the standpoint of the subject, actuality must be infinitely deep. Time is a time that possesses its own autonomy; this world is not merely a material world; all things must be what determines the self itself expressively. But to say that thing itself determines itself expressively is not to say that the thing as such disappears; it is not to say that the world loses its materiality. The thing becomes a thing in an ever more profound sense. And it is therein that we can conceive the life-world. But what is called biological life can moreover be thought to be within physical space. But it does not for that reason possess objectivity within itself. It can even be conceived as the projection of the subject. What I call the life-world is the creative world. The true world of the thing-in-itself must be creative. From that very perspective the world of the laws of physics, too, must be the world of creation. But that world is the world of the recurrence of the same epoch. Even the world of physical principle is within the actually existing historical world. Even so-called material substance is, in fact, a historical fact. Physics's knowledge is necessarily the self-expression of material substance itself in the historical world. From the standpoint of the historical world, to say that a thing acts is to say that at some time, somewhere, someone intuits in the manner of external cognitive perception–qua–internal cognitive perception; perhaps one can even say that it is so before the birth of what is called man. Physics's thinking comes into being in that it belongs to internal cognitive perception. What is called action is the fact that the subject determines the objective and the objective determines the subject; it is on the basis of action that we see things. In the historical world, to see the thing is that at the same time the thing acts and that the self is active. It is in this sense that even thought is a kind of intentional action.

To say that in the world of historical actuality the thing is seen in the manner of internal cognitive perception–qua–external cognitive perception and external cognitive perception–qua–internal cognitive perception is to say that the thing acts; it is to say the self is conscious; it is to say the thing is seen on the basis of intentional action. This is so because in the historical actually existing world, as the self-determination of the dialectical universal, time completely possesses its own autonomy, and the thing is what completely itself expresses itself. For this reason our selves are thought to be characterized by will and understanding. The affirmation of the negation of the historical world is thought to be the operation of the understanding. In such a world the seen thing must be the unity of subject and object; it must be artistic in the broad sense of the term. Our action is necessarily always characterized by expressive activity. To see is to make; to make is to see. The subject determines the objective, and the objective determines the subject; this is to create things in the manner of the unification of subject and object: all is poiesis. Our action does not come forth from the depths of the abstract conscious self; in the manner of the unity of subject and object, singularly, it comes from the world that itself determines itself; it comes from the depths of the world that itself determines itself expressively. That is the activity of the self-determination of the historical world; it is the historical world that, in action, itself determines itself. I said that to speak of the interacting of thing and thing is to posit "under certain conditions" and that it can be thought that it is as the self-determination of the whole that the thing acts. In the actually existing historical world it is the thing that itself expresses itself and is necessarily that which acts in the manner of intentional action. It is as the mutual determination of thing and thing that the thing is seen, that the thing is created. Although it is on the basis of the mutual determination of thing and thing, that is, on the basis of the interacting of thing and thing, that the thing is born for physics, that fact must be thought from the standpoint I have just outlined. To say that thing and thing codetermine each other is to say that the mediation of the continuity of discontinuity—that is, place—determines itself; that place itself determines itself is the fact that thing and thing codetermine each other. To say that we act intentionally is to say that the thing appears historically. To say that we act is not to say that the subject, such as is conceived from the standpoint of the opposition of subject and cognitive epistemological object, constructs the objective; it is to say that thing and thing codetermine each other expressively. The self becomes world; the world becomes self. The body is born of the world. But it is not the body alone that can be said to act intentionally. The self of intentional action is born from the depths of the actually existing historical world that itself expresses itself. When one speaks that way, what we call our free will may well become a problem. But in the world of the affirmation of absolute negation, the world of the continuity of absolute discontinuity, the singular thing absolutely possesses the significance of a freedom that itself determines itself. (A detailed explanation will have to be undertaken another day.)

The world that itself determines itself dialectically, as time-qua-space, space-qua-time, is the world that itself absolutely expressively determines itself. It may be that phenomenologists consider this to be merely the world of objects for the understanding, but to speak of determining the self itself expressively is to speak of reflecting the self within the self—more, it is to speak of seeing the self within the self—and that is to say that the thing truly acts, that the thing creates the thing itself. The expressive operation that expressively determines the self itself can be thought as our intentional action; all of our intentional action belongs to expressive activity. This, then, is the fact that the expressive world itself determines itself. What we call our active self is a singularity in the historical world; our intentional action arises from the depths of history. To act is to see; to see is to act. Even the creative activity of art must be in this sense a kind of intentional action. Even the fact that a thing acts physically must be thought from this standpoint. There is no such thing as a physical world apart from the historical world. The world of acting things can be conceived as the affirmation of negation in the dialectical world. The world of the simultaneity of instants can be conceived as the world of material substance. Something like reflective consciousness can be thought as its affirmative aspect. But even physical phenomena, as factual things that appear in the historical world, are objects for the understanding and thereby for thought. There is no senseless actuality whatever. What belongs to the understanding exceeds what belongs to thought, being greater in scope and more profound. Our intentional action arises from the depths of what belongs to the understanding. The world that infinitely itself expresses itself is the infinite world of understanding; it is the world that sees the thing in the mode of intentional action. Conversely, the world of active intuition is the world of expression, the world of the understanding. Even so-called nature is no more than something seen on the basis of active intuition. Yet it is only the person construed as the eye that sees the self without thinking the self from the perspective of the acting self who can conceive that the world of the understanding does not determine the self. However, the self of the understanding itself must be already within the world of history. To understand the history of the past is also to understand from the actually existing present. From the perspective of the present of active intuition, the world of expression, the world of understanding, can be conceived as the direction of its self-negation; the world of intentional action, the world of acting things, can be conceived as the direction of its affirmation. So the world of the intuition that sees things on the basis of intentional action can be conceived as the actual world in which the actually existing present always determines the present itself.

I think that even everything that can be conceived as the activity of consciousness is not to be conceived from the standpoint of the mutual relation of opposition of subject and what is objective; it should be thought from the standpoint of the self-determination of the dialectical world; that is, I think the world is to be conceived as the activity of giving form that gives form to the world itself. It is from such a standpoint that we must try to think the various differences and relations of our activities of consciousness. Just as it can be thought that in self-awareness the self sees the self in the self, at the heart of the activity of consciousness there must be thought to be a local determination. Thus, what is called "place" indicates that what we call the activity of consciousness cannot be isolated from the world; to the extent that it is thought to be actually existing, it must be the temporal aspect of the temporospatial world.

3

From the perspective of the knowing self, the actually existing present is conceived to be incessantly moving; the biological world is thought to develop from the physical world, the world of consciousness from the biological world, and the world of spirit from the world of consciousness. But the world of consciousness does not emerge from the physical world. It is moreover impossible that the world of biological life emerges from the physical world. It might be thought that it would be possible under certain conditions, but it is impossible under any conditions whatsoever. To speak of "under certain conditions" necessarily implies totality. Physical totality and biological life must be different. Contrary to this idea, I conceive what is called consciousness as the dialectical world's affirmation of negation; I conceive the biological world and the physical world alike to be within the world of history. Perhaps, to those who think of what is called consciousness only in terms of the consciousness of the individual person, such a conception might be thought to be contrary to the systematic order of development. But the fact that the discontinuous continues is the fact of consciousness; it is necessarily at the same time the fact that a thing acts. That which truly exists on the basis of itself is dialectical; dialectical actuality is necessarily conscious. Were that not the case, we could not speak of the absolute dialectic. Even the so-called physical world can thus be thought of as dialectical, but it is so as the infinitesimal minimum of the self-determination of time. Consciousness is therefore conceived to be something like a reflecting mirror. What itself acts by itself must be dialectical. The world of the mutual determination of singularities, the concrete material world, must be a world in which time, as time, possesses its autonomy absolutely. The thing that acts must be utterly linear; it must be conceived to emerge from nothing and to pass into nothing, as determination without that which determines. Considered in this way, perhaps the thing that acts might be construed as something like a merely personal self, but whatever the case, such determination must be conceived to be expressive. The individual person does not exist of itself. The individual person exists as the self-determination of the world of the continuity of discontinuity. Therefore, the individual person exists only on the basis of acting. And to say that it acts thus from the depths of nothing, to speak of nothing-qua-being, is not merely to speak of physical acting; it is necessarily to say that it expresses the self itself. To say that a singularity determines the singularity itself is necessarily to speak of acting expressively; our intentional action necessarily belongs to expressive activity. The mediation of the continuity of discontinuity must be expressive mediation; the space of the historical world must be expressive space. The world of historical actuality is that which itself determines itself expressively; it is that which, being nothing, itself determines itself. The true concrete material world must be comprehended subjectively. That which is conceived as the affirmation of absolute negation, and thereby as consciousness, is of the understanding. What is thought as consciousness's activity of understanding comes into being on that basis. Even something like a round triangle, as an object of the activity of our understanding, arises from the world of historical actuality that itself expressively determines itself; it arises from the depths of nothing. We usually conceive only the world determined as an object of knowledge to be the actually existing world. The world of expressive historical actuality is infinitely more profound, however, infinitely larger. It necessarily subsumes the object of understanding as well; so, too, our understanding selves must be therein.

We can thereby say that, as dialectical universal, the world of historical actuality that itself determines itself, itself expressively determines itself. What I have called the expressive universal necessarily means precisely this. It can be thought both that each singularity in the field of consciousness is independent and that all singularities are one. What is conceived as our unity of consciousness must be something like this. But in our unity of consciousness, each thing, moreover, is not truly independent. This is because the unity of consciousness is conceived subjectively. In the field of expression each thing must be independent; each thing must be a discontinuity. It is as the continuity of discontinuity that what is called expressive activity comes into being. Therefore, to say that a thing acts is to say that a thing itself expresses itself. And to speak of internal perception–qua–external perception, external perception–qua–internal perception, must be to say that the world expressively determines the world itself. In the artistic world all things express the self itself, and in the sense of emerging from nothing and entering into nothing, the artistic world is infinitely linear, temporal. The artistic world is the world of temporal space; therein, time is a simultaneous world. Moreover, that is not the simultaneity of instants; rather, therein time possesses the independence of time itself; it is spatial time. Even color must possess depth, even a line must be rhythmic. More, all that is, in the world of temporal space, must be rhythmic. It is as the self-determination of such a world that artistic expressive activity comes into being. It could only be from this standpoint that Fiedler conceived artistic expressive activity to arise from pure vision. The world of pure vision is a world in which the entire body has become the eye; it is the world of vision's expression. To pursue this further, we can consider what Riegl called "artistic will." What is called the world of artistic expression is not divorced from the world of historical actuality; on the contrary, the former is within the latter. Even what is called artistic expressive activity comes from the self-determination of the historical world that itself expressively determines itself. When we conceive that in the world of time-qua-space and space-qua-time, time is absolutely time, emerging from absolute nothing, entering into absolute nothing, to say that a thing acts is to say that a thing itself expresses itself; as the self-determination of expressive mediation, the world is necessarily a world that itself determines itself expressively. What is thought as the self-determination of such a world is, in terms of external perception, called understanding, in terms of internal perception, intentional action. This is at the same time to say that to see the thing on the basis of action is to speak of active intuition. To say that therein the thing is seen implies, as well, the sense of reflecting the thing. We speak of reflection as attenuated seeing. Understanding and action are the mutually opposed directions of expressive activity. But it is a matter of internal perception–qua–external perception, external perception–qua–internal perception; just as it is thought that divorced from internal perception there is no external perception, and divorced from external perception there is no internal perception, concretely there is no action divorced from understanding, and there is nothing of the understanding apart from action. Just as with internal perception and external perception, action and understanding are something like the inside and outside of expressive activity. Our intentional action does not arise from the so-called world of experience [*keiken*] but from the world of corporeal experience [*taiken*].[13] Thus, what is called the world of corporeal experience is the world of understanding. The world of mere understanding is an attenuation of the world of corporeal experience. Contrariwise, though we speak of the world of mere meaning or the world of mere understanding, these must nevertheless be intentionally active. Although one speaks of mere expression, it is that expression which provokes our action; it is that which affects us. One construes such worlds as divorced from historical actuality only from the abstract standpoint of the knowing self. The world of concrete historical actuality is the world of corporeal experience, the world of understanding, the world of action. So the world of things seen on the basis of action is the world that itself expresses itself. What is called free will is attenuated action; it is expressive activity bereft of expression, active intuition bereft of intuition. The world, centered on the active intuition that expressively determines the world itself, in the direction of its self-negation, in the direction of discontinuity, can be conceived as understanding that has attenuated active intuition; in the direction of its self-affirmation, in the direction of continuity, it can be conceived as something like what is called free will. It is at both extreme points of the self-determination of the historical world that mutually opposed englobing worlds can be conceived. So it is as the world of seen things that the world of phantom images, the world of visions and dreams, is seen. The historical can subsume even the world of dreams within itself. That, however, is absolutely not to lose the sense of active intuition. Understanding is that which attenuates the sense of action from active intuition; will is that which attenuates the sense of intuition from active intuition. Understanding and free will are therefore not mutually divorced from each other. When we call the world the affirmation of absolute negation, in the depths of negation the world of mere understanding comes into being; in the depths of affirmation, the world of free will comes into being. Thus the world of active intuition becomes the world of divine expression, the world of God's creation. We can say that it is only what belongs to free will, what leads astray, what bears the burden of original sin, that is God's greatest creation. It is because we hear the word of God in this world that we can speak of rising above the contradiction of the self and truly live. We say that the historical world possesses a circumference, but the transcendent is qua immanent, and the immanent is qua transcendent. What we call active intuition is absolute negation-qua-affirmation, absolute affirmation-qua-negation. That is to speak of the continuity of the absolutely discontinuous, the mutual determination of singularity and singularity; it is to say the many are the one. The thing that acts in the world of historical actuality is not merely what belongs to external perception but is necessarily what itself expresses itself; it is necessarily what expressively itself determines itself; it is necessarily what acts historically. Such a thing must possess infinite connections and affinities; from absolute negation it must enter into affirmation; it must traverse the world from one end to the other and is therefore conceived as temporally singular. Just as the instant is thought to touch upon eternity, so, too, the thing must be thought always to touch upon the depths of the world. What actively intuits possesses infinite connections and affinities.

What is called the world of actuality is the world of the mutual determination of singularity and singularity; to speak of the mutual determination of singularity and singularity is to speak of the self-determination of that which mediates the continuity of discontinuity. To say that a thing acts is perforce to say that the totality changes. To say that a singularity determines the singularity itself, to say that the thing acts, is to say that the thing affirms itself on the basis of itself negating itself. To say that the thing affirms itself on the basis of negating itself is necessarily to say that the thing first of all itself reflects itself. Although we usually speak of thing and thing mutually determining each other, that is not yet to conceive thing and thing as true singularities; it is to conceive of the continuous change of the mediation. That is not truly the affirmation of negation. That a thing acts and that a thing itself reflects itself are therefore thought to be absolutely different. The aspect of the self-determination of the dialectical universal, the aspect of the continuity of the discontinuous, must possess the sense of something like a reflecting mirror. To speak of reflection is to say that the absolutely other is the self; it is to say that the figure of the self is the self. And so, without positing that, as absolute negation-qua-affirmation, seeing the self in the absolutely other, there is nothing to call the self; that is to say, without acting there is no thing. There is no acting thing without reflecting the figure of the self itself, without seeing the self itself. It belongs to the mutual interaction of thing and thing that a phenomenon appears; to say that a phenomenon appears is to say that thing and thing interact. Thus, the fact that a phenomenon appears is that the mediation of the continuity of discontinuity, characterized as time-qua-space, space-qua-time—that is, physical space—itself determines itself. It is not that there is no experiential world without the thing in itself but that without the experiential world there is no thing in itself. It is the case that the actually existing world is the world of experience, and it is the world of the thing in itself. To conceive a world of acting things apart from the experiential world is metaphysics, which is no more than a kind of dream. In this sense even the natural-scientific materialism that negates consciousness is metaphysical. It is in fact for this reason that even in our common sense we think the world of material substance to be the actually existing world. But the world is a world of internal perception–qua–external perception, external perception–qua–internal perception. To speak of internal perception–qua–external perception, external perception–qua–internal perception is to speak of time-qua-space, space-qua-time. It is to speak of continuity-qua-discontinuity, discontinuity-qua-continuity. It is because a thing reflects the thing itself—more, that a thing sees the thing itself—that a thing acts. This is to posit phenomenon-qua-actuality, actuality-qua-phenomenon. The fact that the subject determines the objective and the objective determines the subject is the fact that the thing acts; conversely, that we see things on the basis of intentional action is active intuition. And that is the self-determination of the eternal now as time-qua-space, space-qua-time. Being nothing, creative activity itself determines itself. What is usually conceived as material substantial activity, however, is a conception of actuality as merely spatialized. The singularity that itself truly determines itself must be that which itself determines itself expressively; it must be that which acts expressively. To say that singularity and singularity mutually determine each other is to say that they mutually determine each other expressively. Singularity and singularity mutually determine each other on the field of expression. Conversely, it is as the self-determination of the expressive mediation that what is called the mutual determination of singularity and singularity is constituted. What is called the mediation of the affirmation of absolute negation is necessarily expressive. The self-determination of such an expressive mediation, the self-determination of the expressive world, is called intuition, the fact that things are seen on the basis of action. It is therein that the thing is created. This is the world of poiesis. I have frequently drawn on the example of artistic creative activity to clarify this characteristic of such determination. In saying this, I am not saying that the singular things that themselves expressively determine themselves exist a priori and then as their mutual determination constitute intuition. Without discontinuity there is no continuity. That intuition constitutes, that the thing is seen actively, is the fact that innumerable things expressively mutually determine each other. Because intuition is usually conceived merely subjectively, the fact that a thing acts and the fact of intuition are conceived to be heterogeneous facts. But intuition is, subject determining the objective, the objective determining the subject, to see the thing actively; and that is the fact of internal perception–qua–external perception, external perception–qua–internal perception, the fact of phenomenal appearance–qua-actuality, actuality-qua–phenomenal appearance. The world of expression, oriented toward external perception, toward discontinuity, can be conceived as the world of understanding; oriented toward internal perception, toward continuity, it can be conceived as the world of the will, the world of the abstract self. Therefore, the expressive world is not, as is usually thought, grounded in the physical world characterized as internal perception–qua–external perception, external perception–qua–internal perception; rather, the physical world is grounded in the expressive world. Nature is within history. The world of the truly concrete actuality of phenomenal appearance–qua-actuality, actuality-qua–phenomenal appearance of necessity is the world of the self-determination of the eternal now, characterized as absolute time-qua–space, space-qua–time. It is something like Pascal's infinite sphere without circumference in which everywhere becomes the center. In this sense even the physical world, characterized as internal/external perception, can be conceived as the actual world. Conversely, even what I call the world of the self-determination of the eternal now that itself expressively determines itself, in its self-negation, is utterly physical; it is the dialectical world of material substance. What is called the world of material substance for external perception is its dialectical significance reduced to its minimum; it is expressive sense reduced from expressive determination to its minimum. There is, however, no external perception that is not internal perception. So it is to the extent that it belongs to internal perception, to the extent that it is historical, that is to say, that it is necessarily expressive. It is in the world of concrete actuality, in the world of history, that the singularity itself determines itself expressively. Such is both of the understanding and is active. It belongs to corporeal experience in the fact that, emerging from the nothing, it enters into the nothing. That is thus actively to see the self itself. In expressive activity, acting is seeing, and seeing is acting. When, from expressive activity, seeing in the manner of internal perception is reduced to its minimum and seeing is conceived in terms of external perception, then seeing is conceived as mere reflection. Therein internal perception is conceived to be simply something like a reflecting mirror, and the field of expression becomes the field of consciousness. Because those who take up the standpoint of the knowing self do not think the self as being already the self-determination of the dialectical world, and construe the self as merely something like a seeing eye divorced from the world, they conceive the self as merely something like the field of consciousness of internal perception and think merely of the likes of the world of expression or the world of understanding. But it is necessarily from the present that one understands even the history of the past. The self is in the actually existing present. There is no world of understanding floating in the ether. In the world of history even dreams are actual. That they are thought to be not actual is because only nature is considered to be actual. Even the various illusions and mistakes that accompany our free will arise from the historical world. In the world that itself expressively determines itself, in emerging from the nothing we enter the nothing. Therein is what can be thought to be our free will, as determination without that which determines.

That, as the continuity of discontinuity, singularity and singularity mutually determine each other is the fact that they mutually determine each other expressively. That is the fact that thing and thing mutually determine each other historically; this is the fundamental significance of the fact that a thing acts. Even the fact that material substance acts does not escape this historicity. And thus the mediation of the continuity of discontinuity itself determines itself. Subject determines what is objective, and what is objective determines the subject; the subjective/objective world itself determines itself. A thing is formed subjectively/objectively. In terms of the subject, it is on the basis of our action that we see the thing; in terms of what is objective, the thing comes into being historically. The thing in the dialectical world, being itself absolutely temporal, is thought both as emerging from the nothing, entering into the nothing, and as absolutely in opposition to the spatial. When one thinks this way, both time and space are unmediated, self and thing cannot mutually relate, and what is called acting is impossible. There, we think of the tool. Usually, self and thing are thought to be actual, and the tool is merely a tool; but what we call a tool possesses the essence of the dialectical mediation of negation-qua-affirmation, affirmation-qua-negation. The tool is at once subjective and objective. So if we posit that without intentional acting, there is nothing we might call the self, then without instrumental mediation, there is no self. This is because without the body there is no self. In short, the world of the thing is the world of the tool. But it is only that which itself expressively determines itself that can possess the tool. That which possesses the tool, as the continuity of discontinuity, as the self-identity of what is absolutely mutually opposed, is necessarily that which itself determines itself. Animals are merely corporeal being. But it is necessarily the case both that man is corporeal being and that man's body is a tool. The self-determination of that which possesses the tool lies in seeing the thing on the basis of expression. And that, conversely, is the fact of the self-determination of the expressive world. Artistic creative activity is necessarily something like this. Fiedler's claim that artistic expressive activity arises when the entire body becomes eye must bear this sense. To say that, unlike animals, we possess the body as tool is to speak of human being; to say that we possess the body as tool is to say that we possess a thing that stands against the self as tool, which is, conversely, to say that the thing is corporeal. To say that thing and thing mutually oppose and determine each other is to say that they mutually determine each other corporeally. So it is only on the basis that our selves possess/ are merely instrumental bodies that there is the acting self; and it is only because there is the acting self that there is the self.[14] There exists the self only as the self-determination of the expressive world qua continuity of discontinuity. To say that a thing acts must be conceived from the fact that something acts. To say that something acts is to say that something acts in opposition to some other thing. Thus to say that thing and thing mutually determine each other is to say that totality as mediation itself determines itself. The singularity that itself determines itself dialectically, what truly acts, perforce itself expresses itself. To say that it expressively determines itself is to say that it possesses the thing as tool — that is, it possesses the self's body as tool — and conversely that the thing is corporeal. Thus it is as subject-qua–what is objective, what is objective–qua– subject that the mediation of the continuity of discontinuity itself determines itself, that the dialectical world determines the world itself, and the present determines the present itself. It is thus as the self-determination of the world that the thing appears. When we say we act, when we speak of the self expressively determining itself, there must always therein be the singularly determined world. Were that not the case, we could not say we act. The singularly determined world is the world of the unity of subject and the objective; it is the world of intuition. To speak of the intuitive world of the unity of subject and the objective is not merely to speak of something like a single work of art. It is to speak of the world of the dialectical unity of singularity and singularity; it is to speak of the world of acting things; it is to speak of the world of affirmation-qua-negation, time-qua-space. Artistic creative activity, as well, comes into being as the self-determination of such a world. We are already in such a world when we act. When we possess tools, already there is the world of the unity of an absolute rupture, the world of internal perception–qua–external perception. When we speak of seeing a thing cognitively, we suppose there is nothing of a tool involved; but our bodies are immediately tools.

Knowing and intentional action are thought to be oriented in opposite directions, but they are both oriented in opposite directions and yet must dialectically be one. From the standpoint of knowing, we regard our bodies as tools. To say that we regard our bodies absolutely as tools is to say, conversely, that the thing becomes corporeal. We cannot but say that, at the limit, the world becomes our body. But that is at the same time to say that what we call our bodies disappears; it is to say, that is, that the self disappears. There, the world is thought as the mere world of things. I have said, however, that the activity of our consciousness, as local determination, comes into being out of the self-determination of the dialectical world. I said that the fact that the thing acts as the continuity of discontinuity is the origin of consciousness. From the standpoint of the intentionally acting self, what is called the world of things is the world from which the self has disappeared, in the sense that the world has become our body; moreover, it is possible to say that because it is utterly corporeal, we are born therefrom, that the origin of our consciousness resides there. Our selves are absolutely what themselves expressively determine themselves; our selves come into being as the self-determination of the expressive world. Thus the expressive mediation must be corporeal. We are born as the self-determination of corporeal mediation. And therein the origin of consciousness is subsumed. Even the fact that material substance acts is rendered consciousness at the extreme limit of the self-negation of such corporeal determination. Therefore, the fact that material substance acts already possesses expressive significance. Even the world of material substance is actual as the self-determination of the historical world. On the basis of the mediation of the continuity of discontinuity, a singularity itself determines itself; the fact that a singularity acts is the fact that the thing becomes tool; conversely, the thing becomes our body. Thus the true singularity affirms itself on the basis of absolutely itself negating itself; each singularity is necessarily the affirmation of absolute negation. Having said that, it is necessary to delve ever deeper into the notion that we conceive the world of material substance at the extreme limit of the self-negation of corporeal determination. The internal perception–qua–external perception, external perception–qua–internal perception of which I have frequently spoken is the way of seeing from the standpoint of knowing; from the standpoint of intentional acting it is necessarily that the thing becomes the tool of the self and that, conversely, the thing becomes the body of the self. It is thus that we can truly clarify the significance of the continuity of discontinuity. That at the extreme limit of the self-negation of corporeal determination the material substantial world is rendered consciousness is moreover the fact that it is localized in terms of external perception and, furthermore, that it is captured in the standpoint of knowing. In the standpoint of truly acting the self is necessarily the affirmation of absolute negation; it must in emerging from nothing enter into nothing. When considered in this way, what is rendered consciousness at the extreme limit of the self-negation of corporeal determination is not something like the so-called world of material substance but must be the world of expression. Thus, what is conceived as external perception becomes the activity of understanding. I do not however thereby claim that what is called material substance disappears. The material substance that is being conceived here is dialectical substance. It is material substance conceived to be in the depths of the historical world. We can even say that the world of historical actuality is the acting of such material substance. Although a commodity is material substance, it is only from this perspective that we can say it is, in fact, a commodity. So external perception thus becomes the activity of understanding, and the activity of self-determination of a singularity that itself determines the singularity itself comes to belong to the will. Internal perception is what becomes the will. From the standpoint of knowing, knowing and acting are simply opposed, but in truth a singularity that itself determines itself, a singularity in the historical world, necessarily both belongs to the activity of willing and belongs to the activity of understanding. To say that we act is to say that a singularity itself determines itself; to say that a singularity acts necessarily is always also to say that the totality itself determines itself. Usually, when it is said that the self understands and the self wills, what is called the self is construed abstractly, but the self is not divorced from material substance or the body; even in understanding and willing, material substance and body do not disappear. And that is necessarily because the thing becomes the tool of the self; and, conversely, the world becomes the body of the self. Our selves come into being as singular determinations of the historical world. Our selves exist as dialectical singularities in the dialectical world. As I have said, it is because we possess our bodies as tools that there is already the affirmation of absolute negation; there is the reason why our selves are conceived as dialectical. What is called the acting self must possess the body as tool. Thus, there is nothing called the self that is not acting. What is called the tool is usually thought to be without relation to the self; it is thought that we can possess tools absolutely freely. It perhaps may thus be understood that when I say we possess our bodies as tools, the self is divorced from the thing. If one thinks that way, however, then the sense of "possessing" disappears, and that is nothing other than to lapse into an argument on the parallelism of mind and body. What we call the body is both the being of the self itself such as with animals and, in that it is a tool, is the being of the acting self. The self that is divorced from corporeal being does not exist. I say so because neither is the self merely corporeal being. The body is both thing and self. That is to possess the body as tool. We possess other tools as extensions of the body. In the historical world what we call the body is the body become one with the tool; it is the body of expressive activity; it is the artistic body. And that does not just begin anywhere but necessarily always emerges from the body of the self. Our personal bodies, being of the activity of understanding, as well as something like the moral body, must also be in this sense corporeal and material.

In the world of the self-determination of the continuity of discontinuity, in the world of historical actuality, a singular thing that itself determines itself, itself expressively determines itself. To express the self itself is to see the self in the other. That is the sense of "reflection." But to see the self in the other is not merely to reflect; it is to constitute the other; it is to render the self objective. This is necessarily to say that therein we possess the thing as tool, that we possess our bodies as tools, and, conversely, that the thing is corporeal. It is as the affirmation of the negation of such corporeal determination that the fact of seeing the thing comes into being. That is active intuition. The thing must be that which absolutely stands opposite the self. To constitute the thing must already be the affirmation of absolute self-negation. The fact that we act is that we are continually constituting the thing corporeally. But the self-determination of the singularity that absolutely itself determines itself comes into being on the basis of the self-determination of the mediation of the continuity of discontinuity; it comes into being from affirmation-qua–absolute negation. Corporeal determination itself comes into being from the self-determination of the world of the continuity of discontinuity, from the self-determination of the expressive world. At the extreme limit of corporeal determination it can be thought that the world becomes the body of the self and that the self itself loses the self. It is in such an affirmation of absolute negation that the fact of seeing the thing comes into being. Therefore, to see a thing is that the self sinks into the world, that the self disappears, and, at the same time, the self is born therefrom. We therefore know our bodies from outside; we know them from out of the expressive world. We do not know the expressive world from out of the self. When a singularity, as the continuity of discontinuity, itself absolutely determines itself, then, as I went on to say, we necessarily possess the thing as tool and, conversely, the thing is necessarily corporeal. In the fact that we possess bodies lies the existentialist dialectic. But that is not yet the true absolute dialectic. To say the dialectic merely belongs to practice or intentional action cannot escape the limitations of this standpoint. In the absolute dialectic we must say that the self, being the continuity of absolute rupture, is born of the world of things. However far one may take the observation that biologically a child is born of parents, it never reaches the point of speaking of being born of things. To speak of being born of things is to say the subject is born of the objective. That is to speak of intuition; it is to speak of truly seeing the thing. What I call "determination without that which determines," or the "determination of the absolute nothing," means nothing other than this; I am not simply saying that being comes out of nothing. Usually when we think of seeing the thing, we think the self is simply passive, but a "passive activity" is the relation of mutual determination of the thing and the thing construed in terms of an epistemological object; already, the self is rendered a cognitive epistemological object. There must be an absolute rupture between subject and the objective. Moreover, there is the fact that, as the affirmation of absolute negation, we see the thing. In that we see things, there is the affirmation of absolute negation. The thing must be a thing seen before it becomes a tool: the thing must be a thing. Something like the thing in itself is not a thing; it is no more than a negative limit concept. We construe the fact of seeing a thing as merely passive because we conceive the thing in terms of physics. But a concrete thing must have a historical actuality; reality must be historical actuality. Just as we think the instant touches on eternity, so, too, the self is born when we see things. The acting self is the seeing self. Perhaps it may be thought that in speaking thus, what are called our selves are thought to belong, instant by instant, to the thing and that there is no independent quality of being of the self; but to think so is already to be thinking in terms of physics. The thing must be a historical thing; the thing must be expressive. To speak of seeing historical expressive things is to say that the self is a historical singular thing that absolutely itself determines itself singularly. What is expressive is what affects the self. Even the fact that we possess bodies dialectically comes into being on that basis (even what is called "impulse" comes into being on that basis). Our action begins there, and it ends there. Historical actuality is the alpha and omega of our action. If one posits that the self is temporal and the thing is spatial, and that subject and the objective, self and thing, as the self-identity of what is absolutely mutually opposed, are unified dialectically, then maybe self and thing are unified in something like circling an infinite boundary; but, in fact, we possess bodies; we see things on the basis of action; things affect us; seeing is acting; the world of the most common-sensical actuality is the absolute dialectical world: it is from there that we can conceive the infinite boundary of space and time. Even what is called the universe must be conceived from here. The antinomies of the world are not at the boundaries of the world: they are "here." Already, in internal cognitive perception–qua–external cognitive perception, external cognitive perception–qua–internal cognitive perception, there is the unity of absolute contradiction. Thus it is therein that there is the body; it is necessarily to see the thing on the basis of action, it is that the thing is seen. Already, that is the self-determination of expressive mediation.

THE ACTIVITY OF OUR CONSCIOUSNESS is not, as is usually thought, the acting of an abstract self divorced from this world but is that which necessarily comes into being as the self-determination of the dialectical world of time-qua-space, space-qua-time. Contrariwise, as I said above, the fact that a singularity determines the singularity itself, the fact that the thing acts, is that the thing makes the thing itself appear, that the thing reflects the thing itself; the coming into being of the material world is already conscious.[15] But even such dialectical determination should be thought from the actual world of seeing the thing on the basis of action.

In actuality, the singularity that itself affirms itself on the basis of itself absolutely negating itself, first of all itself determines itself corporeally. But corporeal determination is not the affirmation of absolute negation. When we speak of the affirmation of absolute negation, the thing is not a tool; the thing appears from the thing itself; it is necessarily that it itself expresses itself. The thing is born therein, and it is there that there is creation. It can be thought of as something like the activity of artistic creation. But of course the activity of the self-determination of a singularity that itself determines itself does not arise from the independent thing itself. It comes into being as the self-determination of the mediation of the continuity of discontinuity; it comes into being as the self-determination of the world that itself expressively determines itself. We can even think that, as Bergson said, our bodies are the traces left by the flow of élan vital that has broken through material substance. From my standpoint élan vital is nothing other than the self-determination of the expressive world. Our bodies themselves are formed from élan vital as expressive self-determination. What we call the tool has already come into being as the process of self-determination of the world of the affirmation of absolute negation. This is why I say the self is born when the thing is born. What the artist has made is not simply his own creation. It must be divine inspiration. Seeing is therefore acting, and acting is therefore seeing. We think of thing and self as unrelated because we see from the standpoint of knowing. From the standpoint of acting the thing is necessarily *pragma*. All of cognitive perception must be of such a nature. That we possess things as tools is conversely that thing becomes body, that world becomes body, which is the fact that the self loses itself. The thing, from the standpoint of the affirmation of self-negation—that is, conforming to the standpoint of the corporeal determination of the world—is what is seen. Conversely, our bodies come into being as singular determinations of the world of cognitive perception. The self-determination of the world of cognitive perception can be conceived as impulsive. Impulsive force constitutes our bodies; the thing for cognitive perception is seen "impulsively." Of course, in such a case I do not know whether it is accurate to call the thing a tool. In such a case the tool is like an organ. If we pursue such a corporeal determination of the world even further, then we possess bodies as tools, and the thing becomes *pragma*. Even the

creative activity of the artist is born as the affirmation of absolute negation at the extreme limit of such determination. It is what possesses the
significance of the singular determinations of the expressive world.

I do not say, however, that the dialectical world of the affirmation of
absolute negation, the world that itself absolutely determines itself expressively, is thereby merely the world for cognitive perception. It follows
that the world of historical actuality that itself expressively determines
itself is not artistic. In the absolutely dialectical world, a singularity that
itself determines itself must be that which itself determines itself absolutely. That singularity does not simply belong to cognitive perception
but necessarily belongs to action. That at the extreme limit of the self-
negation of corporeal determination even artistic intuition, as the affirmation of negation, comes into being is, of course, because our selves are
active. Corporeal determination, conceived as the mediation of the continuity of discontinuity, as the mediation of subject/objective, is not what
is ordinarily conceived of as our bodies. The singularity that itself determines itself in the absolutely dialectical world is not something like a singularity as conceived according to a simply abstract logic; when posited
from the perspective of the thing itself, it is necessarily that which first
of all and absolutely itself determines itself corporeally. The fact of the
self-determination of a singularity itself is first of all necessarily the fact
that thing becomes tool and the fact of an infinite labor in the imperative
becoming-self of thing. That is necessarily an infinite labor. And therein
is the fact that we possess bodies. The body as conceived in the world
of cognitive perception, which is also what is usually called the body,
is not merely a thing. It follows that even though we speak of the self-
determination of a singularity in the dialectical world of the affirmation
of absolute negation, it does not escape such corporeal determination.
On the contrary, it is only in mediating such determination that it can be
said to be singular determination in the absolutely dialectical world. Even
what we call speculation or the will are not divorced from such corporeal determination. When the body of knowing and perception that we
usually think of as the body, being a singularity in the historical world,
becomes the historical body, then it belongs both to the understanding
and speculation, and also to will and action. And there we can say that
our bodies belong to expressive activity, and man can be said to possess

the *logos*. Necessarily: *homo faber* qua *homo sapiens*. I think it interesting that the Hebrews could not conceive of the being of individual personal life apart from the flesh and were, moreover, sensible of the necessity of the body, even in the personal existence of the world to come, and finally arrived at a conception of something like the body of the soul. Man is a singularity mediated by the mediation of the affirmation of absolute negation. In man, therefore, there is the fact of seeing as absolute negation-qua-affirmation, so we can say that to see is to act. When we see the dialectical world from the standpoint of the self-determination of only one singularity, then merely the body of cognitive perception is being conceived. When we take up this standpoint, then the thing that stands over against the self on the basis of the mediation of the continuity of discontinuity is the tool, and, conversely, the thing is conceived as corporeal. The acting self and the world of things comes into being. That which pursues this standpoint as far as possible is practical life activity. Of course, even this is an aspect of the self-determination of the dialectical world. The fact that we possess tools is already dialectical. But that is the dialectical world seen from the standpoint of the self-determination of only one singularity. Seen from this standpoint, there is no Thou, and there is no passage from the I toward the Thou. Were the I and the Thou to become one, it would be nothing other than the I and the Thou each itself negating itself and, as material substance, becoming one. In terms of knowledge, what is usually called the world is the fact that multiplicity is based on the standpoint of the self-determination of one singularity. Such is the world seen on the basis of the self-negation of the world as the extreme limit of the expansion of a single corporeal self. Although the term *negation* is used, it is nothing more than the self-negation of simply one singularity. Artistic intuition, as well, is nothing more than intuition qua affirmation of absolute negation consequent on corporeal determination in the dialectical world such as I have discussed above. Yet the world of the absolute dialectic is the world of the mutual determination of singularity and singularity, the world of the self-determination of the mediation of the continuity of discontinuity. In such a world simply one singularity must itself absolutely determine itself. Although we speak of artistic intuition as objective, that is rather because it is conceived to be subjective and individual. Of course, I am not thereby saying that art is merely individual. Artistic intuition comes into being in the affirmation of absolute negation. That is already to have come into being in the self-determination of the absolute dialectical world itself. It is from that world that the artist's body is born. It is said to belong to knowledge in conforming to the corporeal determination that is a moment of the self-determination of the dialectical world. (I defer discussion of artistic intuition to another day.)

In the self-determination of the dialectical world, one singularity absolutely itself determines itself, which constitutes the infinite labor of the singularity. It, moreover, comes into being as the self-determination of the dialectical world. The fact that we possess things as tools comes into being as already dialectical determination. That a thing acts is the fact of the self-determination of the mediation of the continuity of discontinuity. From the standpoint of the singularity, that is conceived as self-affirmation; from the standpoint of the self-determination of the world, it is self-negation oriented toward discontinuity. The affirmation of the self-negation of the dialectical world necessarily surpasses even artistic intuition. Intuition does not end simply with artistic intuition. What, as the affirmation of the self-negation of the dialectical world — that is, what is seen on the basis of active intuition — is the Idea. We can say that the Idea is the content of the self-determination of the expressive world: it belongs to the *logos*. Greek philosophy conceived the world of such Ideas to be the actually existing world. As the content of active intuition, the Idea is not limited to the artistic. Be it ethical or logical, it is the content of *nous*. What is conceived as the self-determination of the expressive world is reason. When what we call our bodies, as the self-determination of the singularity subsumed within the self-determination of the dialectical world, are historical, they come to belong to expressive activity. Thus, in seeing the thing in terms of expressive activity, the thing itself expressively manifests itself. It is therein that we possess consciousness. As I said at the beginning, consciousness is grounded in the affirmation of such negation of the world itself. The historical body, however, belonging to expressive activity, does not stop at "being conscious of"; as the affirmation of absolute negation, it necessarily belongs to the understanding. Therein the expressive world that has surpassed the knowing body comes into being. And so it is as that which possesses the character of the affirmation of the world of absolute negation that it can first be conceived to reflect the world of things. Therein the world of phantom images, the world of phenomenal appearances, comes into being. In such a case we wonder if the self has been divorced from the body, because we surpass the cognitive body. The fact that it is considered in this way is only because what we call our bodies are conceived according to an idea of the materialist body. Our bodies must be conceived according to an idea that belongs to activity. The true body is necessarily that which is born and dies in the historical world. Even a dream is still a historical fact. Ideology, as well, is necessarily a historical product. In this sense ideology, too, is actual. We can differentiate between whether actuality is seen as merely nature or is seen as historical on the basis of whether the body is constrained by cognitive perception. All of what is seen expressively from the standpoint of the self-determination of a singularity, itself enveloped within the dialectical world, are phantom images. Because, however, the self-determination of such a singularity comes into being on the basis of the self-determination of the dialectical world, in its affirmation of absolute negation it is always intuitive. Therein it can be conceived, as self-determination of the eternal now, to touch upon what is eternal. What counts as apodictic evidence for knowledge must be intuition in this sense. Seen from the standpoint of the self-determination of the singular thing, even knowledge can be conceived as tool. Knowledge, however, is not merely tool; as the self-determination of a singularity, enveloped within the self-determination of the dialectical world, conversely we become the tool of knowledge. Just as the body of the artist is art's machine, so, too, the body of the scholar is scholarship's machine. The life of the artist resides in beauty, the life of the scholar in truth. Even what is called the activity of thinking is not divorced from our bodies. To the extent that thinking is conceived as activity, it cannot come into being apart from the self-determination of a singularity. Knowledge comes into being as the self-determination of a singularity. That is necessarily its facticity. Otherwise, it would not be knowledge. Knowledge, however, is not simply that. Knowledge comes into being because what is singular is conceived as the self-determination of what is universal. Of course, in speaking this way I am not saying that our bodies are merely a relation to beauty or truth. Our corporeal activity, as the singular determination of the dialectical world, is characterized as antivalue. Having said that, however, it is also the case that neither is our corporeal activity merely characterized as antivalue. The corporeal self is a self-contradictory singularity. Necessarily, it belongs to corporeal experience. If we posit the idea of beauty as what is seen in the affirmation of the self-negation of our bodies in cognitive perception, then the idea of the good is that which is seen all the more profoundly in the affirmation of the negation of the body of expressive activity. In the sense that we possess the thing of cognitive perception as tool and conversely the thing becomes body, the idea seen in the affirmation of self-negation of our historical bodies is the idea of nature. Here, *nature* does not mean the material world of substance, as in physics, but means intuitive nature as it is ordinarily conceived. It is nature seen by means of the body; "nature" for the artist is the culmination of such nature. But the thing in the world of dialectical history is not simply the thing of cognitive perception. The thing is social; our bodies, too, are social: everything is *Gemeinschaftliche*. What is seen in the affirmation of the negation of such a corporeal self is the moral idea. Even something like the idea of philosophical truth is an idea seen in the affirmation of the self-negation of the human body. That, however, is not to say it is either nonhuman or ahistorical. It is what is seen from the standpoint of the affirmation of the negation of the totality of historical man. It is therefore not something unchanging. The self-determination of the historical world moves dialectically from epoch to epoch. Although the idea of art, as the affirmation of the negation of the body of and for cognitive perception, is natural, that is not to say that art does not reflect a people or an epoch. Our bodies of and for cognitive perception are both biological and, to the extent they are conceived as expressive activity, necessarily historical. It is as such that for the first time we can see the artistic idea as the affirmation of its negation. But an exhaustive treatment of the differences and relations of various ideas is not here and now my purpose.

Seen from the standpoint of the singular determination that itself absolutely mediates itself, the dialectical world is the world that determines the self itself from an infinite number of singularities; seen from the standpoint of each singularity, the world is the world of tools. But the singularity is a singularity because it is a singularity as against other singularities; the world of the mutual determination of singularity and singularity is the world of the self-determination of the mediation of the continuity of discontinuity. A singularity comes into being as the self-determination of what is universal. We can say that the self-determination of an infinite number of singularities is the self-determination of the world, the forming activity of the world. Furthermore, one can call the corporeal self the machine of the self-determination of the world. Thus, such a world can be conceived as the world of active intuition in which subject determines the objective, and the objective determines subject, a world in which we see the thing on the basis of intentional action, and the thing determines our action; it can be conceived as the world of the self-determination of the eternal now, the present determining the present itself. That is the world of our everydayness, the world of phenomenal appearance-qua-actuality. As singular determinations of such a world, we possess bodies. As singular determinations of such a world, our bodies are historical bodies. As such corporeal selves, we possess consciousness; we both see infinite expression in our exteriority and possess infinite freedom in our interiority; we belong to both the understanding and the will. Even the history of the past can be conceived from here. Even the past is within the eternal now. The practice of physics happens here; the projects of the future begin from here. What is called reason is the activity of self-determination, the forming activity, of such a world. In that the present determines the present itself, the world belongs to reason; reason is the mutual determination of expressive thing and thing. We can even speak of the self-determination of the expressive world. Even what is called reason is not distanced from the self-determination of the historical world. In this sense actuality belongs to reason; reason is actual.

4

What is called the absolutely dialectical world is a world in which a singularity absolutely determines the singularity itself. To say that the world, as negation-qua-affirmation, affirmation-qua-negation, itself determines itself, that is, that the world subjectively/objectively, singularly itself determines itself, must at the same time be to say that an infinite number of singularities themselves determine themselves. Logically speaking, to say that a singularity determines the singularity itself is to say that the singularity itself absolutely becomes the mediation of itself: self becomes world. Thus to posit that as actually material determination is necessarily to speak of possessing the thing as tool, and conversely to say that thing becomes tool. Such corporeal determination of a singularity, however, comes into being as the singularity's determination of the dialectical world; it comes into being from the self-determination of the world. When we speak of a singularity itself determining itself, we necessarily speak of the world in that determination. There is no such thing as a simple singularity in isolation. From the standpoint of the self of intentional action, we corporeally affect the thing by our intentional action; we create the form of the thing, subject determines object. The thing that has been formed, however, is something divorced from our intentional action; the thing possesses its own independence; thus, conversely, the thing affects us; object determines subject. Furthermore, the thing is not simply formed by our intentional action; the thing is born of the thing itself. Thus, even what we call the body is a thing; even what we call our intentional action does not merely arise from our selves but is necessarily born of the world of things. Our selves are necessarily born of the world of things. That is the self-determination of the dialectical world. That is what we in our common sense call the world. The truly concrete world must be this sort of thing. Still, we have not truly been able to think through what is given to us to think in the concept of the world in which we live. Even the fact that we possess tools is already necessarily dialectical. Perhaps one may conceive the physical world to be the world, but our selves are not born of the physical world. It is precisely the scientist's world that is conceived abstractly.

It must be thought that when a singularity dialectically and subjectively/objectively itself determines itself, it itself corporeally determines itself. But our bodies are not born of simply one individual self. Our bodies are born of our parents, and our parents in turn are born of their parents. Such determination is what I conceptualize as the mediation of the singular thing itself absolutely determining itself. But that corporeal life must already be grounded in the self-determination of the expressive world. Even corporeal life must already be that which makes form; it must already be the activity of forming. There must be shape or form in life. There must already be the eidetic in life; there must be intuition.

What we call our life does not merely flow from past to future but comes into being as temporospatial local determination; it comes into being as the self-determination of the eternal now. Something like what Bergson called life is no more than mere internal continuity. Without seeing form, life is no more than something like a strong feeling. Concrete life must be like sculpture and the plastic arts. Life is frequently conceived to be musical, but music, as well, must possess form. In the differentiation between form and substance, form is conceived to be abstract and subjective, but that is an idea rather than form. Form is necessarily that which possesses force. A thing is that which possesses form. Even what are conceived as the impulses of the flesh are necessarily constituted as the singular determinations of the expressive world. When our bodies are conceived as physical scientific synthesis, then even something like "impulse" is necessarily meaningless. Yet as the self-determinations of singularities in the absolutely dialectical world, our corporeal bodies are necessarily infinite labor; they are necessarily "impulsive." Thus even the thing is not merely physical scientific substance, but the object of desire. We therefore live as members of the biological world. Our biological comportment is the activity of forming of the biological world. Of course, because what we call the biological body is not an absolute singularity, it is perhaps necessary to conceive that in the depths of the biological body there is that which is called material substance that both negates and gives birth. Such material substance, however, is not something like what physics calls substance but must be something like "historical substance." Substance for the natural sciences is that which, as much as possible, excludes its very singularity from the corporeal determination such as discussed above; it is, as it were, a body that possesses no tools. From the standpoint of the historical world, physical or material activity is conceived beginning from the fact of corporeal determination. This is usually conceived as the personalization of nature. But that does not project subject into object. All singularities that in the historical world themselves determine themselves possess the significance of corporeal determination.

Corporeal determination, constituted in thing-as-tool and conversely the thing becoming-body, is not necessarily limited to our biological bodies. Our bodies are necessarily historical. Our bodies are constituted as the self-determination of the absolutely dialectical historical world, and they possess the characteristics of its singular determination. What is called life is constituted as the affirmation of absolute negation. That is the forming activity of the historical world. Although we speak of biological life, life is, in fact, nothing other than this. Even what is called the biological body must be that which is formed by the self-determination of the historical world. To say that we are born historically is not simply to say that our conscious selves are born historically but that the self which possesses a body is born; the corporeal self is born. Neither is it to say that the conscious self is appended to our bodies. What forms the body is what forms the conscious self; what forms the conscious self is what forms the body. Our bodies necessarily belong originarily to expressive activity. Conversely, the activity of consciousness is nothing other than the affirmation of absolute negation. What lives possesses consciousness, but only we humans make conceptual differentiations (here, the term *consciousness* is being used, as at the beginning of this essay, in its most fundamental sense). Our corporeal selves, our actual selves, are not born of the biological world; they are born of the absolutely dialectical historical world. Therefore, our selves are thought to be constituted socially; they are always socially determined. Just as our individual bodies are not conceived to be constituted as merely individual bodies but are constituted as single links in the chain of biological life, so, too, our individual selves are not constituted as merely individual selves but as members of historically constituted societies. "*Gemeinschaft*" could well be called the "species" of the historical world constituted by historical life (Tönnies's *Gemeinschaft* as social organism). Just as an animal is thought to be within a "species," and to be within a "class," so, too, we are within a *Gemeinschaft* and are, moreover, thought to be within an epoch. We see things on the basis of intentional action; conversely, things determine us; as the self-determination of the historical world in which we are born of the world of things, we must first of all conceive the world of living things in which we possess things as tools and conversely the thing becomes body. It is in the world of living things that we must conceive our selves to be born. But if that were all, there would be nothing of seeing. The historical body necessarily both acts and sees. It is only thus that we are able truly to speak of the singularity that in itself negating itself affirms itself. Thus the world that, when we see the thing on the basis of intentional action, historically determines us is not merely biological but necessarily social. This is not to say that the biological world disappears; on the contrary, it is entirely nature. But nature must, as the world of the affirmation of absolute negation, be thoroughly expressive; conversely, it must belong to the understanding. Primitive man behaved in accord with the *Gemeinschaft*, understood in accord with the *Gemeinschaft*, and saw things in accord with the *Gemeinschaft*. Therefore it is thought that the historical world begins with *Gemeinschaft*. It may be that materialists conceive nature on the basis of society, and idealists on the basis of spirit, but both society and spirit must together be constituted as the self-determination of the historical world of acting intuition. The fact of seeing is the self-determination of the historical world rendered infinitesimal and is conceived as the biological world. Conversely, our practical life activity can also be thought as the extension of biological life.

WHEN THE WORLD of the mediation of the continuity of discontinuity itself determines itself, then the world both absolutely itself determines itself universally and itself determines itself singularly; it both itself mediates itself spatially and itself mediates itself temporally. It is therein that the *Gemeinschaftliche* can be conceived. The animal "species" can be conceived in that way, but in biological life time is possessed of no autonomy. What concretely exists as the self-determination of the dialectical world is neither merely a singularity nor simply the universal. It is necessarily both singular and universal, temporal and spatial. It is for this reason that although we speak of the material substantial world, to the extent that it is dialectical, it logically must possess "social" characteristics. To speak in this way might be considered to create a groundless analogy, but as I said at the very beginning, acting reflects the self; in this sense the material substantial world too is conscious; that which renders infinitesimal the expressive determination of the world that itself expressively determines itself is the material expressive world. Society, however, must in one aspect be material and substantial. An extensive singularity must be a singularity that itself absolutely determines itself; as the world of the continuity of the absolutely discontinuous, the world that itself expressively determines itself is what itself socially constitutes itself. Conversely, the world that itself socially constitutes itself is the world that itself expressively determines itself. In this sense, even the world of animals can be said to be social. The world of animals comes into being neither merely as the self-determination of the material/substantial world nor merely as the self-determination of the world of consciousness but necessarily also as the self-determination of the expressive world. The body, too, possesses the significance of the self-determination of a singularity in such a world. It may be thought that I conflate animal and man even with regard to the immaterial. I do not say they cannot be differentiated; still, I would attempt to think the differentiations of the abstract world beginning from the concrete world. Even the variously differentiated worlds are within the world of history. It is beginning from the world of history that its differentiations and relations must be clarified.

To posit that the world determines itself is necessarily to posit that the world itself changes itself; it is necessarily to posit that it moves by itself. To say that a thing changes or that a thing moves is necessarily to say that opposing things become one. The more that opposing things are necessarily thought to become one, the more we must say the thing moves. But what sort of thing might such a unity be? Of course if we merely think of things as arranged in a row, then we cannot conceive of a moving world. Indeed, that cannot even be a generic unity. Even though we conceive of a graduation of specific differences after the manner of abstract logic, that is not the moving world.[16] The essential principle of differentiation is not a truly moving essential principle. In the moving world there is nothing that is merely particular. When many people think about what is called the development of the world, they conceive it according to a biological concept as teleological. This is to think unity as a singularity. When the independence of the particular is negated and the particular is subsumed under the unity of the logical subject, something like the *Ding an sich* is conceptualized; but when we conceive that the particular possesses its independence, and moreover bears the significance of totality, a teleological unity is conceptualized. But it goes without saying that in the world of the *Ding an sich*, and in the teleological world, as well, each thing cannot be independent. It cannot be said to be a world of the self-identity of opposed things, nor is it a world that includes absolute negation within itself. It is not a world that moves by itself. The world that moves of itself must be a world that includes absolute negation within itself; it must be a world of the unity of absolute contradiction. What itself determines itself within such a world must be the *Gemeinschaftliche*. Both temporal and spatial, spatial and temporal, it itself determines itself temporal-spatially. What, as the unity of contradiction, actualizes itself must possess the characteristics of such local determination. What, as self-determination of the eternal now, *is*, must be the actually existing present that itself determines itself. It is that which possesses the characteristics of what I call the world of active intuition; it is the world that corporeally determines the thing; it is the world of seeing the thing corporeally. The body I speak of here is not simply the biological body; it is the body of expressive activity, which means the historical body. Of course, that is not to say that it is no longer biological. The essential will must be biological, corporeal. The singularity that itself determines itself is necessarily utterly corporeal. I have said that to posit that the singular self in the absolutely dialectical world itself absolutely determines itself is to say that, possessing thing as tool, conversely thing becomes body; to posit that at the extreme limit, world becomes body is that the self loses the self, and that it is therefrom that the self is born. Therein we are inconsistent with creative activity. We must think so from the standpoint of the intentionally acting self. Thus, creative activity, conceived to be absolutely in the profound depths of the historical world, as the self-determination of the absolutely dialectical world, is necessarily that which creates so-called material substance. What is made on the basis of such creative activity—that is, what is determined as the self-determination of the dialectical world—must be thought to be *Gemeinschaftliche*. As the self-determination of the expressive world, it possesses the significance of seeing the thing in itself. It is the world that possesses one kind of *paradeigma*. In the world of active intuition, the thing must be both tool and *paradeigma*.

In the self-determination of the dialectical world, that is, in the affirmation of its negation, what is singular is thought first of all itself to determine itself corporeally; that is, in possessing something other as tool, conversely something other becomes body. But that must already be both the affirmation and the negation of the self itself. In its ground it must be inconsistent with the genesis of biological life; it must be inconsistent with élan vital; it must be inconsistent with that which gives birth to life. Therein, the linear must already be circular; élan vital is not simply something flowing but is necessarily that which we should call the self-determination of the eternal now. It must have something of the nature of the model. Creative activity is necessarily form-giving activity. But there is no seeing in biological life processes. The affirmation of absolute negation is necessarily to see the thing on the basis of intentional action; thus, to see is necessarily to act. The true body must belong to expressive activity. Therein, we possess consciousness. Consciousness, however, does not begin here; consciousness does not issue from the body. As I said in section 2, consciousness is necessarily the affirmation of absolute negation. To say that a thing acts is necessarily to say that a thing reflects itself. From the perspective of the opposition of subject and object, what is called acting and what is called consciousness are conceived as complete and separate things. But from the standpoint of the world of historical actuality, acting is necessarily to reflect: necessarily, phenomenal appearance-qua-actuality. But even though we speak of reflection, that is not yet seeing. It is nothing more than an abstract affirmation that belongs to merely corporeal determination. In order for us to speak of seeing the thing on the basis of intentional action, there must be a single world that itself determines itself. The affirmation of the self-negation of the absolutely dialectical world is not merely biological but must be social. That is what we call the self-determination of the historical world; therein our bodies are expressive activity. As the affirmation of self-negation of a singularity in such a world, that is, on the basis of intentional action, we do not merely constitute the self—that is, we do not merely live biologically—but we make things objectively; we see the idea objectively. We see the idea corporeally. In such a world the thing is not merely tool but *paradeigma*. What I call social determination is not, as is usually thought, something like the constitutive principle of society abstracted from its historical basis. It is the activity of self-determination of the world of the affirmation of absolute negation. Even what we call myth is not merely subjective but the constitutive principle of such a world. Durkheim said that society is not a kingdom within a kingdom but a part of nature, its highest manifestation; but that must be thought exhaustively in its most profound sense. To call society nature is necessarily the significance of historical nature. Ordinarily, society is considered something like a kingdom within a kingdom, but considered from the standpoint of the activity itself of the self-determination of the dialectical world, the world might well be said itself to determine itself concretely and socially. The dialectical world, which is the affirmation of absolute negation, on the one hand can be thought, in that it is corporeal, to be the flow of life that infinitely itself determines itself, as élan vital; and on the other hand, it is the fact of being absolutely able to see the self itself and of being able to see what, as social determination, belongs to the idea. Thus, it is in the direction of the absolute negation of such a world that the world of material substance can be conceived; its affirmation-qua-negation can be thought to be reflecting consciousness; contrariwise, in the direction of its absolute affirmation, the personal world can be conceived. Even what is called the world of "personality" is established according to social determinations. When the world is seen merely as perceptual or epistemological object, then the world of material substance is conceived to be the most universal, the primary world, and something like the biological world or society is conceived to be merely a particular, secondary world.

From the standpoint of a singularity determining itself, the self-determination of the dialectical world is necessarily corporeal. But it is fundamentally necessarily creative; our bodies live on the basis of élan vital. Thus, what is called creative activity necessarily comes into being as the self-determination of the eternal now. The fact that a thing is made can be conceived neither as an effect of material necessity nor on the basis of a teleological causality. When each discrete actual present touches upon eternity, it is necessarily subsumed within the eternal now; the circle must be said to determine itself. The self-determination of the world of affirmation-qua–absolute negation must be this kind of thing. Élan vital must therefore have something about it of the model. On this point I differ from Bergson, who thought space to be merely negative. Just as when we conceive biological life to belong to élan vital, it is necessarily conceived as already the self-determination of the eternal now, so to conceive that our bodies are expressively active and to conceive of the development of historical life, it is necessary to conceive them as the self-determination of that which is absolutely eternal. It is thus that we can say the world of history is truly creative. Each discrete thing that exists in such a world, as actually existing presents that themselves determine themselves, is necessarily that which possesses the characteristics of a single world. *Gemeinschaft* is necessarily such a thing; it must be formed on the basis of the forming activity of the world of history. The animal's species is also such a thing. Still, it never goes so far as expressively determining the self itself. Just as species opposes species, *Gemeinschaft* opposes *Gemeinschaft* and must be thought to exist simultaneously in the eternal now. That is not the particular conceived as the determination of the universal; we should say, rather, that the particular itself determines itself. As Goethe conceived the development of living being as metamorphosis, so we must think even the development of the historical world. Still, true creative evolution is neither teleological development nor pure duration. True creative activity is necessarily that which creates such a world. The self-determination of the world of the eternal now must be the true creative activity. It is necessarily that which determines what itself infinitely determines itself; of necessity, it is the fact that what is made, makes; it is necessarily to say that what is enveloped is equal to what envelops. A single species of animal is thought to be continually developing of itself, but in fact it is the development of the teleological world. A species can mutate, however, in a flying leap at a certain time, as in De Vries's explanations of sudden mutations.[17] We can think that therein is a kind of creative activity. Of course, we probably should not consider the sudden mutation of an animal as creation altogether, but in the true development of life there must always be such creative activity. This is not simply to say that what is merely potential becomes manifest. It appears to go against reason, but we must say that what is not implicated is implicated; it is the fact of the self-identity of what is independent, the simultaneous existence of temporalities. Therein we must conceive the originary structure of creative life. I call the process of such creative evolution "metamorphosis." It is in this sense that we must conceive the activity of forming, life; or, rather, the activity of modeling. Of course, what I am calling "originary structure" is not that which can be known conceptually; it can only be seen. It is what is seen on the basis of acting, as in artistic creative activity; or rather, acting is the self-manifestation of the originary structure itself. Perhaps when we speak of structure, it might be thought to be something like a mere pattern, but it is creative activity itself. Were we to say how teleological development and creative evolution differ, we would say that in the former, a one contains the others or contains the totality; a one itself harbors infinite potential in the depths of itself; a one possesses infinite possible directions; but in creative evolution, what exists is that which is absolutely determined; it is what is made; it is a single limit and can be conceived to be moving from limit to limit. What I call the self-determination of the dialectical universal must be conceived in this way. What exists is determined as a single limit of the dialectical world. It is for this reason that the more what exists is determined, the more singular it is, then the more global it is, that is, the more universal it is. The more singular it is, the more it can be thought to be therefore free. Because the self is that which, being a single limit of the entire structure of the dialectical world, is determined, the fact that the self moves is the fact that the world moves, the fact that the world moves is the fact that the self moves. But that is not to negate the independence of a singularity. In the dialectical world a singularity must be conceived itself absolutely to determine itself. It is necessarily both that which, being a single limit, is determined and that which is possessed of a single tendency that determines the entire world. In the absolutely dialectical world, that which is formed is that which forms: form-qua-force. Moreover, to speak of determining the entire world from a single determined limit is necessarily to say that a singularity itself negates itself. If a certain single determined world itself absolutely determines itself, the fact that it renders itself singular necessarily means that at the same time it is dying. The world progresses on the basis of moving from limit to limit. That is dialectical process. If what is called dialectical process is conceived as something like merely temporal progression, then there is no necessity to conceive of something like originary structure. But if we are to conceive dialectical process as the self-determination of the eternal now qua affirmation of absolute negation, then we must conceive that there is something like originary structure there. It is in such a structure that species, each of which itself determines itself, confront each other.

The dialectical world is the world of active intuition. The self makes things on the basis of intentional action, but the thing is both that which is made by the self and something distanced from the self and thereby determines the self. Furthermore, the thing is born of the thing itself, the thing is nature; and thus the self as well is thing; our intentional action, too, is born of the world of things. What I call the world of active intuition is necessarily this sort of thing. This is what we conceive as our world. In such a world the thing itself corporeally determines itself. At the root of corporeal determination there must be thought to be that which belongs to élan vital. We can say that the dialectical world, as the infinite flow of life, itself determines itself. But the dialectical world, of course, must be the affirmation of absolute negation. It is necessarily the world that, as the self-determination of the eternal now, itself sees itself absolutely expressively. Even our corporeal determination is not simply biological but necessarily belongs to expressive activity. To posit that, making things on the basis of intentional action, the made thing is distanced from the self, and that, conversely, it determines the self, is to posit active intuition; the coming into being itself of such active intuition is necessarily the affirmation of absolute negation, necessarily the self-determination of the eternal now. It is in such a world that for the first time we can speak of being born of the world of things. We are therefore both biological and more than biological. The world both belongs to élan vital and does not merely belong to élan vital. The world itself determines itself in the manner of the *Gemeinschaftliche*. We are both a species of animal and what actualizes itself in a *Gemeinschaftliche* manner. Thus *Gemeinschaft*, as self-determination of the eternal now, always possesses the characteristic of seeing what is of the Idea. In itself it is formative, the activity of modeling. *Gemeinschaft* exists to the extent that in itself it is formative. There is one world to the extent that we see things on the basis of intentional action. Thus *Gemeinschaft* exists concretely as self-determination of the eternal now; as particularities that themselves determine themselves in the eternal present, *Gemeinschaft* and *Gemeinschaft* oppose each other, and thus possess the significance of simultaneous existence in the eternal present. A *Gemeinschaft* therefore always possesses an other. So a single epoch is constituted on the basis of self and other mutually determining and mediating each other. A single epoch in history is what is called the "world." As the determination of the eternal now itself, that is, as absolute local determination, it is what sees the content of the eternal, that is, what is of the Idea. *Gemeinschaft* exists in a place. Cultural will is the *entelechia* of the epoch. A single age, as I have said, is what we should call a single limit of original structure. History continually moves from epoch to epoch. Moreover, it constitutes the system of the eternal.

When the dialectical world itself determines itself, it is corporeal as the affirmation of negation. The singular thing itself determines itself corporeally. The dialectical world is conceived as the infinite flow of life. We are species of animal. But in the dialectical world our bodies are not merely biological but are characterized by expressive activity; they are historical. We are not merely a species of animal but a people. A people is a biological species in the world of the affirmation of absolute negation, in the world of history. This biological species does not yet however possess the significance of the self-determination of the eternal now; of itself, it is still biological. There is necessarily the self-determination of the eternal now in the depths of the historical world. It is when a people possesses the significance of the self-determination of the eternal now that *Gemeinschaft* comes into being. *Gemeinschaft* is what possesses the cultural significance of a people. In that, we are distanced from the significance of being merely a biological species. What unifies a *Gemeinschaft* is the mythic. It is said that totems are not necessarily relations of blood relatives. In that fact, cultural will is already at work. Without tradition there is no culture. Thus, tradition begins with myth. It is within *Gemeinschaft* that we become a species in the world of the eternal now. The *Gemein-schaftliche* is in one aspect biological and racial and, in itself negating itself, sees the ideal; that is, it itself universalizes itself, globalizes itself. It is society's process of becoming-rational. Therein is the origin of morality and law. In one aspect *Gemeinschaft* is utterly biological, even material; in a word, it can be said to be natural. Just as it is thought that there is no self without the body, one might well say that what is called an economic formation is the basis of *Gemeinschaft*. But historical nature must of course be expressive. In exactly the same way as there is no body without spirit, there is no *Gemeinschaft* that does not possess cultural spirit, in whatever sense of the term. As self-determination of the eternal now, it includes contradiction within itself; it is itself continually determining itself dialectically; that is, it is seeing the ideal. It might be thought from the standpoint of merely corporeal determination that even the ideal is instrumental. But, contrariwise, from the standpoint of the self-determination of the eternal now it is the corporeal that is instrumental, material. As self-determination of the eternal now, the *Gemeinschaftliche* can by no means be thought necessarily to come into being from one location. Various animal species and various *Gemeinschaften* would well be thought to arise from various places. Species confronts species, *Gemeinschaft* confronts *Gemeinschaft*. Because the coming into being itself of *Gemeinschaft* already includes self-contradiction, it could well be thought that it is in itself moving dialectically. It is on the basis of the fact that one *Gemeinschaft* mediates other *Gemeinschaften* that it itself develops itself (of course, in time, for the sake of that development, the *Gemeinschaft* itself may well destroy itself). Thus a single historical world, as the self-determination of the eternal now, comes into being; what is called an epoch comes into being. Therein culture, as the manifestation of world spirit, comes into being. Because the coming into being itself of the *Gemeinschaft* is based on the self-determination of the eternal now, the self-determination of the historical world, the *telos* of *Gemeinschaft* itself can be said to lie in the constitution of culture. What is called a single epoch in history is the becoming-nature of history itself; as the self-determination of the eternal now itself, the epoch comes into being in the coimmanence of history-qua-nature. We should probably say that it is therein that the expressive world determines itself. Therein, as subject-qua-object, object-qua-subject, the world possesses its individuality. Therefore, when a single epoch itself determines itself, various cultures are established. Conversely, when various cultures express the spirit of the age, they may be said to possess the same kind of "stereotype."[18] What is called art, with regard to history-qua-nature as affirmation of absolute negation, is established in conformity with the side of nature; it is the becoming-nature of the spirit of the epoch. We therefore speak of the cognitive body's affirmation of absolute negation. In the self-determination of the historical world, as the self-determination of the eternal now, there is always necessarily the coimmanence of history and nature; the epoch must be thought to determine the epoch itself. Therein, our bodies are not merely biological but belong to expressive activity. When the world is corporeal, the self itself loses itself, and we are born of the world. And that is inconsistent with élan vital. Therefore, our bodies, characterized by expressive activity and being historical, are born of the self-determination of the expressive world. Our cognitive bodies see the thing in the manner of expressive activity. Such active intuition is artistic intuition. When we see the thing artistically (in the broad sense), then as self-determination of historical nature, our expressively active bodies are born. The thing is not merely utilitarian but ideal. What we call culture, therefore, as the self-determination of the expressive world, as historical nature, always possesses the significance of art. There is no cultural people that does not possess some kind of art. This is not merely to say that art is culture, nor is it simply to say that artistic intuition is cultural activity. Our bodies, as singular determinations of the dialectical world, are both utterly biological and utterly belong to expressive activity. "Historical nature" is both to the furthest extent nature, and utterly expressive. That world that itself expressively determines itself, itself determines itself as nature. "Nature" is the side of the self-determination of the eternal now itself. It is where the thing is born and goes toward death. As the historical present, we possess therein a single epoch. In historical nature we see things actively, as internal cognitive perception–qua–external cognitive perception, external cognitive perception–qua–internal cognitive perception; and what is called active intuition comes into being. Artistic intuition comes into being in conformity with the natural side of historical nature; and, as the self-determination of the eternal now that itself expressively absolutely determines itself, is what can absolutely see the ideal, that is, see the dynamic idea. This can be conceived as the moral idea. In the affirmation of absolute negation of corporeal determination, we are born not merely biologically; we are, at the same time, born in our belonging to *Gemeinschaft*; we are born historically. Therein we possess expressively active bodies. *Gemeinschaft* comes into being as already historical nature. The historical-natural, itself belonging to forming activity, absolutely possesses the tendency to see the ideal. Spatially, it is to see, by means of external cognitive perception, the artistic idea; temporally, it is to see, by means of internal cognitive perception, the moral idea. Various legal systems necessarily all give form to moral ideas. It is as concretizations of moral ideas that for the first time the state can truly be called a state. *Recht* does not emerge from *Macht*. Of course, one aspect of *Gemeinschaft* is biological and material. Historical nature is in one aspect material nature. The absolutely dialectical world, as the affirmation of absolute negation, is the world of infinite life, the world of force. Therein is the being of the *Gemeinschaft*; the state, too, is that which necessarily possesses life and force. But the world of mere life, the world of mere force, is no more than the mere world of living things. The world of historical nature is the world of force, the world of life, and also necessarily the world of actively seeing the idea, necessarily the world of the activity of forming. The true state resides in seeing the idea actively. The state comes into being in active intuition. The state is not merely the cognitive epistemological object of the understanding. In the world of active intuition, seeing is acting, which conversely, as historical self, determines our intentional action.

Usually when we speak of nature, it is the nature of natural law of which we are thinking, but from the standpoint of the intentionally acting self, it is necessarily the place where the thing is born, the place where the self of intentional action is born; it must be on the side of the self-determination of the historical world. Even what natural scientists call experience must be this sort of thing. In one aspect it must be absolutely negative and material, and in the other aspect, as self-determination of the historical world, it is absolutely expressive; it is what, as a single world, itself determines itself. What is called an epoch, being historical nature, itself determines itself. The *Gemeinschaftliche*, as the particularity that itself determines itself within such nature, is in one aspect absolutely material and possesses a material structure, but also, it itself expressively determines itself; that is, it sees the ideal. The will of historical nature is what constitutes the *Gemeinschaftliche*. Therefore even something like art is constrained by material conditions; but even something like economic formations do not come into being materially, biologically. But the historical world itself determines itself according to such nature, seeing the ideal, and is also absolutely expressive. One aspect of the dialectical world, as corporeal determination, is characterized by élan vital; it is absolutely creative but also, as the self-determination of the eternal now, is what absolutely itself reflects itself; that is, it is conscious. The self-determination of the eternal now, belonging to the activity of making-form, is the fact that to make is to see, and to see is to make; as nature, it itself determines itself in actuality; but in one aspect it is utterly creative, in the other aspect absolutely conscious, and thus possesses the characteristics of something like a reflecting mirror. At the extreme limit of the latter, it can reflect what is not reflected. This is because consciousness is conceived as intentional or as belonging to the understanding. Therefore, the actually existing world, the world of historical nature as historical present, always is possessed of an infinite circumference. In the historical present, the infinite past and infinite future, centered on the world of actuality of active intuition, are conceived as simultaneously existing as circumference. Therein, the world of knowledge comes into being. Our knowledge, characterized by judgment, takes the world of actuality as logical subject and possesses what is infinitely predicative. The world of knowledge comes into being in seeing historical nature as merely the self-determination of the expressive world. Even knowing is a species of active intuition, but it has forfeited the sense of artistic creative activity and making things in transduction.

What I call here historical nature as the self-determination of the eternal now is frequently conceived as second nature. But I, on the contrary, conceive it to be first nature; and I would consider the so-called nature of the laws of nature to be on the side of first nature's self-negation. To the extent that we see actively, to the extent that the thing is thought to cause us to move, that is nature. Even what is called material nature, to the extent it is thought to possess a sense of the principle of things, can be called nature. It is unlikely that we can legitimately call something like the material world, merely conceived on the basis of a matrix, nature. Historical nature, as determined in absolute negation-qua-affirmation, always includes contradiction within itself. The world of material substance is conceived abstractly in the direction of its self-negation; in the direction of its self-affirmation, it is abstractly conceived as the world of consciousness. But, as subject-qua-object, object-qua-subject, it itself subjectively/objectively forms itself; that is, it is utterly creative. So we can conceive biological nature in the negative direction of such creative nature, and in its positive direction we can conceive the world of so-called second nature, the world of custom. If we begin from the opposition of subject and object, it might be thought that both differ entirely in character, but if we take the creative nature that itself dialectically determines itself as the true actually existing world, then there is therein a single constitutive force. Even what is termed animal instinct cannot emerge from a merely material world. And what constitutes our customs is not mere consciousness. Something like what we call animal instinct comes into being as the self-determination of the dialectical world. And something like what we call second nature comes into being in our biological bodies and, moreover, in expressive activity. Maine de Biran distinguished between active custom and passive custom; but to the extent that it is thought that a single world itself constitutes itself on the basis of active intuition, that is, as the self-determination of the eternal now, one can say that the content of the eternal is reflected therein, and the ideal is seen. From the standpoint of the self-determination of the historical world, what is called active custom should be conceived as active intuition. That is what is conceived as the development of historical life. But even active custom becomes virtually passive historically. Thus, contrariwise, it is what constrains the development of our lives; at the limit, it renders us material substance. That as self-determination of the eternal now a thing is formed historically, that is, that the thing is actively seen, is not to say that the thing appears by chance, and in that fact there is necessarily what we call custom. The self-determination of the topological world, as time-qua-space, space-qua-time, we can call customary constitutive activity. Being static, custom is dynamic; being circular, custom is linear. Halting, it moves; moving, it halts: such is not a merely linear progress. We are moreover unable to conceive there to be any kind of fixed thing in itself at the heart of custom. Were one to think so, that would negate custom. Custom must be said to be the self-determination of that which is nothing in terms of the thing in itself. What of greatness that has appeared historically is felt to come from a great accumulation of custom; it is also that which is fated to perish. As *Stil* becomes *Manier*, it forfeits historical life. Custom is continuous, but it is not mere continuity. As technics begets technics, it is creative, discontinuous. Of course, the prior does not merely disappear, nor is the subsequent simply the continuation of the prior. The historical world of such customary determinations moves from limit to limit. Of course, to speak of moving from limit to limit means that the limit becomes transition. The self-determination of the historical world is that, as customary constitution, as a singular historical nature, it itself determines itself. It is a single determinate world. Determinate such as it is, it is an eternal world. But it is at once that which is determined and that which itself determines itself. Custom is not merely stones in a river becoming rounded by means of friction. In man custom is both active and passive, and it can be so conceived in what is truly historical. Even what is conceived as the nature of natural law can be conceived as the unchanging custom of the historical world. What, being spatial, renders infinitesimal the temporality of custom that itself determines itself temporally, can be conceived as unchanging custom. Contrariwise, when it is thought to possess temporality, it is both active and shackles itself, and necessarily finally destroys itself. That is conceived as becoming-material, but custom neither emerges from nor returns to material substance. Even the material world is one species of custom in the historical world such as delineated above. Even something like animal instinct can be conceived to be nature's custom. Still, it is only that which possesses an expressive body that truly possesses temporality and sees the idea on the basis of active custom. The ideal is seen on the basis of active custom. The world of the eternal now, customary being as it were, itself determines itself by way of custom. So as determination of that which is undetermined, it is both absolutely determined and absolutely undetermined: it possesses an infinite circumference. It is both passive and active. Being nothing, the world of the affirmation of absolute negation, the world that itself determines itself must be this sort of thing.[19]

5

On the basis of concepts such as I have considered above, I should like also to try to understand even the activity of judgment as expressive activity in the historical world; even knowing is grounded in active intuition. In the world of the affirmation of absolute negation, the singular thing itself determines itself corporeally; we possess the thing as tool, and conversely, the thing becomes body. The self becomes that which itself mediates itself, a singularity that itself absolutely determines itself; being temporal, the self is thought to be the inner self; but time is spatial, and when the self-determination of such a singular thing is con-

ceived to come into being as the self-determination of the mediation of
the continuity of discontinuity, it is necessarily corporeal. Our selves are
actual because we possess bodies. The fact, however, that we possess the
thing as tool, and, conversely, the thing becomes body, is the fact that
thing becomes self, self becomes thing, and the self disappears. What is
called our corporeal comportment necessarily comes into being as the
self-determination of the continuity of discontinuity. That is the fact of
being born. Even our bodies are born of the world of things. Therein we
conceive the flow of life, élan vital. Élan vital, the infinite flow of life,
must absolutely be characteristic of one aspect of the dialectical world.
But because that is necessarily the affirmation of absolute negation, our
lives cannot be merely biological, nor can they be simply pure duration.
They are necessarily characterized by forming activity. Our lives are not
merely the fact of acting; they are also the fact of seeing; acting is necessarily seeing. As I said at the beginning, the fact of acting, as the affirmation of absolute negation, is the fact of reflecting the self itself. In
the world of phenomenal appearance-qua-actuality, we must necessarily
conceive it so. To form in the manner of the activity of the plastic arts is
to see the self itself. Considered simply in terms of élan vital, it is likely
that the self is not that which is seen in its absolute objectivity. But it is to
the extent that it is formed objectively that there is something called the
self. Of course, we can probably imagine that, abstractly, behind what is
formed there is absolutely a self that forms. But that is no more than to
think that, just as the thing is conceived to be transcendent in its exteriority, the self is conceived to be transcendent in its interiority. Yet our intentional action, as the fact that what transcends internally is what transcends externally, is established on the basis of the fact that interiority is
exteriority. What we call our bodies have already come into being in such
a standpoint. The body is the seen self. Again, that is—immediately—
seeing: internal cognitive perception–qua–external cognitive perception,
external cognitive perception–qua–internal cognitive perception. What
is seen is what sees. The spatial is the temporal, and the temporal is the
spatial; the spatial-temporal forms the self itself. To say that the spatial
is temporal is to say that a thing acts. It may be that because this is an
infinite forming activity, it is thought that the self cannot be seen. But
the self is that which necessarily is always seen. There is an inclination,

when discussing forming activity, to consider the self-determination of
a singularity to be principally merely temporal; but forming activity is
not that which should be considered merely temporal. Being spatial, it is
necessarily temporal; it is of necessity the acting of the spatial. Without
seeing, there is no forming activity. And in order to see, there must be
the spatial. What is called forming activity therefore happens as the self-
determination of the eternal now. Forming activity comes into being on
the basis of the fact that spatial-temporal things oppose each other and
interact in the eternal now. From the standpoint of a singularity, the fact
that a thing is possessed as tool is because forming activity is already characteristic of our bodies. It is on the basis of seeing the self-determination
of the eternal now as temporal that the flow of life characterized as élan
vital is conceivable. The historical world is what itself constantly determines itself in the manner of forming activity; it is what constantly itself
sees itself. Thus we are able to say that it itself determines itself in custom. What, being passive, is dynamic is custom. All things are inert. But
in the historical world, the concrete is not merely inert; it is what actively
forms things, what sees things.

The body is neither only nor merely a moving machine; it is what itself
sees itself. It is both that which is acted upon by other bodies and that
which acts. Form can be seen where active and passive are one. That is a
single forming activity. Forming activity is not that form constitutes material substance, as the Greeks thought, but that what is formed, forms.
Such activity comes into being only as the self-determination of the dialectical world. To say that an infinite number of things interact is to say
that the mediation of the continuity of discontinuity itself determines
itself; to say that the mediation of the continuity of discontinuity itself-
determines itself is to say that an infinite number of things interact.
Those who consider form to be active take substance to be raw material.
But in such thinking, as in Greek philosophy, the way in which form
itself negates itself is not clear; what is conceived as raw material then becomes nothing. With regard to what I call the self-determination of the
dialectical universal, the fact that an infinite number of things interact is
the fact that, as the world of the continuity of discontinuity, the world
itself negates itself; the fact that the world itself affirms itself is the fact
that the thing is seen, the fact that form appears. What exists in the

present, as the self-determination of such a world, is always something formed; it is both determined and determines. Even to posit that a thing acts must be thought on that basis. What we call our bodies are acting singularities in the world that itself forms itself, that is, in the historical world. To say that a thing acts is necessarily to say that the mediation itself forms itself. Whatever itself forms itself necessarily forms itself as the self-determination of the world that itself forms itself. The historical world, which is the self-determination of the eternal now, itself determines itself as historical nature; it itself determines itself as the world of active intuition. To put it subjectively, the world of the actually existing present is determined in custom. What is called custom is the self-determination of mediation itself. Our bodies are determined as intentionally active custom of the historical world.

The historical world, as self-determination of the eternal now, is the world that is itself continually forming itself; it is the world that itself is continually seeing itself. Thus, as the affirmation of absolute negation, it is not a world that merely develops in the mode of continuity but a world that moves from epoch to epoch, a world that moves from limit to limit. The world of the determined present, being always one single limit of the world, possesses an infinite shadow. It always possesses the look of its original structure. Thus the shadow always extends in opposite directions. At the extreme limit in the direction of its negation, it can always be conceived as the world of substance; at the extreme limit in the direction of its affirmation, it can always be conceived as the world of the personal. Our bodies as well, being things that act in the determined historical present, that is, being intentionally active custom, possess both of the two infinite directions. They are both knowing and willing. The world of knowledge is conceived as surpassing actuality, albeit in conformity with actuality; that is, it is conceived as surpassing the epoch, in the negative direction seeing the original structure of the world; the world of morality is conceived in seeing the original structure of the world in the positive direction. Thus the world, as self-determination of the eternal now, continually itself determines itself in the manner of nature; we continually see the ideal by way of active intuition; we continually see form. What is called truth is no more than the original structure of a certain epoch seen in a negative direction; it is the world seen from a single limit. Of course, original structure is absolutely that which is not known, yet knowledge absolutely takes it for a cognitive epistemological object. Although it speaks of knowledge, what is called science does not necessarily take the original structure itself of the world as cognitive epistemological object. I have said that when we, as historical bodies, ourselves determine our selves, and possess the thing as tool, conversely the thing becomes body. Something like the knowledge of the natural sciences grasps the significance of the tool, as the utilitarians say. But although natural scientific knowledge speaks of the thing as tool, the thing is not merely tool. The thing is both tool and *paradeigma*. And only as such can it be characterized in terms of original structure. Particularly when it comes to something like biology, even our bodies themselves are taken as cognitive epistemological objects. But still, biology is not a discipline undertaken from the standpoint of the historical body; we can probably say that the typological *Geisteswissenschaften* make of original structure a cognitive epistemological object from such a standpoint. Still, a knowledge that sees original structure in the negative direction of the actual world is grounded in the fact that we see the ideal by way of active intuition. Historical life itself sees itself in terms of élan vital, and that is infinite forming activity. It is always in the world itself determining itself that the ideal is seen. The idea is the content of historical nature. Even the worldview of the proletariat is no more than a kind of idea. And that is not to be explained scientifically. That the idea is seen as self-determination of the historical present, that we see the idea in the manner of active intuition, means that the idea is seen from a variety of standpoints. As the content of the self-determination of the historical world, that is, as the content of the eternal now, ideas are of identical character; but, the historical world being the dialectical world, they differ in the manner of their dialectical manifestation. Being historical actuality, the dialectical world always itself determines itself; past and future exist simultaneously therein and belong to original structure. The artistic idea is seen on the plane of the dialectical world's determined present, as it were. But the historical present, as one limit of original structure, as the present that itself determines itself, is possessed of an infinite shadow that extends in the two directions of negation and affirmation. As the present of negation, the idea for knowing is seen; as the present of affirmation, the moral idea is seen. In active intuition, the artistic idea is seen in conformity with the affirmation of the negation of its instrumental corporeal determination; the idea for knowing appears on the negative side, in conformity with the affirmation of the negation of its expressive corporeal determination; the moral idea appears on the positive side. Philosophy is the expression of the idea for knowing. It is the gnoseo-logical expression of historical life. The determined content of original structure, as a single epoch, appears in the art of an epoch as the idea of beauty; it appears in the systematic legal morality of the epoch as the idea of the good; and it appears in the philosophy of the epoch as the idea of knowledge. In this sense philosophy is the study of ideas, the study of worldviews. Although science, as knowledge, corresponds to actuality, and even claims to see original structure in its negative direction, it is a standpoint that has transcended the actuality of active intuition. The cog-nitive subject bespeaks this standpoint. It is an abstract standpoint. How might it ever be possible to transcend the present within the present? The present is always the historical present; as the self-determination of the eternal now, it is a determined present. The standpoint of negation must absolutely be subsumed therein. Characterized by expressive activity, our corporeal selves are both utterly self-negating and self-affirmative. At the extreme limit of self-negation, the self becomes something like universal consciousness. Of course, such an abstract subject does not exist inde-pendently. It is nothing more than what is conceived as the negative mo-ment of active intuition. And, in fact, it always conforms to the present. Therefore science, too, is historical. What is called epistemology is the philosophy of such scientific knowledge. Philosophy is not the study of an objective cognitive epistemological object but is necessarily the study of active intuition. The content of our lives is what becomes the object of philosophy. There must be a profound intuition of life in the depths of philosophical systems.

Judgment is the self-expression of what is actual. All of historical actu-ality is what itself expressively determines itself. Acting within history is to express the self itself. Even to say that material substance acts, to the extent that it is conceived as acting within the historical world, does not escape what I said at the beginning. Acting, being the affirmation of absolute negation, is to reflect the self itself. Here is the true significance of saying that all things are judgment. What becomes the logical subject of judgment is necessarily what is actual. What is truly actual is neither something like nature construed as cognitive epistemological object nor something like so-called subjective spirit. It is necessarily what itself historically determines itself, necessarily the historical thing in itself. It is, of necessity, the historical thing in itself that truly becomes logical subject but not predicate. Something like Aristotle's singular thing is still no more than that which is determined at the extreme limit of an abstract universal. Of course, the historical world that itself always expressively determines itself always possesses the expression of the self that is determined as itself in the present; it is what is determined as universal. History always possesses tradition; without tradition there is no history. So tradition determines us. In terms of knowing, it is a single conceptually determined world. From this we are able to make various rational deductions that are subject to dispute. But truth is not established on the basis of inferences and deductions subject to dispute. Truth must be grounded in experiment. To experiment is actively to see the thing in the historical world. The reasoning of actual knowledge must be inductive. Laws, being the expression of actuality, must follow experiment. However long a tradition may last, it necessarily follows experiment and changes in time. There is no such thing as eternal unchanging scientific law. Only those who conceive so-called objective nature to be actuality itself think so. As the expression of historical actuality, even scientific law changes historically. But in saying that, I am not simply negating what is called nature. It is always as nature that the historical world that is the self-determination of the eternal now itself determines itself. So-called nature is subsumed within the historical world; it is necessarily subsumed as one of its moments, as it were. In this sense even the syllogism is subsumed within dialectical logic. Inductive logic must at its core be dialectical. We can say that all things are syllogistic, in the sense that the historical world, as nature, itself always determines itself. The fact that the thing itself expressively determines itself is the fact that, as the affirmation of absolute negation, it itself determines itself dialectically: that is concrete logic. That actuality itself determines itself in the mode of the *logos* is dialectical logic. It is on the basis of that dialectical logic that so-called syllogistic logic is established and, therefore, possesses the significance of the tool.

Perhaps it will be said that to speak in that way is not logic but phenomenology. But I think that historical actuality is an actuality that is of the *logos*; a phenomenology of historical actuality becomes, in effect, dialectical logic. But Husserl's phenomenology is simply a phenomenology of the world of consciousness, and Heidegger's phenomenology is a phenomenology of the world of the understanding. What is called *Dasein* is not historical actuality. Even "fundamental ontology" cannot be conceived to be fundamental. Man is necessarily man that acts intentionally. Thus expressive activity is necessarily characteristic of intentional action. Because historical actuality is of the *logos*, in one of its aspects it is a cognitive epistemological object of understanding; and it is from that standpoint that even something like hermeneutic phenomenology comes into being. It is further likely that because historical actuality also possesses an aspect of itself consciously representing itself, what is called a phenomenology of consciousness comes into being. Thus, phenomenology can be conceived as the study of mere description. But the concrete cannot be conceived from an abstract standpoint.

Dialectical logic is not necessarily limited to active intuition. Artistic creative activity is also dialectical, as is moral intentional action. Historical actuality in its entirety itself dialectically determines itself. Historical actuality is always determined as a single limit of original structure. It casts an infinite shadow in the two opposite directions of its self-negation and its self-affirmation. Yet the standpoint that negates actuality while being commensurate with actuality is the standpoint of knowing. The standpoint of knowing, while being commensurate with actuality, is the standpoint that surpasses actuality in the direction of actuality's aspect of negation. Our corporeal selves are not merely biological but are necessarily characterized by expressive activity; that is, they are necessarily historical bodies. In our corporeal determination, we possess the thing as tool, and, conversely, thing becomes body. In such corporeal determination, as the already dialectical self-determination of a singularity, the fact that thing becomes body is the fact that the self loses the self. It is necessarily established as already the self-determination of the dialectical universal that we might well call "generative nature." Yet that is not the world of the affirmation of absolute negation. In the historical world of the affirmation of absolute negation we see the thing divorced from such biological corporeal determination. The thing is something divorced from the biological body, but what is seen determines what sees; we see the self in the thing. In such a concrete world, expressive activity is necessarily characteristic of our corporeal determination. Thus the thing is not merely a tool but that which shows something; it is objective manifestation. In this case our corporeal determination becomes the activity of judgment. That the thing shows something is a fact that, in the world of the affirmation of absolute negation and centered on active intuition, we might pursue exhaustively. Therein the world of mere understanding is conceived. Such is the world where the thing is no longer seen. The absolutely dialectical world, the world of the eternal now, as nature, itself determines itself. But that is not merely biological nature; it is necessarily historical nature. The self-determination of such nature, being of the activity of the plastic arts, is that we see the thing actively. In the world of this active intuition, however, the thing is what absolutely shows something. In one aspect thing must be word. That is, in one aspect it must be a world of the *logos*. At the point at which the thing absolutely shows something, original structure appears in the mode of the *logos*. That is the world of objects for knowledge. And that in one aspect must be the standpoint of the self-negation of what is conceived as our biological bodies. It can be thought that therein forming activity loses forming activity itself; form loses form itself. That is the unseen world of ideas, a world where life has lost life itself. But that, too, always appears as one aspect of the world of actuality, one aspect of active intuition. Just as it can be thought that our biological desires arise as the self-determination of biological nature, so, too, our epistemological desires arise as the self-determination of historical nature. As Aristotle said, all humans seek innate knowing. Thus all problems arise in this historical actuality, and it is in this historical actuality that they are decided. And that is because historical actuality is one limit of the original structure of the world. It is in the self-determination of the historical present conceived as the present determining the present itself, and as the forming activity of the identity of subject and object, that the idea is seen, and the original structure itself is seen from one limit. Therein, historical life itself sees itself. Philosophy is the expression by way of the *logos* of such ideal content. Philosophy, therefore, as students of worldviews say, possesses content different from that of science and identical to that of art or religion (but I think I will attempt a consideration of religion separately). Dialectical logic differs from the logic of cognitive epistemological objects and is necessarily the expression, in the mode of the *logos*, of historical life itself. Scientific method and dialectics are not to be confused with each other.

It can probably be maintained that the cognitive epistemological objects of science, as of course being historical actuality themselves, are dialectical; scientific knowledge, as well, can be said to be dialectical. But scientists are in fact scientists in determining a certain specific standpoint. Science is established in determining what is dialectical nondialectically. Of necessity, science comes into being by positioning the acting self outside the world. Scientific cognitive epistemological objects, as historical actuality, are necessarily both absolutely objective and subjective. That can be said even of the cognitive epistemological objects of physics. Particularly when it comes to something like contemporary quantum mechanics, it can be said that it is already inconsistent with the world of the dialectical universal. But it is precisely the dialectical world that has rendered the subject infinitesimal. When it comes to the social sciences, because its cognitive epistemological objects are already concrete and belong to historical actuality, social science can likely be conceived to be dialectical. But social science, too, is science on the basis of determining a certain standpoint. For example, it is on the basis of circumscribing what is called the economic world that economics comes into being. Although something called the historical self is conceptualized in economics, it does not touch upon the self it has rendered a cognitive epistemological object. This is not to say that scientific knowledge is not dialectical. But dialectics does not occupy a certain determined standpoint. The standpoint of the dialectic is necessarily a concrete standpoint, necessarily a standpoint without a standpoint, as it were. Logic clarifies the fundamental structure of actuality itself. To the extent that actuality is conceived as nature rendered cognitive epistemological object, logic is syllogistic. Logic is conceived as a tool from the standpoint of the opposition of subject and objective, but all things are necessarily first of all things before they are tools. Yet even the self is logical actuality, and even the thing is logical actuality; there is no actuality without logic. To conceive logic as merely a tool is to conceive acting as merely supralogical.

But to say that thing and thing act is necessarily to speak of the continuity of discontinuity. It is as the self-determination of the dialectical universal that what acts can be conceived. Because syllogistic logic is the logic of objectified nature and is not a logic of concrete actuality, even when nature is thought to be historical, it is thought to be nothing other than merely a tool. And that is not to determine actuality itself. Contrariwise, scientific logic is dialectical. But, as I said before, it has determined a certain standpoint. The question, concerning what sort of thing what we call logic is, requires an elaborate discussion, but a logic of cognitive epistemological objects is not dialectical. That is a logic of a determined universal. It is the dialectical universal seen from the standpoint of universal determination. Though we speak of scientific logic and knowledge as inductive, the fact is that because it is dialectical, it absolutely anticipates such a universal and therefore cannot determine it. Of course, I do not reject the logic of cognitive epistemological objects. In the dialectical universal, the universal determination must itself be absolutely universal. Dialectical logic is dialectical logic on the basis of making the logic of cognitive epistemological objects a moment of dialectical logic. Still, the cognitive epistemological object, as self-determination of the expressive world, is necessarily that which is seen actively. This is to say that knowledge is the expression in the mode of the *logos* of actuality; logic is the structure, characterized as *logos*, of actuality. Even the logic of cognitive epistemological objects is in this sense logic. In spite of the fact that when actuality is conceived to be merely material, and the *logos* is conceived to be merely an object of the understanding, historical actuality necessarily is characterized by *logos*.

HUMAN BEING

("NINGENTEKI SONZAI," 1938)

1

The world of historical actuality is the world of production, the world of creation. Although to speak of "production" is to say we make things and that the thing is something made by us, it is nevertheless the case that the thing, as an utterly independent thing, conversely affects us and, indeed, that the acting itself by which we make things is born of the world of things. While thing and self are utterly opposed and utterly contradict each other, the thing affects the self and self affects thing; as contradictory self-identity, the world itself forms itself, moving in active intuition from the made to the making. As productive elements of the productive world, as creative elements of the creative world, we are the possibility of production. So it is in respect of the fact that we are historically productive that there is the true self. The world is therefore a world of difficult labor; man is the contradictory existence of freedom and necessity. Were this a contradiction merely for thought, there would be neither any imperative "should" nor suffering. We both must and cannot think that in the world there is a beginning. This is self-contradiction. But perhaps it would be well to leave that question to the philosophers. Because contradiction is the fact of actually existing life, there is for us infinite effort, infinite labor. Even the infinite "should" issues from that fact. Contradiction is the fact of human life. It is the problem of our life and death. So it is in that contradiction there is historical actuality.

To the extent that it is thought that the self depends on the self, there is no dialectic. It is merely internal development. Yet neither is there any dialectic even when one says the self depends entirely on the external.

Even to posit that self and thing, being entirely mutually opposed, co-determine each other—more, that they mutually negate each other—is not an absolute dialectic to the extent that self and thing are thought to be merely spatial, merely atemporal. The standpoint of the absolute must be the opposition of past and future. The past is what has already passed; the future is what has not yet come. Therein there must be an absolute interruption or rupture. Moreover, time, as absolute self-identity, is continually moving from past to future. What I call the eternal now that itself determines itself is that absolute contradictory self-identity. It is because the present determines the present itself that time comes into being. That the absolute dialectic is necessarily the movement from the made to the making is the fact that the thing is made; it is necessarily the fact of what is called creation. To say that a thing is made is not to say that the thing appears causally, nor is it to speak of teleological development. In the world of causal necessity there is no production; neither is there production in the world of teleological development. Something like production has not heretofore been thought from the standpoint of philosophy, but the world of historical actuality must be a world of production. Without speaking of production, there is nothing to call the world of historical actuality. The world of historical actuality must be thought from the fact of production. And that is a standpoint one can reach neither from the standpoint of the cognition of objects nor from the standpoint of the activity of introspective contemplation. Therefore, a person is frequently thought to be uncreated, unmediated—a miracle. But even the activity of the intellect must, as intentional action in the historical world, be mediated by the historical world.

One can think there to be neither causal necessity nor internal development at the heart of production. When we posit that one cannot make anything from the depths of consciousness, we might seem actually to be talking about something like simple natural generation. But that does not bear the significance of making. What I have called the activity of forming is frequently regarded as the same as the activity of artistic creation. The activity of artistic creation is also a kind of historical activity of forming. But it is no more than a particular kind of historical forming activity. The historical activity of forming must be differentiated from merely natural generation. Its standpoint is precisely opposite. In historical activity there is no continuity that is merely given. Natural generation is not forming activity. The made is what has been surpassed; it is a dead thing. So one cannot speak of moving to the making. Therein, neither spatially nor—it might almost go without saying—temporally is there continuity. To the extent that one might think so, then one is not thinking of historical forming. It is for this reason that I say there is nothing simply given in history; the given, I maintain, is something made. The movement from the made to the making is necessarily the continuity of absolute interruption or rupture. If so, what sort of thing is this "continuity of absolute interruption"? It must be conceived as our expressive activity. The self-identity of the movement from the made to the making is neither within the made nor within the making. Neither is it in any sense within the so-called immanent world, such as is thought to be the case in natural generation. It must be transcendent. The self-identity of absolute contradiction is not what is within "this world." It is possible to speak of the movement from the made to the making only in the world of transcendental self-identity. To say that what is transcendental is immanent is necessarily to speak of expressing the self itself.

When speaking of expressive activity, people think in terms of a movement from the subjective to the objective, but it must always also be conceived in terms of a movement from the objective to the subjective. Subject and what is objective must be utterly mutually opposed. And indeed, this opposition must be conceived not merely as a spatial opposition but as a temporal-spatial opposition. The objective absolutely does not issue from the subjective, and the subjective absolutely does not issue from the objective. There must be an absolute interruption or rupture between them. Moreover, insofar as the thing is formed as the self-identity of an absolute contradiction, there must be expressive activity. It is not only that expression cannot issue from the merely objective; neither can what is called expression issue solely from the subjective activity of temporal continuity. Expression is based neither on internal mediation nor on external mediation; nor yet again is it based on so-called natural generation. The self-identity of the world that itself continually constitutes itself expressively is not immanent in that world; it is necessarily transcendental. It is therefore from there that a truly objective "should" emerges. Although this world is utterly determined causally, what is given, as what is made, is made in order to be negated. What is made is what is constantly in the process of being destroyed. In the historical world there is nothing whatever that is eternal and unchanging. There is at the heart of the historical world in no sense whatever any self-identity remaining that might be conceived according to a logic of the cognitive epistemological object. Insofar as there is, there is nothing of form-making. When one thinks simply from the standpoint of a logic of the cognitive epistemological object, it is probably impossible to differentiate between natural generation and historical form-making activity. Consequently something like historical form-making goes unthought.

OUR INTENTIONAL ACTION does not arise merely subjectively. On the contrary, it must be that which arises objectively. But of course, even though we say it arises objectively, that is not to say it arises from the abstract idealist notion of the objective, conceived in its opposition to the subjective. Our intentional action arises as historical form-making activity. It is thus true objective intentional action that makes things historically; it can thus be praxis. There is no intentional action, no praxis, that is not productive. Anything that is not production is no more than abstract will. For this reason I maintain that intentional action arises intuitively. This is to say, it is necessarily corporeal. Intuition does not imply that the self is merely passive. The self is subsumed dialectically within the world of things; the subjective is subsumed within the objective. Therefore, intuition is always active intuition. From the standpoint of abstract logic, action and intuition are considered merely a mutual opposition; something like "active intuition" might even be thought to be a contradictory concept. It is thought that action disappears when one is speaking of intuition. But to say that intuition is merely passive, to say that the self completely disappears within the thing, is not intuition. Where there is no self, neither is there intuition. To speak of intuition is to say that the self, as the self-negation of the world of things, is born of the world of things; the thing provokes our action. I therefore maintain that even something like the instinctive activity of animals is already active intuition. The world of historical actuality is the world of the movement from the made to the making, the world of form-making activity. To the extent that, as the self-identity of absolute contradiction, it possesses self-identity in what is absolutely transcendental and to the extent that it is the form-making activity of the movement from the made to the making, it is actively intuitive. Dialectically, to see is to act, and to act is to see. To the extent that even the instinctive activity of animals is historically form-making, it is actively intuitive. To say that dialectically to see is to act is neither to say that acting and seeing become one nor that acting disappears. To speak of the form-making activity of the movement from the made to the making is to say that the thing, as the self-identity of what is absolutely opposed, is made and that, being self-contradictory, what is made is continually being destroyed, and that what is being destroyed itself becomes a condition, which is to say that a new thing comes into being. Absolute negation, therefore, becomes mediation; absolute nonbeing becomes mediation; the thing is mediated by life and death. This is neither to say that it is mediated externally nor that it is mediated internally; nor is it to say it is mediated as the unity of the subjective and the objective. Were it mediated by the unity of the subjective and the objective, that would be being, not nonbeing. It is necessarily mediated by what is absolutely transcendental. To say that it is mediated by the absolutely transcendental, to say that it is mediated by absolute nonbeing, is to say—positively—that it is mediated by the creative expression of the historical social world; it is mediated, as it were, by the concrete word. Our historical life is called forth by objective expression. Our life is necessarily mediated by objective expression. Objective expression is not merely that which is to be interpreted. There is nothing called life that is not mediated by objective expression. What is absolutely transcendental, what—mediated by absolute nonbeing— appears creatively, is objectively expressive. There has heretofore been no profound consideration of the fact that the thing comes into being in terms of expressive activity. Seen merely from the perspective of a logic of the cognitive epistemological object, it is associated with the abstract way of seeing of the activity of artistic intuition as something like the unity of subject and object. However, the thing coming into being in terms of expressive activity must be conceived as the thing coming into being as the contradictory self-identity of the absolute past and the absolute future, that is, as the contradictory self-identity of two absolutely opposed aspects; the thing must be conceived to come into being in historical space. That is necessarily and truly to speak of the movement from the made to the making. In speaking this way, it might be thought to be unmediated or immediate. But it is quite the contrary. Therein there is nothing whatever that is given. Expressive activity does not come into being on the basis of what is merely given. The given is what is made; the made produces on the basis of itself expending itself. One's body produces on the basis of the body itself expending itself. Even biological life is the contradictory self-identity of consumption and production. This is not to say the self itself negates itself. That is simply a contradiction. One cannot speak of the movement from the made to the making as the self itself negating the self. It must be based on the other. In order to speak of the movement from the made to the making, it must be mediated by absolute negation. To the extent that the movement from what is given is thought as a natural coming into being, there is nothing of expressive activity. That which is objectively expressive in the depths of the self is what confronts the self. When we say we make things, it is always with respect to what is objectively expressive. What is in this sense objectively expressive is reason. The *logos* is characteristic of poiesis. Because our lives exist in making things objectively expressively, because our lives are mediated by absolute negation, life is self-contradiction; life is entirely labor. There is no life in the immediate or the unmediated.

To say that a thing is made in the historical world is to say that a thing is given form in expressive activity. That is, what exists, as what is given, produces on the basis of itself expending itself; it is born in its dying. In the historical present—that is, in the historical space that is the simultaneous presence of past and future as absolute contradictory self-identity—it is on the basis of the self negating itself, on the basis of a continuous expenditure, that is, on the basis of entering into the past, that something new appears, which is to say a thing is created. That is, what is made becomes what makes; what is created becomes what creates. That is further to say that the thing acts in historical space; therein is what is called intentional action. Even in the instance of physical space, to say that a thing acts might be to say that the thing negates the thing itself. To say that a thing acts is to say that a thing expends force. But in physical space, a thing does not exhaustively expend itself. Consequently, one cannot truly speak of acting in physical space; there is no singularity that itself truly determines itself. What therefore truly acts must be that which is both being born and going toward death. Historical space must be the place of life and death. There is nothing that is mediated on the basis of the self and what stands in the same line as the self. It must be mediated by what is absolutely transcendental; it must be mediated by objective expression. Historical space must be the place of expressive activity.[1]

In the actually existing historical world, what is seen in active intuition is necessarily what has been formed in expressive activity. What is seen intuitively on the basis of absolutely contradictory self-identity is necessarily mediated by absolute negation; as immediately objective expression, it is necessarily what calls to us from the depths of death. To speak of making things expressively, mediated by absolute negation, is to speak of the self passing away; conversely, the fact that a thing appears expressively is that the self is born: therein the acting of the self is summoned forth. Our life exists in making things; what is called productive life must be grasped from expressive activity. Expressive activity has heretofore only been conceived from the standpoint of the conscious self. Expressive activity has been conceived as the conscious self making the self objectively appear in its presence. But the activity of consciousness itself, of course, develops from historical production. What we call the activity of our consciousness develops because our production is mediated by absolute negation, that is, because it is mediated by objective expression. The given, as that which in the dialectical world is given form on the basis of absolute contradictory self-identity, that is, on the basis of what is formed on the basis of historical life, is what must be seen in active intuition. Thus it is necessarily that which immediately brings forth our intentional action. And that is because the instinctive activity of the animal is already actively intuitive. To say that an animal sees a thing is to say that it sees instinctively; seeing is immediately acting. Because it is thought that nothing like judgment enters into that seeing, it is thought to be merely immediate, merely unmediated. However, even then there must already be the mediation of expressive activity. Even the instinctive life activity of the animal must be mediated by historical life. Therefore, as Schopenhauer said, even the world of the animal is the world of labor.

It is already a world mediated by absolutely contradictory self-identity. Even our conscious intentional action has developed from that world.

What we consider to be the body, as contradictory self-identity, is already that which acts. To act is to see; to see is to act. The action of the body is already expressive. To say that the body acts is not merely to speak of natural generation. The plant does not possess a body. Where acting and seeing are unified, there is the body. Where the thing is seen active-intuitively, there is the body. What is seen calls forth our action. Our life emerges where what is seen is what is desired. There is the body where what is continually moving temporally—that is, what acts—is mediated by absolute negation, mediated, that is, by objective expression. What we call our bodies are therefore already self-estranged being. Thus, because our bodies are mediated by absolute negation, because they are mediated by objective expression, conversely they are bodies that are to be utterly negated. Therefore, from the body emerges the intentional action that negates the body. This also establishes the standpoint of the conscious self. Therein, even the mere imperative "should" is conceived as action. Such action must, however, come into being grounded in the dialectical development of the historical body. The historical body cannot be negated, but were it to be negated, what is called action would disappear. What exists within history cannot negate history. Even to speak of negating must be from the standpoint of history. It is the movement from the made to the making. To speak of the movement from the made to the making is not to invoke nondialectical movement; on the contrary, it is to make of absolute negation the mediation. It may be that when one speaks of the mutually opposed directions of what is called the body from the standpoint of a logic of judgment, both directions become one unproductively, but being mediated by absolute contradictory self-identity, the body is self-contradiction; it is both being and nonbeing. Because our historical life, being productive, emerges active-intuitively, and because, being expressive, it is mediated by objective expression, what is called language emerges within our historical life. Linguists say that naming arises from production. *Logos* emerges from poiesis. This is why I speak of something like a "logos-body."[2] The more our historical life, as the movement from the made to the making, is creative, the more does it belong to reason. Reason, therefore, is not immanent in our productive corporeal self but confronts us from outside; one can speak here of command. Moreover, to say that our historical life is productive, to say that it is mediated by objective expression, means that the ground of what we call our "life" is social. It means our action is mediated by forms that have been given form objectively. What we call society is constituted centered on some kind or another of objective expression. Society cannot be constituted without some kind of ideology. Because what we call our corporeal life is self-contradiction, because it negates itself mediated by objective expression, it is in the self-negation of the self that what is called society comes into being. It must, however, come into being to the furthest extent as the negation of corporeal life from within corporeal life. Were that not the case, it would be no more than merely abstract being. I therefore characterize society as historic-corporeal. So when the historic-corporeal species, that is, *Gemeinschaft*, is thought to be, mediated from corporeal life by absolute negation, constituted by objective expression, itself mediated entirely by negation and when, at the limit of that process, we confront absolute contradictory self-identity, and what is called corporeal life is entirely negated and we confront absolutely objective expression, it can be thought that we then confront, as it were, the word of God. What, being created, creates—that is, the created thing—is thought to confront the creator. Therein, we are separated from our corporeal ballast and are thought to become (like Kant's universal of consciousness or practical reason) merely subjects of reason. Objective expression is thought as an infinite "should." What is thought to be intuition is negated therein. But then there is absolutely no movement from the created to the creator. We are entirely what, being created, creates; we are what, being made, makes. We are mediated by absolute negation; we make things by negating the self itself; conversely, the thing, in being seen, acts. Fundamentally, at the limit of expressive historic-corporeal action, we contradict the infinite "should." This is not to negate what is given; on the contrary, it is to affirm what is given and what has been made in the historical present that is the simultaneity of an infinite past and an infinite future; that is, it is to affirm the infinite past. It is not to negate the historic-corporeal development that is the movement from the made to the making; on the contrary, it is necessarily absolutely to affirm it. Perhaps it is possible to conceive abstractly of a simple negation, but negation must be negation because it arises from that affirmation. It is to see the given as the past. It is, however, to see it as the past in the historical present. Therefrom arises the demand toward the historical future. The singular self-determination of the historical present that makes of absolute negation the mediation is of reason; and that can be thought as the infinite imperative that confronts our conscious selves.

Just as it is said that man is the last created, so, too, man is the limit of the movement from the created to the creating. Here, it can be thought, man's action is mediated by judgment, and action is conditioned by the moral imperative. Even man, however, as the movement from the made to the making, is necessarily continually developing historically. Our action is necessarily what is demanded by the world of things seen active-intuitively. When we are productive, we confront objective expression. To say that a thing is seen active-intuitively is to say it is mediated by absolute contradictory self-identity; it is to say that seeing is acting; and thus is our action demanded, in terms of expressive activity. Active intuition is making form qua intuition. From an epistemological perspective, it might be thought that expression is merely the object of understanding. Or again, in speaking of production, it might be thought that something like the work of art is merely the object of aesthetic appreciation. Objective expression, however, provokes our action as expressive activity. It is for that reason that what is called the body exists. The body is self-contradictory being such as I have described above. That is, mediated by absolute negation, mediated by objective expression in the movement from the made to the making, it self-contradictorily itself continually gives form to itself: that is, it is actively intuitive. Conversely, the active-intuitive activity of making-form is corporeal. The instinctive life activity of animals, as well, to the extent that it is form-making activity, must be such a thing. That is, it is necessarily already mediated by absolute negation. That "in the beginning was the word" is to be experienced, and, as for Faust, is to be translated neither as meaning nor as force nor as act. And that is why I use the phrase "active intuition" to indicate the extremely profound totality of life. From the standpoint of abstract logic, intuition and activity are thought to be simply mutually opposed, and something like active intuition is considered to be nondialectical. But what we call our life resides in making things active-intuitively. Therein is what is called the self (one might well say *ambulo ergo sum*). Thus, the process of such historical life is truly an absolute dialectic. What is called abstract thought is constituted at the limit of the historical life that is the movement from the made to the making. When the significance of form-making activity is excluded from expressive form-making activity, there is what can be conceived as the activity of judgment. It may be that one can say judgment is not intuition, but there is no judgment that is not based on active intuition. Even in the instance that we see things with our eyes, we see active-intuitively; seeing is already mediated by objective expression (as Lachelier says, to see is to create).³ There is no judgment that is not characterized by form-making activity. Were this not the case, judgment would be without content. Even what has heretofore been conceived as activity has been thought to be situated at the interface of abstract history; it has not been conceived as a process of historical development; it has not been thought to be situated in temporal-spatial concrete historical space. Intuition and judgment must necessarily be the two extreme poles of expressive form-making activity mediated by objective expression as the movement from the made to the making—in other words, of historic-corporeal activity. The dialectical does not emerge from the nondialectical. Our lives develop out of animal life; however much our lives negate animal life, they nevertheless possess animal life as one pole of human being. Yet on the basis of the fact that the lives of animals possess human life at one pole, the lives of animals are life. This is not to say that man simply developed from animals but that the human is one extreme limit of the animal. In this particular sense human life and animal life oppose each other. Concrete life is always in the middle. Historical life, mediated by absolute negation and as the continuity of rupture, always possesses an aspect of the neutral. At the limit of the human there is the aspect of consciousness. One can conceive of a merely passive intuition from the standpoint of the conscious self, but then expression is conceived as the object of understanding; it is conceived as mere meaning. But even that kind of conscious self must be constituted at the furthest limit of the self-negation of the corporeal self. The very fact of thinking must itself be historic-corporeal. Therein, already, expression and activity are unified dialectically.

WHAT IS CALLED THE DIALECTIC cannot be conceived from the standpoint of the so-called logic of judgment. From that standpoint, thought must be utterly continuous. Thought cannot go outside thought. From that perspective it might even be thought that the dialectic, as the unification of what cannot be unified, must of necessity be imperative. But to speak of the imperative, one must first of all recognize the self-identity of the self. The self-identity of the self must be, like that of *cogito ergo sum*, the self-identity of object and acting as absolutely mutually opposed; it must be contradictory self-identity. For this reason the self, as self-contradiction, is continually moving from the made to the making. In that movement is the self. Such contradictory self-identity is what I call active intuition. Therein, activity is provoked from what is absolutely negative with respect to acting; that is, it is necessarily called forth from objective expression and is necessarily mediated by absolute negation. If not, it would not in fact be the actually existing self. The self must therefore be corporeal. To say that activity is mediated by absolute negation, that is, that it is mediated by objective expression, it must be that it is affirmed on the basis of utterly negating the self itself. Probably, if it is seen only from the side of the acting, it can be conceived as being merely the imperative. But the imperative is not immediately the self. What is approached on the basis of the imperative is necessarily that which is given to be negated. But again, if that were all there is to it, there would be nothing called the self. What is negated must be, again, that which negates. It is such an expressive-active subject that can be said to possess the imperative.[4] Such contradictory self-identity is probably unthinkable from the standpoint of the logic of judgment. It is thinkable, however, in the self of the person who knows contradiction, that what is mutually contradictory is unified. Even the imperative of the logic of judgment must be constituted on the basis of such a contradictory self-identity. But because it is merely abstract and formal, it can conceive nothing of active intuition. Furthermore, there is no actually existing self that is not corporeally mediated by active intuition. In what is not mediated by active intuition, there is neither action nor praxis. A true objective imperative is necessarily what confronts the self as the objective expression of the world of historical life to which we are bound productively and corporeally. Even in what is called scientific knowledge, the sensible that is its ground must be grasped active-intuitively, historic-corporeally (because the object, actuality, and sensuousness must be grasped subjectively as sensuous human activity, as praxis).[5] Even what is called scholarly knowledge is not constituted from the standpoint of judgment of the abstract self. Objective cognition is possible for us only as expressive active elements of the world formed expressively and actively. Thought is constituted as the furthest limit of the historical form-making activity of the movement from the made to the making. It is necessarily from there that the concepts of the abstract and of negation arise. Where what is called the self is summoned forth from the world of things, there is the dialectic.

It may be that when I speak of the historical world as expressively form-making, I could be thought to see the historical world in a merely contemplative way, like a work of art. But expressive form-making is to come into being, to bring into being, to create. What gives form to the self-itself expressively must be that which answers to passion, it must be the daemonic. The world of historical life, from the instinctive life activity of the animal to the religious life activity of the saint, must be a world that answers to passion. Hitherto, expression has only been conceived to be objective sense as an epistemological object, and no thought has been given to expressive form-making. But what I am calling the expressive activity of form-making is neither mechanical nor biological; it is the movement from the made to the making. So what makes the activity of historical production, in fact, the activity of historical production lies in its expressive form-making. It may be thought that I lapse into irrationalism when I say, as above, that what gives form to the self itself expressively is passionate or daemonic. But to give form to the self itself expressively is not to act blindly. The fact of expressive form-making is the fact that a thing is given form objectively. Such objective form-making activity may be conceived as reason. Concrete reason is the self-formation of the passionate (*Les grandes pensées viennent du coeur.*) Hegel, the advocate of an absolute rationality, said that nothing great could ever be accomplished without passion.

2

The actually existing world is a world of the mutual determination of singularities; it is what I call the world of place, the world of the dialectical universal. That a singularity itself utterly determines itself, that a singularity is mediated internally that is to say, and that a singularity is a singularity only in opposing other singularities, means that the singularity is necessarily mediated self-contradictorily, internally-*soku*-externally, externally-*soku*-internally (*soku* means: contradictory self-identity).[6] The world of the mutual determination of singularities is a world that itself determines itself in the manner of internal-qua-external, external-qua-internal. And that is the world that itself determines itself in the activity of making-form; it is the world that itself gives form to itself. Form-making activity is not merely the fact that the self mediates itself internally; it is not to speak of something like the activity of biological development. The world that itself gives form to itself cannot be a merely autotelic world. This is not to say, of course, that it is a world mediated merely externally, a mechanistic world. The noumenal cannot be conceived to be either internally or externally the ground of the form-making active world. Were anyone to think so from either perspective, it would not be form-making activity. It would of necessity be either mechanistic or autotelic. The world that is continually moving in the manner of form-making activity is not a world mediated either merely internally or merely externally, as might be thought in terms of abstract logic. That is to say, what is given is given as what is made; it must be a world continually moving from the made to the making; it must be a world in which the subject [*shutai*] continually makes the milieu, and the milieu continually makes the subject. We therefore speak of mediation without that which mediates; we speak of the world as absolutely dialectical.

It follows that such a form-making active world must be, as I said in the preceding section, a world of expressive form. It is necessarily impossible to speak of the movement from the made to the making in terms of formal logic. What has been made is what has passed. The past does not come again. What has passed must be nothing. Moreover, it is as the movement from the past to the future that there is time. For what is called time to come into being, past and future must in some sense be simultaneous. It is for this reason that time comes into being on the basis of the fact that the present determines the present itself. But if the present is conceived to be merely spatial, then there is no such thing as time. That would be nothing other than the negation of time. Time, therefore, must be conceived as a continuity of rupture. Truly objective time is not mediated internally. Time conceived to be mediated merely internally is utterly subjectivist. But to say this is not to say that time is mediated merely externally. Mediated neither externally nor internally, time transcends both internal and external mediation and is necessarily mediated by the transcendent; that is to say, it is necessarily mediated by absolute negation; it is mediated by creative expression. Time is therefore thought as singular. The world that is continually moving temporally-spatially (even the physical world) is necessarily a world mediated by the transcendental. Even what is conceived as so-called physical space already belongs to expressive activity. It is necessarily what I call "historical space."

The world of contradictory self-identity, conceived as a world in which a singularity is necessarily an internally mediated singularity and, at the same time is a singularity mediated externally by other singularities, is a world that is itself constantly and absolutely giving form to itself in the movement from the made to the making. That is what is called historical life. To say that the world, as the movement from the made to the making, is creative is to say that a singularity becomes, in fact, a singularity in that it itself mediates itself; to say that a singularity becomes a singularity is to say that the world becomes creative. In the development of such a world, on the one hand, as what is made, as what is given, and utterly mediated externally, the material physical world can be conceived to be made but not making; on the other hand, as the made and the making, the world may be conceived as infinite life. (Even the material physical world, as the historical world, is not simply the made, but . . .) So to speak of the movement from the made to the making is to speak of expressive active form-making; to speak of what transcends activity is to speak of being mediated by objective expression. This is why I say that our life is called forth by the material word. When I say that even the instinctive life activity of animals arises from active intuition, I am saying nothing other than this. Active intuition is the fact that action is provoked by objective expression. (Poiesis is characteristic of *logos*; *logos* is characteristic of poiesis.) Animal life is animal life because it possesses human life as one of its limits; human life is human life because it possesses animal life as one of its limits. To say that the world develops creatively as the movement from the made to the making is to say that a singularity forms in expressive activity; it is to speak of entering the world of social production from the world of instinctive activity, to enter the world of the historical body from the world of the biological body (and therein what is called consciousness emerges). At the extreme limit of such a development, what is given, as what is made, is given as that which is to be utterly negated; when the world itself falls into self-contradiction, the singular thing, itself negating itself, becomes self-aware; that is, transcending activity, it comes itself to know itself. The activity of production becomes intellectual; it becomes a productive activity without production. It can be conceived as *cogito ergo sum*. To speak of the movement from the made to the making is, of course, self-contradiction because to say that what is given as the basis of acting is the made and is therefore to be utterly negated is to say that the self negates its own acting, and that is to lapse into self-contradiction. Such a fate is implicit in the very beginnings of the life of what, being created, creates, in the very beginnings of historical form-making activity. It is for that reason that I maintain that the life of animals possesses human life as one limit and that human life possesses animal life as one limit. Thus, to say that our life at its extreme limit falls into such a self-contradiction is to say that, as the movement from the made to the making, mediated by absolute negation, our life contradictorily falls into absolute negation; it is to say that in that process it infinitely contradicts what expresses the self itself. And it thereby contradicts the Absolute, which is said to possess new life on the basis of the fact that we die. Because it is mediated by the objective expression of the absolute infinite, the world becomes personal. Thus, I am I only in confronting the Thou. The mutual determination of singularity and singularity becomes the mutual determination of the I and the Thou. Our personal self-awareness is necessarily born of the world of infinite historical form-making. The personal continually develops from the historic-social production of our corporeal selves. The development of our individual self-awareness must be premised on the basis of the self-contradiction of historic-social formation as the movement from the made to the making. Individual self-awareness does not come into being as separation from the historically form-making activity of the movement from the made to the making; it comes into being as its ultimate limit. Were that not the case, individual self-awareness would likely be no more than something conceived merely ideally, as something like abstract will. Therein it would be impossible to discover any sort of praxical significance.

In this essay I have made statements to the effect that historical form-making, characterized by expressive activity, is mediated by objective expression, or that our life is called forth by the word. Because such locutions may invite misunderstanding, here I find it necessary to go back and articulate my thinking more clearly. It is not that I think that meaning provokes activity, or that the world is a world of meaning. It is the world of historical actuality that is the world of expressive things; it is the world of material expression. What I call "objective expression" means material expression. In ideality, thing and expression are not conceived to be linked. Thing and expression, however, must be linked in historical actuality, and historical actuality is therefore dialectical and is therefore, in fact, historical actuality (the world of things is merely conceived negatively from such a world). To say that the thing is expressive or to speak of material expression points to the fact that the world is already self-contradictory. Thus, what we call our intentional action is the fact that we make things; what we call production is constituted in the manner of expressive activity. Our action is called forth from the world of material expression. Therein is the intentionally acting self. To say that the thing confronts the self expressively is to say that it presses upon the self as the present self, the self given to be negated. That which is to cause us to move, that which is to provoke our intentional action, is that which presses upon us. When a person faces the "I," it is neither as mere material substance nor as mere meaning. It is the same, even in the instance that food faces the animal. If food does not confront the animal as material substance, neither does it do so as meaning. To say that the thing is expressive is to say that the thing is seen in terms of expressive activity; to say that we act intentionally, to say that we act, is to say that we make things in expressive activity. It is thus that self and thing mediate each other through absolute negation. In the historical world of expressive activity, person and thing codetermine each other dialectically. The fact that we are born in this world, therefore, is the fact of labor, the fact of hardship. And that is, at the same time, creation. What I call the objective expression that mediates expressive form-making activity is such material expression. This is to say that, from a transcendental standpoint, the activity comes into being and is negated at one and the same time. It is to speak of the word, something in the sense in which the Christians speak of the "Word of God." The *logos* in Christianity is not identical to the *logos* in Greece. It is that upon the basis of which we live and according to which we die. It is that which is possessed of creative significance. But I do not speak from the standpoint of religion, only from the standpoint of a logical analysis of historical form-making activity. In the world of historical form-making, the transcendental is at work immanently. Of course, what is transcendent cannot be immanent. That is, it acts expressively (symbolically or semiotically). (It is in this sense that meaning is something actual.) But when I say that form-making activity is mediated by the transcendental, I am not saying that it is mediated in the manner of a deus ex machina. What is called internal contradiction and what is called intuition-qua-form-making are one as the two sides of the thing. It might well be called contradictory self-identity. We move from internal contradiction to intuition; that is, form appears transcendentally from internal contradiction (of course, they are simultaneous). When the active self is thought to have disappeared on the basis of internal contradiction, form has appeared in the manner of active intuition; and it is on that basis that the self lives. In this case we say that the activity is mediated by the transcendental. It is when we know self-contradiction within the self itself that there is already at work that which transcends the self itself (the movement from the made to the making). The form that is seen is what transcends the activity. That is what is expressive, and what exerts a force, suffusing symbolic or semiotic expression. That is absolutely never divorced, however, from activity; rather, it is what is self-contradictorily linked to activity. To say that form is seen on the basis of the contradictory self-negation of the active self is also to say that form is seen as that which is to be negated. To say that the thing provokes activity is to say that the thing negates the thing itself. Such a self-contradictory instance is called active intuition. From the standpoint of symbolic logic, such an instance is thought to be merely unmediated and direct, and thing and self are somehow thought to become merely one. Thereby, there is nothing that might be called seeing. To speak of seeing concretely or materially, the active self must, self-contradictorily, be enveloped therein. The historical actuality of active intuition is the place where the self is enveloped self-contradictorily; there, we always face absolute negation; there, we are mediated absolutely by objective expression, by creative expression. Thus, that is at the same time the fact that the present includes its own self-negation; one can even say that the present determines the present itself. Therefore, our active intuitive historical life essentially includes the moment of self-alienation. Were that not so, there would be nothing to call life. This is why I say that the animal possesses the human as limit and that the human possesses the animal as limit. Even something like the cognitive subject comes into being at the extreme limit of the active intuitive self. Facing absolute negation, and absolutely mediated by objective expression, the active intuitive self at the extreme limit of self-negation becomes the mere knowing self. We can say that our life is expressive active form-making because we are essentially self-alienated; our very coming into being is already radically logical. We can say that without the logical moment there would be no such thing as life. Concrete logic must be a logic of expressive active form-making.

It might be said that when one characterizes the world of historical form-making as one of expressive activity, the world is thought to be immediately hermeneutic or is seen as artistic. But even what is called cognitive activity does not see the world from outside the world. Even the knowing self is not merely something like an eye that sees the world from outside the world. Even the activity of cognition comes into being at the extreme limit of the activity of historical form-making in the manner of the movement from the made to the making, as discussed above. Cognition itself belongs to the activity of historical form-making. It is within the world of becoming and on the basis of movement and becoming that there is knowing. It is for this reason that what is called cognition is even possible. Were it something merely outside of that world, what is called knowing would be impossible. What is called the activity of historical form-making, as I have already argued, is always already mediated by the transcendental. In the world of historical form-making, the expressive is the actual. At the extreme limit that is a creator's creation, what is given, as what is made, is that which is to be utterly negated; then, the activity of historical form-making, in the sense that it utterly negates and transcends the corporeal, becomes semiotic expressive activity. That is the activity of intellection. The historical corporeal self, at its foremost point, becomes intellectual. The world seen according to the self-contradictory negation of such an intellectual self is the so-called world of objects of cognition. In the sense that it is seen on the basis of the self-contradictory negation of the intellectual self, it is the world of an intellectual imperative "should." It is not a world constituted subjectively but a world that appears objectively. It is what confronts the intellectual self as command. We do not recognize this because the intellectual self self-contradictorily negates the self itself. Therein, what is "corporeally intellectually aware" is negated, and one might plausibly think that it would be impossible even to speak of something like seeing. To see in terms of expressive activity is the fact that the activity is dialectically enveloped within the world of things. Even when one speaks of the physical world, at the extreme limit of the self-transcendence of the historical corporeal productive self, there must be the world seen on the basis of semiotic expressive form-making. What is seen on the basis of the pure self-form-making of the semiotic expressive self might be thought to be the world of number. It is thought to completely transcend what is corporeally given (of course, even mathematics is something that develops historically from the historical world, but . . .). Contrariwise, the world according to physics always proceeds from that which is corporeally given.

Yet to see this world as expressive form-making is not to see this world subjectively. The absolutely dialectical world of the mutual supplementarity and complementarity of subject and object must to the furthest extent be the world that itself forms itself expressively. That is a world that utterly transcends our subjective activity; it is a world thought as one in which what is called our subjective activity emerges from the movement of that world. The world that merely confronts us as cognitive epistemological object is not the truly objective world. However far one might pursue such thinking, the world would never be more than a merely external world; it would necessarily be no more than something like a world of the Kantian thing in itself. The truly objective world must be a world that absolutely negates us but at the same time is the world from which we are born. It must be the world of the historical-social thing in itself. Our intentional action develops from the dialectical self-identity of what is called seeing and what is called acting; it develops in terms of expressive form-making activity, it develops productively. Historical-social matter must be possessed of expressivity. It moves neither mechanically nor teleologically; rather, it moves expressively and in form-making. To the extent that the thing is seen expressively and in terms of form-making, the thing shows or manifests the thing in itself. Outside of this, there is no hidden world of the thing in itself. Therefore, what appears is qua-actuality. A materiality that is not possessed of the essential quality of expressive form-making is nothing more than a thought materiality. To the extent that the thing forms the self itself expressively — that is, to the extent that it appears in actuality — it is actually existing.[7]

AS CONCEIVED BY HISTORICAL MATERIALISM, the world of matter is a world that neither moves mechanically nor develops biologically. It is necessarily a world that is continually itself forming itself in expressive activity, which is to say, in production. Thus we can say that, from the beginning, man makes the milieu and that the milieu makes man, and one can speak of a world of the relations of production, a productively active world. Historical matter is neither what merely moves nor what merely grows but necessarily that which possesses expressivity; it is that which necessarily moves in expressive activity. What is conceived as physical force in the world of historical matter should better be called the force of expressive form-making. It is the forces of production and, therefore, the force of creation. To say that the thing possesses expressivity is to make appear the self-contradictory nature of the thing. To say that the thing itself expresses itself is to say that on one side it itself absolutely negates itself; it necessarily becomes nothing (which is not to become merely latent or dormant). Moreover, the very fact that it itself negates itself is also at the same time that it itself makes itself appear; one must necessarily say that the thing sustains the thing itself—which is necessarily to say that there is a thing. In the historic-social world, the thing is necessarily that which expresses itself productively in expressive activity. And it is as such that it possesses its existentiality. (I wonder if the fact that contemporary physics conceives the contradictory unity of physical substance and waves is not based on this principle, derived from this concept of self-contradictory being.) The dialectical world as conceived heretofore has not been conceived as a dialectical world that truly takes absolute negation as mediation. Expression, therefore, has been subsumed within subjectivist activity; it has not been conceived objectively as the essence of the thing itself. The historical world is neither mediated externally, nor is it internally mediated. Neither do I maintain that it is unmediated in the manner of the unity of subject and object. The unity of subject and object conceived from the standpoint of the logic of judgment in terms of the grammatical logical subject of a statement or proposition is no thing whatever outside of a static unity. Continually moving from the making to the made and from the made to the making, the world is necessarily constituted in the self-identity of absolute contradiction. It is a world mediated by the absolute nothing, a world mediated by absolute negation. Thereby, what acts, what mediates itself internally, must negate the self itself—rather, must be negated: the self must be mediated externally. To say that the self is mediated externally is to say that the self is negated. To say that what makes is itself something made is to say that what makes is negated by this world. Everything is thereby determined by the past; it is a world of the past only. Therefore, to speak of the movement from the made to the making is necessarily to say that the making is born of the depths of absolute negation, from the depths of nothing. And that is to say that the thing acts in expressive activity; it is to say that in the world of historical movement, the thing is possessed of expressivity. To this point I have spoken of the movement from the made to the making, but to speak of the made is to speak of what has entered into the past. To speak of "from the past" is to speak of necessity, from which the making cannot emerge; therein there is no freedom. To say "from the made" is the negation of life. It is in such an affirmation of negation that there is historical movement. It is neither mechanical nor teleological. Although the past is what is utterly determined, it is given as that which is to be negated. To say that the past is negated within time is to say that the future is born. That is not to say, however, either that the future is subsumed within or is immanent in the past or that what has appeared as the acting makes of the past raw material. The past is the past because it utterly negates the future; the future is the future because it utterly negates the past. Time is constituted as such contradictory self-identity. To say that what is given as past (that is, what as external mediation negates us) is given as that which is to give birth to the future on the basis of negating the self itself is to say that it is given as that which is to be seen in expressive activity (in the historical space of the simultaneous copresence of past and future). In the dialectical world, which is external mediation–qua–internal mediation in the manner of contradictory self-identity, the thing is seen in expressive activity; the thing mediates the self itself in expressive activity. Our productive intentional action arises from seeing the thing. Our life arises from seeing the thing dialectically. Except that at the extreme limit of such life we think we act intentionally from an abstract self divorced from the activity of historical form-making. But however far one carries this abstraction, our intentional action is never separated from the activity of historic-social constitution. Though it be moral intentional action, it is nothing but a continuation of historic-social constitution. One might therefore even think "should, therefore can." Indeed, it is because historic-social constitutive force is expressively active and because the thing is possessed of expressivity that one can perhaps say that actuality is logical. It is not that concrete actuality becomes the cognitive epistemological object of logic but that logic is at work within actuality. To say that the thing acts in expressive activity is to say that the thing acts logically. One can say that actuality moves in terms of a dialectical logic. What is called abstract logic appears at the extreme limit of dialectical logic's negative mediation. Expressive activity makes mediation of negation. When, at the extreme limit of its negative mediation, the acting itself is thought to be negated, expressive activity becomes the activity of judgment (therein, what is simply semiotic can be thought to become the cognitive epistemological object). It is, however, on the basis of making mediation of absolute negation that the life of expressive active form-making comes into being. And that one can say that what is called the activity of historical form-making is necessarily social might itself well be understood from the fact of the expressivity of historical matter.

The world that comes into being on the basis of the self-identity of contradiction, the world that is continually itself constituting itself in expressive activity, is a world in which seeing is acting and acting is seeing; that is, it is a world that, centered on productive historical actuality, continually moves from the made to the making. Where the world is productive, there is historical actuality; there is where history lives. That a thing has been made is the fact that it has entered into the past; the made thing is the dead thing. In historical space, however, it is not that the thing simply becomes nothing but that it has become something seen; it has entered the expressive world. Thus, it is as something seen that it provokes the activity of expressive activity; the thing is what moves productively; it is the movement from the made to the making, the movement from past to future. And that is to say that this world is utterly mediated externally. Were the thing not to enter into the past, nothing at all could be born; without any sort of change no thing whatsoever could emerge; without cause there is no effect. For this reason the world of historical actuality, which itself constitutes itself in expressive activity, is to the furthest extent a world of cause and effect, the physical world. Although we speak of the physical world of causality, it is necessarily a world seen entirely in expressive activity. Physical substance must be possessed of expressivity (physical substance is necessarily in one aspect wave motion). As I said above, the actuality of production in expressive activity, historical corporeal actuality, is constituted on the basis of absolute contradictory self-identity; it must be entirely mediated negatively. Were that not so, there would be no actuality that itself determines itself. To speak of being entirely mediated negatively is to say that the body becomes utterly *logos*-like; it is to say that the thing becomes utterly nominal. It is when it is thought that actuality passes, that is, when actuality is what is to enter into the past, when it is thought that actuality comes into being as the effect of the movement from the past that is the utter negation of actuality to the future, that—transcending actuality—the physical world, expressed merely mathematically (formally), can be seen. Even an experi-

ment in physics is to see in expressive activity. What is called mathematical form is the form of the activity of expressive form-making in which
seeing is acting and acting is seeing; it is the pure form of the dialectical
self-identity of cognitive epistemological object and activity. One might
even consider mathematical processes to be the semiotic form-making of
the contradictory self-identity of seeing and acting. Although the world
according to contemporary physics is said to transcend actuality and to
be nonintuitive, it is nevertheless necessarily and completely constituted
from the world of actuality on the basis of experimentation. Historical
actuality is that which is formed in expressive activity; it is that which
itself gives form to itself in expressive activity; because it is mediated by
that which is absolutely transcendental, it can be thought to transcend
the self itself and to be mediated by what is not actual. As above, to say
that the thing is made in historical actuality is to say that the thing, mediated by absolute negation, is seen; it is to say it appears, which conversely is to say that activity is provoked; the physical world is conceived
as the movement from the made to the making—that is, as the movement from the past to the future. It is only as that which is to be negated
by the future, however, that the past is the past; without the past there
is no future, but neither is there any past without the future. When the
future is thought to be within the past, then it is a teleological world that
is being conceived. But even though it is a teleological world that is being
conceived, it is not a world of productive actuality. It is not a world of
form-making activity; therein there is nothing of making. Therein there
is nothing of the autonomy of activity; it is merely that activity is subsumed within the cognitive epistemological object and the seeing within
the seen. It is not a world of the contradictory self-identity of seeing
and acting. Be it a mechanistic world, or be it a teleological world, it is
a world conceived in abstraction from the movement from the made to
the making. Even in teleological activity the future is merely subsumed
within the past. The world of productive actuality must be a world of the
movement from the made to the making; it is necessarily a world of the
contradictory self-identity of the made and the making. It is of necessity
a world mediated by absolute negation. What is made is that which enters
into the absolute past, and one cannot speak of the movement from the
made to the making. That is a contradiction. Moreover, the world of pro-

ductive actuality is that which is continually moving, in expressive activity, from the made to the making. From the standpoint of the logic of
judgment, this can neither be called being nor can it be called nothing. It
is nothing other than self-contradictory being-qua-nothing and nothing-
qua-being. It might almost go without saying that a teleological world,
though it be called the world of matter, is necessarily a made world. In the
historical world there is nothing that is merely given. What is given must
be what has been made. It is because it is what has been made that it can
become the making. Without having been made, it cannot become the
making. Even in the case of the material world, it is only as being made/
making that it can become entirely the milieu of the historical world.
Thus, it is vis-à-vis historical becoming that it can possess the quality of
past-as-ground. In the world of our active intuition, it is only from the
aspect of the past that there is the seen.

The world of historical actuality such as I have discussed above is a
world that, being self-contradictory, itself continually transcends itself;
insofar as it always itself transcends itself, it is a world that possesses the
very quality of actuality of the self. To say that insofar as it transcends
the self itself it possesses the actuality of the self itself means that it is
established on the basis of absolute self-identity, that it possesses self-
identity in the absolute other; it means that it is not within the self
itself that it possesses self-identity. The world that possesses self-identity
within the self itself is not a world that transcends the self itself from
within the self itself. It might almost go without saying that the physical
world as it has heretofore been conceived, even as a teleological world
of biological life, is not a world that transcends the self from within the
self; it is not a world that possesses the self in self-negation; it is not a
world that from within the self destroys the self. It is merely a world of
spontaneous generation. It is only when the self transcends the self, with
the self going outside itself into the world that one can say for the first
time that it itself is self-contradictory being; it is only then that one can
speak of the self continually transcending the self from within the self,
self-contradictorily. The world that, on the basis of the contradictory
self-identity of seeing and acting, forms the self itself in active intuition
is not a world that possesses self-identity within the self itself. It neither
possesses self-identity on the side of the seen thing, nor does it possess

self-identity on the side of the seeing. If it is not a world that is medi-ated externally, neither is it a world mediated internally. Although it is that which is utterly determined as that which is made, as that which is mediated by absolute negation, it is that which always transcends the self-itself self-contradictorily; it is that which is continually moving from the made to the making. It is that which does not possess within the self itself that which mediates the self; that is, it possesses no self-identity. One therefore says that it is mediated by absolute nothing. But that is not to say it is mediated by simply nothing but that it is mediated by what is absolutely transcendental. For this reason I say that in the historical present we touch on the present that cannot touch on the absolute. Self-identity does not exist in this world. It is not merely that the absolute is that which is not to be approached but also that we cannot even confront it. There is no path from the created to the creator. Actuality, however, is always mediated by the absolutely transcendental; it is from the abso-lute that we cannot even speak of confronting that we are shown as that place of confrontation.

The historical actuality that forms the self itself in the manner of ex-pressive activity in the movement from the made to the making is always, as above, the world that transcends the self itself. It is as the active aspect of such a world, that is as creative elements of a creative world, that we possess our lives; our being is therefore self-contradictory. Even the life of the animal is already such contradictory being. To the extent that what might be called animal life is conscious, it is neither merely mechani-cal nor simply teleological; it is necessarily historically form-making. As Hegel said, animals, too, perform the mysteries of the heroic. But animal life conforms to the aspect of the made; it is life that adheres to the sur-faces of things. But the historical actuality that forms the self itself in ex-pressive activity is both that which, as something formed, is utterly deter-mined and that which, as something utterly transcending the self, forms the self itself. Our historical life, mediated by absolute negation, always faces absolute negation. This is to say that it touches on the absolute that absolutely cannot be touched upon. We call the vanguard of such his-torical life human life. It is because in the world of historical actuality we confront the absolute that we cannot confront that we become self-aware. When, at the extreme limit of the self-contradiction of the world of historical life, as contradictory self-identity, continually moving from the made to the making, in acting we confront absolutely infinite objective expression (the so-called word of God), we become self-aware; that is, we become personal. Outside of this there is no true self-awareness whatever. In this way our human life and the life of animals stand at opposite poles of historical life; but I do not thereby say that so-called daily life as such is such life-at-the-limit. Even what we call our daily life is animal in its fleshly aspect; and though we call it mindful or spiritual, it is for the greater part merely customary. Still, constitutive historical life, as absolute contradictory self-identity, possesses both poles (what people usually think of as "daily life" is its informal version). The animal is an animal because it possesses the human as its polar opposite; the human is human because it possesses the animal as its polar opposite. We are truly human only when we situate ourselves at the extreme limit of that life in our daily life activities. Outside of that our lives are nothing more than animal or socioautomatic. As Bergson puts it, the flow of life of creative evolution solidifies in the way an iron ingot hardens. What I call life is not the same as what Bergson called life, but on the basis of the fact that the historical life that continually moves dialectically from the made to the making is inscribed on the surface of what has been made, it solidifies, becoming automatic and mechanical. That is the side of death. Life lives insofar as it is creative in active intuition. That I characterize life activity in its everydayness as concrete is not by virtue of becoming customary or automatic. Only what is concrete is liable to corruption; to speak of being liable to corruption is, conversely, to speak of being able to touch the absolute.

3

What we think of as our actually existing world is necessarily a world that touches on the sensible; more, it is necessarily grounded in the sensible. Heretofore, sense or the sensible has been conceived from the standpoint of judgment to be merely passive. But that is not what grounds our actually existing world. Our actually existing world must be grasped as sensuous human activity, as practice, subjectively.[8] Though I speak of the subject, it is not that there is first of all a subject that subsequently grasps something. "Sensuous human activity" necessarily arises in active intuition. Sensuous human activity arises from the dialectical self-identity of the seeing and the acting. This is to speak of making things; it is to speak of praxis, or practice. What we call our actually existing world, therefore, is a world of productive practice; to the extent that, centered on productive practice, it is continually moving self-contradictorily from the made to the making, it is, in fact, the actually existing world.

The fact that man has appeared in this world is necessarily the effect of millennia of biological evolution. And we must posit a world of infinite physical movement prior to the genesis of living beings. It can be thought that living beings emerged within a certain setup of the physical world. To characterize the historical world's development as expressive activity is not to ignore the laws of the natural sciences; on the contrary, they must, taken together, be the law of the self-formation of the dialectical world of the mutual complementarity of subject and object. Thus, the world that, as contradictory self-identity absolutely characterized by such mutual complementarity, gives form to the self itself, must be the world that gives form to the self itself in expressive activity. The fact that there could be the eye or the ear cannot but be thought as the trace of past millennia of evolution.

As contradictory self-identity, the world that itself forms itself in the movement from the made to the making attains man at the furthest limit of being made, making; man is, as it were, the apex of creation. The given is thereby absolutely that which is made, that which is given to be negated. It is to think the made from the making. This is why it is said that God made man in His own image. Even our bodies, as already belonging to expressive activity, are mediated by the transcendental, but it is at the furthest limit of the movement from the made to the making that we can say we face toward the absolutely transcendental. There is our self-awareness, our freedom. We can think something to the effect that we have been able to break away from historical causality. In the world of historical actuality, the sensible is not merely grasped as sensuous human activity but is grasped entirely as expressive and form-making; it must be grasped as historic-social activity. It follows on the becoming-creative of the world that moves from the made to the making that it necessarily moves from the instinctive to the becoming-social. At the furthest limit of that movement, when it becomes a matter of the movement from the making to the made, because it is mediated by the absolutely transcendental, what is called the world of free man comes into being. What I call the world that itself determines itself idiosyncratically is the world of free man.[9]

As I argued in "The Problem of the Generation and Development of Species," in the historical world the subject determines the milieu, and the milieu determines the subject.[10] Although subject and milieu are utterly opposed, the subject determines the milieu on the basis of idiosyncratically negating the self itself, and the milieu determines the subject on the basis of idiosyncratically negating the self itself. Subject and milieu, by means of idiosyncrasy, in mutually negating each other mutually determine each other; in the movement from the made to the making, the world is idiosyncratically continually itself determining itself. What is called the subject [*shutai*] is the active side of contradictory self-identity; the milieu is the side of the seen thing. To say that the world, moving from the made to the making, is moving idiosyncratically is to say that the world is continually itself forming itself in expressive activity. Thus to say that it is mediated by absolute negation is to say that it is mediated by the absolutely transcendental, by absolute nothing. We can say that at the furthest limit of the movement from the made to the making the world is continually moving from the made to the making centered in idiosyncratic constitution. Because it is mediated by absolute negation, the world is continually moving in self-awareness. This is to say it is characterized by reason. What is given is what has been made, and what has been made is what is given; what determines the self itself syllogistically is what is idiosyncratic.

Therefore, the world of man, as the apex of the movement from the made to the making, and centered on idiosyncratic constitution, can be thought as the conjunction of the utterly mutually opposed aspects of the seen thing and activity. What is called seeing and what is called acting are thought to be utterly mutually opposed. The center of the idiosyncratic constitution by which the world itself determines itself—that is, reason—is the point at which the world, taking absolute negation as mediation, can be thought to be the point of touching on the absolute that is absolutely untouchable, the point mediated by the absolutely transcendental. At this point the given, as that which is given to be negated, can be conceived as the movement from the making to the made. From such a standpoint it is thought that it is something like a cognitive epistemological subject that as expressive constitutive activity utterly transcends what is corporeally given and that, thereby, theoretical reason comes into being. Contrariwise, on the side of activity there is thought abstractly to be the world of the "should." A world of Kant's "practical reason" comes into being. So when, in the opposition of the made and the making, the made is thought to be simply the given, it is considered to be mere material substance. The opposition is thought to be one of form and substance. But in absolutely dialectical historical space, the made is necessarily both the given as that which is to be negated and that which negates the making. The past is not merely that which is given to be negated by the future; it is necessarily also that which negates the future. In historical space as absolute contradictory self-identity, the given is not merely given substantially, or materially, but is necessarily given as quality or character that negates the making; that is, it is necessarily daemonic. It is not simply that which is to be given form but must be that which is to be utterly defeated or overcome. At the extreme limit of the movement from the making to the made, therefore, the self-formation of the world mediated by absolute negation is not the formation of epistemological objects but must be of the imperative "should." At the extreme limit of the self-determination of the world of the dialectical universal that itself utterly determines itself in expressive activity, the world is a world of the personal self-awareness that opposes individual to individual, the I to the Thou; it is necessarily a world that itself forms itself in practical reason. For this reason the true "should" must be conceived not from the standpoint of the self of consciousness but from the standpoint of the practical self of active intuition. It is as creative elements of a creative world that we possess the concrete imperative "should." The imperative "should," as the objective expression of the historical world that itself forms itself in expressive activity, necessarily confronts us from without.

AS I SAID BEFORE, the world of historical life, at the limit of the movement from the made to the making, continually moves centered on idiosyncratic constitution. The world itself constitutes itself idiosyncratically.

That may be said to be reason. To the extent that as idiosyncratic elements of an idiosyncratic world we belong to reason, we are creative. To see the world from this perspective alone is the so-called rationalist standpoint; to see man only from this standpoint is the perspective of an immanent humanism; it is the standpoint of *hyūmanizumu*. That is, as the apex of the movement from the made to the making, it is thought that man himself creates himself. But, as I argued above, man appears at the apex of the movement from the made to the making at the extreme limit of the world that is continually moving from the made to the making. Man absolutely cannot escape from his infinitely profound historical ballast. Were he to escape it, what is called man would disappear. This would leave behind simply something like merely abstract will. Is it not for this reason that one must posit that there is an extreme limit in the world of the movement from the making to the made? I ask this because, as the world that is itself continually forming itself in expressive activity and on the basis of absolute contradictory self-identity, it does not possess self-identity within itself. If in the making the made is transcended, then there is only a world of merely abstract logic. That is merely the direction of dying. There is reason where, as the contradictory self-identity of what is called seeing and what is called acting, we see the thing self-contradictorily. As self-contradictory being we see the thing on the basis of negating the self itself; where, from seeing the thing we act, there is the fact that there is reason (on the basis of acting, we reflect the thing; on the basis of reflecting the thing, we act). What is called reason is therefore not immanent in man; it is on the basis of being mediated by the transcendental that there is what is called reason. To say that man is rational is not grounded in an anthropocentric humanism; on the contrary, it is necessarily quite the reverse. Perhaps it will be thought irrational, but contrariwise it is what shows the transcendental foundation of human being. What is truly rational is necessarily what is mediated transcendentally.

Here I cannot but recall the novels of Dostoevsky. His problem was the question of what sort of thing man is. He pursued the problem seriously and exhaustively. Like the hero of *Notes from Underground*, the impulsive person, like a mad bull, lowers his horns and rams into a wall. But where there is no freedom, there man is not. Natural science says there is nothing of what is called free will or the like, but if man is not a mathematical formula, neither is he an organ stop. The hero of *Crime and Punishment* killed a usurious old woman. But he did so neither in order to take her money nor for the sake of saving someone. Rather, it was to test his freedom, to see whether he could become a strong figure such as Napoleon, to whom all is permitted. Yet it became clear that he was no more than a single louse. Even the famous discourse of the Grand Inquisitor in *The Brothers Karamazov* says nothing other than this. Dostoevsky saw man at the extreme limit; he saw man in relation to his "vanishing point."[11] Nietzsche, too, saw man at the limit. But he saw him from the exactly opposite standpoint from that of Dostoevsky. As I have argued before, it is as the apex of the movement from the made to the making that man is truly human in dashing against an iron wall. There, there are only two paths. Either one could, like Raskolnikov, living without God, bow one's head to the prostitute Sonja and thus enter upon a new life or, like the man named Kirilov, find the way to God from within the "evil one." Nietzsche's notion of the Overman is precisely that. But my sense is this: is it not necessarily the case that his concept of the eternal return rather shows that, from the standpoint of the Overman, he is confronted with a profound desire that he himself cannot on his own transcend? The dwarf says all that is straight is a lie, all that is true is crooked, and time itself is a circle. From the standpoint of the eternal return, even the Overman necessarily at some time becomes a dwarf! The dogs bark when the moon is high (*Vom Gesicht und Rätsel*).[12]

Where there is no freedom, there man is not. But the more man would make himself utterly free, the more he dashes up against the iron wall of the absolute. The more man would be truly man, the more he stands in crisis. Man that has not yet attained that crisis has not, strictly speaking, escaped the animal realm of "living in liquor and dying in a dream." One can therefore say that it is the man who has turned furthest from God who has approached nearest to God. It is in man negating man himself that he truly finds the living path of man. Here I consider there to be true reason. Concrete logic, as the true dialectic, must take up this standpoint. If it is not that man becomes God, neither is it that God becomes man. Nor yet is it that God and man become one in the so-called union of God and man. God and man are necessarily utterly opposed;

alienated in absolute negation, they are mutually opposed; or rather, one cannot even speak of "opposing." In the movement from the made to the making, as absolute contradictory self-identity, there is the opposition of God and world; man, as the apex of the movement from the made to the making, and in being mediated by absolute negation, belongs to reason. To see God only in man's absolute negation, as in dialectical theology, is not therefore truly to know the God of the absolute. There is no path from man to God. There must therein be absolute negation. It is only on the basis of absolute negation, however, that man possesses true life. The phrase "not I, but Christ lives in me" is to speak of being resurrected other than in prolepsis. True culture must be born from there. But I do not speak here of religion. It is not from the standpoint of religious experience that I argue. I speak from an exhaustive logical analysis of historical actuality. Furthermore, I do not merely analyze its structure but seek to clarify its movement.

As I said before, I am not attempting to disparage human reason or freedom; on the contrary, it is quite the reverse. I am attempting to displace its ground from subjectivist man and to posit it in the creative operation of the creative world. I would even seek the ground of moral imperative there. It is to the extent that man is creative as the apex of the movement from the created to the creative that he is of reason, that he is free. I take no part in negating culture from the standpoint of religion. As I said above, however, the world that moves from the made to the making always transcends the self itself; historical actuality is always trembling. Therein is the subjectivity of the world. Therefore, as the apex of the movement from the made to the making, man is always willful. Where reason steps over reason in the direction of reason is where the world of abstract logic is established. To see the world from that perspective is subjectivism. Many have heretofore considered reason or freedom only from this standpoint. Of course, without what is willful, there is no man. Where there is what is willful, there is the religious essence of man. It is not that there is reason where there is nothing of abstract logic. Where there is abstract logic as the negation of the self itself from the standpoint of the self itself, there is dialectical logic. However, that man steps over the self itself in the direction of willfulness is the degeneration or corruption of man; that reason steps over the self itself in the direction of abstraction is to lose the objectivity of reason (that technics steps over technics in the direction of technics is intentional action). It may seem irrational, but, as I said before, man is man because he possesses the animal as the other extreme of his being; the animal is animal because it possesses man as the other extreme of its being. The world of historical actuality that transcends the self itself is always entirely and continually progressing in the direction of transcending the self itself. That is, it is both an advance in the direction of idiosyncrasy and an advance in the direction of degeneration or corruption, the furthest point of which is decadence. A single historical tendency is nothing more than that. In possessing new life, we return to the feeling of creative nature. From there we come to possess a renewed creative power, where a new life is born in us. It is always from there that emerges what is irrational and animal, irreducible to abstract logic. Therein is the great crisis of culture. However, to the extent that as the movement from the made to the making the crisis is constitutive as active intuition, being rational it becomes the creative force of new history. On this basis one speaks of the limit becoming transition, or of metamorphosis. What in the manner of contradictory self-identity is continually constituting in active intuition, in the movement from the making to the made, is concrete logic. What being of the *logos* is natural and being natural is of the *logos*, what is historic-natural, is what is truly of reason. What being immediate is mediate, what being mediate is immediate: what is truly syllogistic must necessarily be this sort of thing. Where we act from seeing and see on the basis of acting without supposition, there truly is what is of reason. To speak of acting on the basis of reflecting the thing, and on the basis of acting to reflect the thing, must necessarily also be in this sense truly of reason. That is to speak of the movement from the made to the making; as mediated by absolute negation, there is necessarily always abstract logic at work therein. Were that not the case, there would be nothing of reason. Were it to lose the sense of being given as the made, it would become merely abstract. The merely abstract is, conversely, the merely irrational. The negation of actuality must always issue from self-contradiction. From the standpoint of abstract logic, the negation of actuality is impossible. Even if it were possible, it would not be possible to constitute objective knowledge. Even the forms of thought that are the ground of scholarly knowledge must be grasped in the manner of active intuition. It is thus that for the first time that historic-social actuality can become the logical and grammatical subject of judgment. Undoubtedly, one can proceed from a certain determinate form of thought in a certain determinate historical period in terms of abstract logic. Therein is what is thought to be the continuity of knowledge. When, however, one takes it to its conclusion, one returns to the root of active intuition; it is necessarily constituted creatively from active intuition. Dialectics is the logic of such creation. It may be thought that one can reach that point if one proceeds in terms of the logic of judgment. But there is necessarily a fundamental idea already grasped in terms of active intuition that is already at work in the logic of judgment. And that is necessarily what has been made historically. It is for that reason that it can be taken to its conclusion. It comes when what has been constituted historically and subjectively is to be negated historically. There is nothing that is merely given in the historical world.

PERHAPS IT CAN BE SAID that Greek culture was a culture that privileged seeing, in other words, that it was subjectivist. Acting was subsumed within the seen thing. It might be possible to think that it was unmediated, historical-corporeal. That is, it was of the polis. In the culture of the Middle Ages, however, God and man were opposed; the immanent and the transcendental were in utter opposition. So culture sought that which transcended man's essence; that is to say, it was a religious culture. It might even be considered to have been dialectical. However, the standpoint of mere mutual negation is not dialectical. It might even be considered that in the Middle Ages it was man that was to be negated. However, one can say that in one aspect God was made human. And that is the secularization of the Church. It is for this reason that the Inquisition seemingly inexplicably emerged in the world of the Middle Ages and condemned Christ. Therein there is nothing of true contradictory self-identity; on the contrary, anything truly religious was lost. Contradictory self-identity, as mere mysticism, was no more than abstractly sustained in monastic practice. But the Renaissance was not merely the restoration of ancient culture but the fact, it is said, that man discovered man. Man returned to the creative self and wrested sovereignty from God. That was humanism. And one can probably say that it was there that the early modern culture of anthropocentrism began. The authority of the transcendental was displaced to reason and experience. Today's culture can be thought to be the effect of that displacement. It may be that we can say that today we stand at the limit of the movement from the made to the making. But the made cannot pass into the making. There is what is called man, as self-contradictory being, at the apex of the movement from the made to the making. We must attempt to return once again to the ground of human being. And we must there once again discover a new man.

The anthropocentric humanism by which man divorced himself from religious authority and rediscovered himself at the beginning of the early modern period, as the development of new historical life, formed the great culture of the early modern period. But the development of anthropocentrism itself necessarily progressed in the direction of humanism and individualism. Reason stepped over reason in the direction of reason. Thereby, contrariwise, man lost man himself. Man does not live on the basis of man himself, nor is that the essence of man. Man necessarily and utterly depends on the objective. Man exists in possessing the life of the self in what has transcended the self itself. In the Middle Ages God and man were opposed. In the early modern period, when man became the center (when man became God), man and nature were opposed. Nature, being milieu, was even something to be used, but nature-as-object was necessarily what essentially negated man. If man did not make nature, then man, first and last, was that which was negated by nature. Even though we speak of the conquest of nature, it is still only because we follow upon nature that we conquer nature. Our hands and our feet alike are things. Even when we consider inner desire, it is that which negates the self. Even when one posits the ego as being utterly negative with respect to nature, that is necessarily nothing other than a formal ego. One does try to find something like the self in nature-as-object. Therein there is only death. It is for this reason that I say anthropocentrism, contrariwise, leads to the negation of the human. The true self is not to be revealed in the constitution of the subjectivist self from the standpoint of the opposition of subject and object; on the contrary, it is necessarily from nature itself being something made that the true self is revealed. In the historical world there is nothing that is merely given. History is a thoroughly self-contradictory dialectical process. It is as the apex of the movement from the made to the making that man exists. What is called man emerges from the self-contradiction of the world itself. What are called our true selves exist, as creative elements of the creative world, in being productive, in being creative. Therefore there is man in the fact that what is truly immanent in the self itself is mediated by the transcendental, and in the fact that what is mediated by the transcendental is truly immanent in the self itself. This standpoint is diametrically opposed to the relation of the transcendental and the immanent in the Middle Ages. In the place of the mystical union of man and God in the Middle Ages, there is productive creation. Undoubtedly, such contradictory self-identity is not conceivable from the standpoint of abstract logic. But the fact of contradictory self-identity is the fact of the movement from the made to the making. What mutually opposes each other in abstract logic are utterly unrelated according to the terms of abstract logic. It is, moreover, for that reason that the world self-contradictorily and dialectically is continually moving from the made to the making. Is it not that in returning once again to the ground of the constitution of man, and as productive-creative man, that a new man must necessarily emerge?

To speak of moving from the immanent anthropocentrism of the early modern period to the objectivism of historical man is not to speak of reverting to the religious mysticism of the Middle Ages. It is to take the standpoint of active intuition, where seeing is entirely based on acting and acting on seeing; it is to assume the standpoint of *homo faber*. Even the scientific spirit, in which it is on the basis of practice that the thing is reflected and on the basis of reflecting the thing that there is acting, is nothing outside of this. From the beginning that the animal is for "man," we have seen the thing on the basis of acting, and we have acted on the basis of seeing. Even what is called science has necessarily developed from the standpoint of *homo faber*. What becomes its cognitive, epistemological object is necessarily historical actuality. Therefore, even the physical world must be one of mutual complementarity. There is no theory apart from practice. But that is not to say that theory emerges from something like so-called intellectually self-aware experience. In historical life, nothing is simply given; the immediate is mediate, and what is mediate is immediate. What is called active intuition is to see by means of historical life. There has been active intuition beginning with the animals. At the limit of such historical life, as the movement from the made to the making, it has come to reason. It is therein that the animal corporeal must be negated. Theory is established where the corporeal self is mediated by absolute negation in expressive activity. But that is by no means to escape from the standpoint of the movement from the made to the making. Were that not so, it would become nothing but abstract theory. In the standpoint of historical creative man, even tradition must be intuitively at work, as T. S. Eliot said. He likened this to the catalyst of literature. In the extinction of the individual, art approaches the condition of science.

From the perspective of historical productive humanism, something that is transcendentally subjective, such as the universal of consciousness or the absolute ego, does not become the center. Although it is said there is that which utterly negates the subjective, neither does anything like the "substance" of the natural sciences become the ground. Historical, social, creative activity becomes the center. As I said at the beginning of this essay, we make things. But, although a thing is made by us, being autonomous, it contrariwise causes us to move. Indeed, upon reconsideration, the fact that we make things, as the movement from the made to the making, arises from the world of things. The development of scientific industry has constituted the contemporary capitalist world on the basis of such a historical process. But, as anthropocentric humanism, that has resulted in class struggle within a country and international strife among nations. That leads to the dead end of historical life, to the degeneration and annihilation of man. This situation cannot be redeemed by anthropocentric humanism (although it would make of the subject the mediation, the problem of man cannot be resolved in the war of subject and subject). What must be sought is a transposition to the perspective of an objective humanism, that taking absolute negation as mediation is historical and productive. This is neither the standpoint of Kantian duty nor of the Fichtean self-realization of the absolute ego. In spite of what Fichte claimed, he did not escape humanism. It is in producing, in his-

torical production, that we see the self; it is by means of historical production that we come to the unification (of person and person, country
and country). And that, moreover, is neither material welfare nor abstract justice. It is a relation constituted in the made thing, in seeing the
made as the objective expression of historical life; it is the standpoint of
the idiosyncratization of the world. As I have already argued, historical
productive man exists as the apex of the movement from the made to
the making, in being mediated by absolute negation. Were that not the
case, man would be merely a troop of ants, as Dostoevsky says (which
is not to ignore the question of material welfare, but . . .). It is said that
early modern capitalism emerged out of Calvinism. In Calvinism, which,
against the humanization of the God of the religion of the Middle Ages,
returned all things to a transcendental God, all that is left to us is merely
the isolated self. That Calvin moreover—and differing from Luther—
negated even an interior unity with God was nothing other than the
establishment of abstract rationalism. I think that, fearful of the relation
of man and God being made one of sentiment, Calvin went so far as to
rationalize and institutionalize that relation. But in Calvin, all that was
to the glory of God. Yet with the death of God, the aspect of "from the
made" developed into something like what Max Weber called capitalism.
Concomitantly, in the aspect of "from the making" we did nothing other
than maintain and sustain the self itself as belonging to practical reason.
I cannot now say anything positively concerning something like the new
humanism. But when I speak of returning to the transcendental, I am
not speaking of returning to an abstract absolute being that is merely
the negation of man; I am not speaking of a return to the world of the
Middle Ages. Rather it is truly to take up the standpoint of idiosyncratic
historical actuality; it is to take up the standpoint of historical reason. It
is to return to the standpoint of the absolute contradictory self-identity
that brings into being a world that, because it is transcendental, is immanent. That is not to say it is irrational. The standpoint of historical
reason is, as I said before, scientific in the sense of reflecting on the basis
of acting and acting on the basis of reflecting. But the seeing must completely and necessarily enter into what is seen; the historical must enter
into what is seen. If not, it is merely abstract. Creation is not the task of

the individual; without what is of a people, there is nothing of creation. Even what is called a people, to the extent that it is creative, belongs to reason.

IT MAY BE THAT the phrase "the transcendental" gives rise to various misunderstandings, but as I have often said, it is as absolute contradictory self-identity that it is transcendental with respect to the self of consciousness and the knowing self. We can say that, contrary to the self of intentional action or the productive self, the transcendental is immediate; it is that within which we are. One might even call it the dialectical noumenon, but that might, on the contrary, run the risk of rendering it metaphysical, something like Hegel's *caput mortuum*. In its appearance as the unity of movement and stasis, it is said to be truly absolute contradictory self-identity. Religion is not a superstition of the past or the opium of the ignorant masses; the religious is always at work in the heart of history. But, as I said before, I am not doing philosophy from the standpoint of religious experience. Quite the contrary. The standpoint of religious experience is that it is in the individual approaching death that the absolute emerges. Therein there is no scope for linguistic ambiguities. In religion there must therefore be a conversion, what is called a change of heart, in life.

From the standpoint of Kantian philosophy one is thought to be outside the scope of speculative thought if one mentions immediacy or intuition. But intuition is neither sensation nor imagination. Even Descartes clearly differentiated them. One might even say that what Descartes called *entendement* is rather intuitive. As in the famous example of the sealing wax, the wax possesses taste, fragrance, color, form, and size. But as they are brought near to the fire, those attributes immediately change. Those attributes are no longer sealing wax; the sealing wax is said to be merely *mentis inspectio*. The Cartesian concept of extension may as it stands be thought to be naïve, but the physical thing, albeit abstract, in some sense cannot be divorced from the geometrical, from the intuitive; one must speak of it as *mentis inspectio*, I rather think. From my standpoint that is the fact that one is continually seeing the thing in the manner of active intuition, in a world of expressive activity. In an insightful reading of this passage in Descartes, Alain said that it is only to imagine the living Descartes, Descartes standing before the thing, Descartes inseparable from intellectual awareness and attention.[13] He said, *"Ce n'est pas ici un homme qui arrange ses ideés au mieux, mais bien plutôt il pense l'univers present."* This is the attitude of the empirical sciences, as well; the experiment necessarily takes place on the ground of the historical world. In part I of this essay I suggested that we might be able to think of Descartes's *cogito ergo sum*, being contradictory self-identity, as seeing the self itself in expressive activity. Our knowledge arises from the fact that we, as singularities in the historical world, see the thing in expressive activity. It is from there that we are continually seeing the thing self-contradictorily. To give form dialectically is to see. We must attempt to return once again to the Cartesian standpoint. Of course, I do not claim Descartes was a dialectical thinker. But the standpoint of the immediacy of that which is indubitable in doubting everything, may necessarily be the standpoint of the self of expressive activity. In Descartes, that self was merely the self of speculative thinking. What is called phenomenology has moved from there in the direction of the standpoint of the merely conscious self. But there might be a path other than that.

NOTES

Introduction

1. These translations have been prepared from the *Nishida Kitarō zenshū* [Complete works of Nishida Kitarō], ed. Abe Yoshishige et al., 19 vols. (Tokyo: Iwanami, 1966–67). The *zenshū* will hereafter be cited as *NKz*. "Hyōgen sayō" [Expressive activity], in *Hataraku mono kara miru mono e* [From the acting to the seeing], *NKz* 4:135–72; "Kōiteki chokkan no tachiba" [The standpoint of active intuition], in *Tetsugaku ronbunshū* 1 [Philosophical essays 1], *NKz* 8:107–218; and "Ningenteki sonzai" [Human being], in *Tetsugaku ronbunshū* 3, *NKz* 9:9–68.

2. *Zen no kenkyū* [An inquiry into the good], *NKz* 1:1–200. A responsible English translation is *An Inquiry into the Good*, trans. Masao Abe and Christopher Ives (New Haven: Yale University Press, 1990).

3. The *Tetsugaku ronbunshū* may be found in vols. 8 through 11 of the *NKz*.

4. The best introduction to this general intellectual and cultural problematic is undoubtedly Harry Harootunian, *Overcome by Modernity: History, Culture, and Community in Interwar Japan* (Princeton: Princeton University Press, 2000). To invoke an age-old concept of philosophy as anarchic force — that is, to conceive philosophy (and Nishida-philosophy) as the affirmation of the essential groundlessness of thinking, an affirmation of the essential singularity of thinking (an affirmation that, as such, is thereby the immediate possibility of thinking) — is not to suggest that Nishida Kitarō was in any way sympathetic to the political actions of contemporary anarchists and communists in Japan or elsewhere. Indeed, there is considerable evidence to suggest a more than incidental complicity between Nishida (and his disciples) and the Japanese state. For introductions to some of the complexities of the issues involved see Christopher Goto-Jones, *Political Philosophy in Japan: Nishida, the Kyoto School and Co-prosperity* (London: Routledge,

2005); many of the essays in Christopher Goto-Jones, ed., *Re-politicising the Kyoto School as Philosophy* (London: Routledge, 2007); and from a very different perspective, Michiko Yusa, *Zen and Philosophy: An Intellectual Biography of Nishida Kitarō* (Honolulu: University of Hawaii Press, 2002).

5. Tiqqun, *Introduction to Civil War*, trans. Alexander R. Galloway and Jason E. Smith (Los Angeles: Semiotext[e], 2010): "*Sense* is the element of the Common, that is, every event, as an irruption of sense, institutes a common" (45).

6. On the essential complicity of modern European philosophy with the state see the text of a lecture Michel Foucault gave in Tokyo in April of 1978, "La philosophie analytique de la politique," in Michel Foucault, *Dits et écrits, 1954–1988*, ed. Daniel Defert and François Ewald, 4 vols. (Paris: Gallimard, 1994), 3:534–51.

7. Christian Marazzi, *Capital and Language: From the New Economy to the War Economy*, trans. Gregory Conti (Los Angeles: Semiotext[e], 2008); Christian Marazzi, *The Violence of Financial Capitalism*, trans. Kristina Lebedeva (Los Angeles: Semiotext[e], 2010); and Bernard Stiegler, *For a New Critique of Political Economy*, trans. Daniel Ross (Cambridge, UK: Polity Press, 2010).

8. Karl Marx, *Grundrisse: Foundations of the Critique of Political Economy (Rough Draft)*, trans. Martin Nicolaus (London: Penguin, 1973), 401n; cf. 305n.

9. Karl Marx, *Capital: A Critique of Political Economy*, trans. Ben Fowkes (London: Penguin, 1976), 1:492–639.

10. See Étienne Balibar, *The Philosophy of Marx*, trans. Chris Turner (London: Verso, 1995), 13–41.

11. See "Zettai mujunteki jiko dōitsu" [Absolute contradictory self-identity], *NKz* 9:147–222.

12. See *NKz* 9:3–7.

13. For an extended consideration of the generation and possibility of sense see "Ronri to seimei" [Logic and life], *NKz* 8:273–394; I am currently preparing a translation of this essay.

14. "Rekishiteki sekai ni oite no kobutsu no tachiba" [The standpoint of singularity in the historical world], *NKz* 9:69–146.

15. See "Ronri to seimei" [Logic and life], *NKz* 8:273–394.

16. See, e.g., Gilles Deleuze, *Expressionism in Philosophy: Spinoza*, trans. Martin Joughin (New York: Zone Books, 1990); Gilles Deleuze, *Spinoza: Practical Philosophy*, trans. Robert Hurley (San Francisco: City Lights Books, 1988); Gilles Deleuze, *The Fold: Leibniz and the Baroque*, trans. Tom Conley (Minneapolis: University of Minnesota Press, 1993); Étienne Balibar, *Spinoza and Politics*, trans. Peter Snowdon (London: Verso, 1998); Antonio Negri, *The Savage Anomaly: The Power of Spinoza's Metaphysics and Politics*, trans. Michael Hardt (Minneapolis: University of Minnesota Press, 1991); Antonio

Negri, *Political Descartes: Reason, Ideology and the Bourgeois Project*, trans. Matteo Mandarini and Alberto Toscano (London: Verso, 2006); Warren Montag and Ted Stolze, eds., *The New Spinoza* (Minneapolis: University of Minnesota Press, 1997); Warren Montag, *Bodies, Masses, Power: Spinoza and His Contemporaries* (London: Verso, 1999).

17. Karl Marx, "Economic and Philosophical Manuscripts (1844)," in *Early Writings*, trans. Rodney Livingstone and Gregor Benton (London: Penguin, 1974), 322–34.

18. Ibid., 328.

19. Ibid.

20. Marx, *Grundrisse*, 491.

21. Ibid., 491–92.

22. Marx, *Capital* 1:928.

23. See Alfred North Whitehead, *Process and Reality: An Essay in Cosmology*, corrected ed., ed. David Ray Griffin and Donald W. Sherburne (New York: Free Press, 1978), 219–65.

24. "Jissen tetsugaku jōron" [Prolegomenon to a philosophy of praxis], *NKz* 10:7–123.

25. See, e.g., "Chishiki no kyakkansei ni tsuite (shin naru chishikiron no chiba)" [On the objectivity of knowledge (foundation of a new epistemology)], *NKz* 10:343–476; "Keiken kagaku" [Empirical science], *NKz* 9:223–304; "Butsuri no sekai" [The world of physics], *NKz* 11:5–59; and "Kūkan" [Space], *NKz* 11:193–236.

26. A serious investigation of these themes would have to include, at the very least, scrupulous readings of "Shu no seisei hatten no mondai" [The problem of the generation and development of species], *NKz* 8:500–540; "Kokka riyū no mondai" [The problem of *Staatsräson*], *NKz* 10:265–337; and many of the essays already cited.

27. Spinoza, *Ethics*, Part III, Prop. 9, Schol., in *The Collected Works of Spinoza*, ed. and trans. Edwin Curley (Princeton: Princeton University Press, 1985), 1:500.

Expressive Activity

1. See Glossary, s.v. "Object." Unless stated otherwise, all notes are by the translator.

2. Emil Heinrich DuBois-Reymond (1818–96), German biologist, author of *Über die Grenzen des Naturkennens* (1872) and *Die sieben Welträtsel* (1880).

3. "Substrate" translates *jitai*, which translates Aristotle's *hupokumeinon*.

4. "What should be" translates *tōi*, which in turn translates *Sollen*.

5. There are many places in this section where I have not exhausted the argument. [Nishida's note]

6. Here Nishida uses the term *jigyō*, a neologism that translates Fichte's *Tathandlung*, itself a neologism. In both cases a "literal" translation would be something like "fact-act" or "fact-deed."

7. "Public place" is undoubtedly an inadequate translation of *ōyake no basho*. *Ōyake* once meant *daimyo* or lord, and only in the modern period did it come to mean "public." In any event it should not be confused with "public" in the senses most common in modern Western political thought. Here, "public place" suggests the radical exteriority of exposure as being situated, and it is as such that it is the condition of possibility for thought.

8. Bernhard Bolzano (1781–1848). Nishida translates *ausgesprochener Satz an sich* as *meidai jitai*, proposition qua substrate or *hupokumeinon*.

9. Konrad Adolf Fiedler (1841–95).

10. See Glossary, s.v. "Action."

11. It might be relevant to recall here that the volume of Nishida's essays in which this one made its second appearance is called *Hataraku mono kara miru mono e*: From the acting to the seeing.

12. See Glossary, s.v. "Place."

13. "Being-at-a-place" translates *oite aru basho*, a locution as awkward in Japanese as in English in this context. *Oite* is the continuative form of the verb *oku*, to put, posit, position; in the very common usage *ni oite*, it is generally quite satisfactorily translated as "in" or "at." *Aru* is generally translated as a form of *to be*, although there is considerable discussion about whether it is a true existential—rather than merely predicative—copula. One is tempted to hear a resonance between the concept of *oite aru basho* and the Heideggerian notion of the thrownness (*Geworfenheit*) of *Dasein*. Such a comparison might well have annoyed Nishida, who was consistently impatient with Heideggerian phenomenology.

14. "Light," *hikari*, is used in the sense of "enlightened" or "illumination"; *denki* is what one turns on and off with the flip of a switch.

15. "Spontaneous presentation" translates *jihatsujiten*, one of Nishida's neologisms, compounded of *jihatsu*, spontaneity, and *jiten*, itself a compound found in no dictionary but consists of two Sino-Japanese characters, "self" and "expand," "develop," or "grow."

16. See Glossary, s.v. "Subject."

17. "Objects of art" translates *geijutsu no taishō*, not *objets d'art* but with what is an object for artistic perception and poiesis.

The Standpoint of Active Intuition

1. "Instant" translates *shunkan*, and "instantaneous" translates *shunkanteki ni*; *shunkan* is literally the blink of an eye, the *Augenblick*.
2. See Glossary, s.v. "Qua."
3. See Glossary, s.v. "Singularity."
4. The phrase is from Aristotle, and has been translated variously as "quiddity," or "what it is to be it," although the history of its translation has been extraordinarily complex and contestatory, perhaps because all of Aristotelian ontology is at stake in the phrase. Jean-François Courtine and Albert Rijksbaron offer an illuminating and pertinent discussion in Barbara Cassin, ed., *Vocabulaire Européen des philosophes: Dictionnaire des intraduisibles* (Paris: Le Robert/Seuil, 2004), s.v. "to ti en enai."
5. Aristotle again, this time in the *Physics* in a discussion of movement. *Phthora*, roughly, is "destruction"; *alloiosis* is "alteration."
6. Here the subject is *shutai*; see Glossary, s.v. "Subject."
7. "Impulsive": *shōdōteki* refers to impulse, urge, or psychoanalytic drive.
8. See Glossary, s.v. "Experience."
9. "Deictic" translates *chokushō*, direct evidence or proof.
10. *Jiyū*, here translated, as is customary, as "free," literally means "based on itself."
11. "Local determination" translates *bashoteki gentei*; see Glossary, s.v. "Place" and "Determination."
12. "Thing in itself" translates *mono jitai*, which in turn translates Kant's *Ding an sich*. "Happens" translates *genshō suru*; *genshō* is "phenomenon," and *suru* changes the noun to a verb. So, "the thing in itself happens" is a perhaps weak rendering of something like "the noumenal *Ding an sich* phenomenons itself."
13. See Glossary, s.v. "Experience."
14. "Our selves possess/are merely instrumental bodies": see Glossary, s.v. "Being." The verb here is *yū suru*. *Yū* is "being"; *suru* transforms it into a verb that is neither predicative nor existential copula. In any event this is where the visual pun on being/having takes on the full force of the philosophical argument. In this sense the entire problematic of the worker's *Eigentum* as articulated in Marx's "Economic and Philosophical Manuscripts" of 1844, and in *Capital* is at stake here.
15. "The thing makes the thing itself appear" translates *mono jishin wo genshō suru*, literally "the thing phenomenons itself" (see note 12 above).
16. "Specific differences," *shusateki dankai*, translates the *differentia specifica* of scholastic philosophy (and Kant).

17. Hugo De Vries (1848–1935), author of the two-volume *Die Mutationstheorie* (1901–3).

18. "Stereotype," *suteiru*, is used here in the technical rather than the pejorative sense; it is one of the later Nishida's most consistent figures.

19. Bergson considered custom the becoming-material substance of life. But I conceive élan vital to be the expansion of active custom. Bergson thought the temporal to be primary and the spatial to follow the temporal. I conceive it to be quite the reverse. If one posits life to be constitutive, then one cannot but conceive it in that way. Life that is not constitutive is neither objective nor historical. It is no more than that which is conceived in the depths of the merely subjective self. When we speak of custom, of course, we probably most often conceive it to be continuous. But that is based on conceiving something of the thing in itself at the heart of custom. And when one thinks in that way, then from where might one try to conceptualize the coming into being of custom? Custom is necessarily the self-determination of that which is, in terms of the cognitive epistemological object, nothing. It is only after having written the present section on custom that quite by chance I happened to read Ravaisson's *On Custom*; I learned that Ravaisson had already thought quite profoundly about custom. He did not go so far as to conceive it in terms of the actuality of the historical world, yet one cannot but say it is a beautiful thinking, rich in insights. [Nishida's note] Jean Gaspard Félix Ravaisson-Mollien (1813–1900) published *De l'habitude* in 1838; a Japanese translation appeared in 1938. — Trans.

Human Being

1. It may be that to speak of the movement of the historical world in terms of expressive activity will be regarded by materialists as idealism. But it is quite the reverse. I am conceptualizing a historical material activity. I therefore consider the subjective activity of consciousness to be within historical material movement. The historically concrete must be possessed of expressivity. Were that not so, one could speak neither of the historical concrete nor of the dialectical concrete. For example, the commodity that is the elementary form (*Elementarform*) of the wealth of capitalist society is the complementarity (*Zwieschlächtiges*) of use-value and exchange-value. It is for that reason that the capitalist world moves dialectically. Without expressivity the commodity could not be said to possess exchange-value. If expressivity did not belong to the essence of the thing, would it not be impossible to say that the world of things is possessed of ideology? What is called society, moreover,

must be originally constituted in terms of expressive activity. To think of the world in terms of a mutual complementarity is not to think subjectively. The objective conceived merely as negative with respect to the subjective is not the truly objective. Even physics does not conceive something like what is called the external world. [Nishida's note]

2. "Logos-body" translates *rogosuteki shintai*. A more facile, but misleading, translation would be "logical body," but that would translate *ronriteki shintai*. Nishida's point seems to be that the body is of the *logos*, that it belongs to the possibility of logic, but is not in the ordinary sense immediately "logical."

3. Jules Lachelier (1832–1918).

4. "Subject": *shutai*. See Glossary, s.v. "Subject." The force of Nishida's argument here seems to be that the subject, as *shutai*, emerges in active intuition precisely *as* the historic-corporeal subject who acts.

5. The reader will detect a certain resonance in the opening lines of the first of Marx's "Theses on Feuerbach": "The chief defect of all hitherto existing materialism (that of Feuerbach included) is that the thing, reality, sensuousness, is conceived only in the form of the *object or of contemplation*, but not as *sensuous human activity, practice, not subjectively.*"

6. See Glossary, s.v. "Qua."

7. There is a visual pun in "to the extent that it appears in actuality, it is actually existing." The first character in the compound translated as "actuality," *gen* in *genjitsu*, is the character for "appears," *arawareru*; the second character, *jitsu* in *genjitsu*, is the first character in "actually existing," *jitsuzai*. The pun perhaps underscores the virtually tautological character of the immanence that is at stake here.

8. See note 5 above.

9. "Idiosyncratically" translates *koseiteki ni*, which more usually is translated as "individually"; I have avoided that translation to avoid certain confusions. Here and throughout the rest of the essay, the reader may find it useful to bear in mind the Greek roots, such that *idiosyncrasy* suggests constitution in and as the separation or divergence that *idios* is: hence "idiosyncratic constitution" later in the essay.

10. See Nishida Kitarō, *Shu no seisei hatten no mondai*, in *Tetsugaku ronbunshu* 2, *NKz* 8:500–540.

11. English in original.

12. The way of seeing Nietzsche's thought of the eternal return as the discovery of a great life-affirming will that goes so far as to affirm the return of life is undoubtedly just, from the perspective of the Overman. But to say that life is eternally brought to return, manifestly cannot but be to say that this is

already the extremity of life. One can even say, with the hero of *Notes from Underground*, that it is to dash oneself into an iron wall. I see this Nietzschean insight outside of Nietzsche, and I embrace this notion. [Nishida's note]

13. Emile Chartier Alain (1868–1951).

GLOSSARY

This brief glossary is intended as a preliminary guide for the reader; it simply indicates certain terms that are problematic in English translation. I hope that it will help the reader avoid some of the less interesting and unproductive misunderstandings and confusions of reading. This glossary is thus not intended to be in any sense an exegesis of the key terms of Nishida-philosophy, nor is it intended to provide an in-depth discussion of the terms included herein. It is intended to help clarify certain recurrent lexical problems in the translation. Problematic vocabulary and constructions that occur infrequently in the text are treated in notes.

ACTION (*hataraki, kōi*) Nishida maintains the distinction, in common usage among contemporary Japanese philosophers, between the most general sense of action, *hataraki*, which is neither necessarily conscious nor even restricted to the animate, and "intentional action," *kōi*. It is critical to Nishida's argument and to his conception of "active intuition" that will and intentionality are not in the first instance attributes of any already existing subject, however conceived. Subjectivity is one of the possible effects or consequences of active intuition; in no case is a subject the transcendental author of will and intention. Intention there is, but I am an effect rather than the cause thereof.

ACTIVITY (*sayō*) *Sayō* refers to the operating, functioning, or, most generally, the "doing" of something, with no necessary relation either to its provocation or its result. Thus, for example, when Nishida speaks of "artistic activity," that activity is not merely a means to an end. Activity is "artistic" not because it produces artifacts but by virtue of the specificity of its "doing."

BEING, TO BE (*yū, aru*) Nishida uses the same Sino-Japanese character for both the verb "to be" (*aru*) and "to have" (*motsu*). This is not Nishida's neologism but a possibility inherited from classical Chinese. There is no lexical ambiguity for the reader of the Japanese text. Nor is it the case that "to be" and "to have" are somehow the same thing. But it does remind the reader both that there is always something of appropriation at stake in being—that "active intuition" is a constitutive appropriation—and that, conversely, being is at stake in all appropriation.

DETERMINATION (*gentei*) The most widespread sense of *gentei* is of a fixed limit or boundary; it is that which determines what is as determinate. The sense of determination in Nishida's texts is by no means restricted to that of causal determination. Indeed, determination can be of many kinds, but it is always that which renders determinate. This sense of determination (or "finitization") is irreducible to any determinism.

EXPERIENCE (*keiken, taiken*) *Keiken* is experience conceived as something that happens to an already existing epistemological or phenomenological subject. *Keiken* can therefore be the object of recollection or anticipation, an object for consciousness. *Taiken* refers to material, corporeal experience (which for Nishida includes thinking), which is not necessarily the experience of a subject, precisely because *taiken* is constitutive. *Taiken* is that experience by which what is comes to be. *Keiken* is, by definition, therefore comprehensible, an object of the understanding; *taiken* is not necessarily even an object for consciousness.

OBJECT (*kyakkan, taishō*) In general, Nishida distinguishes between two senses of object. Although there is a clear and important distinction between them, they are by no means necessarily mutually exclusive (indeed, Nishida speaks of the "objective object" [*kyakkanteki taishō*]). The object as *taishō* is the object of cognition and knowledge; *kyakkan* designates the objectivity of all that to which cognition and knowledge are essentially irrelevant. It is perhaps useful to bear in mind, however, that the difference between *kyakkan* and *taishō*—which is distinguished when necessary in the translation as "cognitive epistemological object"—does not correspond to a presumptive difference between the material and the immaterial. For Nishida, consciousness, perception, and thought are material; conversely, what is most often called materiality is never merely inert substance.

PLACE (*basho, tokoro*) *Basho* is one of the key concepts of Nishida-philosophy. (Nishida's seminal essay is titled "Basho" and was written in 1926, immediately after "Expressive Activity." There is an excellent German translation by Rolf Elberfeld in *Logik des Ortes: Der Anfang der modernen Philosophie in Japan* [Darmstadt: Wissenschaftliche Buchgesellschaft, 1999].) The words *basho* and *tokoro* are in constant use in colloquial Japanese, a fact of no minor importance for Nishida insofar as he is at pains to emphasize that there is nothing out of the ordinary in his usage: his concern is with what is conceptually at stake in that usage. It is important to note that for Nishida, "place" is not a point in abstract (Kantian) space and, correlatively, that time and space mutually implicate each other as their respective necessary presuppositions. The only problem for translation is the adjectival/adverbial form, *bashoteki (ni)*, which I have translated as "topological," being unable to imagine a more colloquial equivalent.

QUA (*soku*) *Soku* has a long, philosophically important history of usage in Chinese and Japanese Buddhist thought; Nishida undoubtedly intends that resonance to be heard in his own usage, which, in fact, is derived from that tradition. It also bears an essential relation to Spinoza's use of *sive* in *"Deus sive Natura,* variously translated as "God as Nature" or "God, or Nature." Nishida frequently uses *soku* as if it were equivalent to the copula. For example, early in an essay he may make the argument that "space is time, time is space," that is later abbreviated to "space-*soku*-time, time-*soku*-space," that in turn may subsequently be further abbreviated to "space/time, time/space." In any event, the *soku* refers to the coimmanence of two terms, that is, to the fact of relation as transduction—the fact that each term implies and is implicated in the other as its own presupposition. In that *qua* is undoubtedly an unsatisfactory equivalent for *soku*, its appearance in the translation must stand as an index of its essential inadequacy.

SINGULARITY (*kobutsu*) *Kobutsu* is frequently translated as "individual thing" or even as "individual." I think this invites the misunderstanding of *kobutsu* as personalogical individual (which in Japanese would be *kojin*). I have avoided translating *kobutsu* as "singular thing" because for Nishida singularity is neither attribute nor predicate. Rather, singularity is "absolute contradictory self-identity" (*zettai mujunteki jiko dōitsu*) in that a singularity is necessarily that which "itself determines itself" and, at the same time, that which is determined in relation to that which it is not. The force of this formulation should register even in the adjectival "singular" (*kobutsuteki*) and the adverbial "singularly" (*kobutsuteki ni*). The term *singularity*, of course, has a wide variety of meanings and usages in mathematics, physics, and meteorology. Indeed, there are increasingly references to a coming "technological singularity." The reader will, of course, be careful not to conflate Nishida's concept of the singularity of the *kobutsu* with these other meanings and usages. That being said, however, it is interesting to note that the concepts of singularity in many of these uses, Nishida's most definitely included, are precisely concepts of a threshold that is at once the possibility and limit of intelligibility.

SUBJECT (*shukan, shutai, shugo, shudai*) The English word *subject* is, of course, a philosophical scandal, conflating within one word epistemological and phenomenological subjects, logical and grammatical subjects, topic and theme, and the object of political subjugation and agency. Japanese usage allows somewhat less ambiguity and confusion (e.g., *shugo* designates the logical or grammatical subject;

shudai designates topic or theme; etc.). Most of these distinctions offer no special difficulty to the translator. But the distinction between *shukan* and *shutai* does, and the difference is critical to Nishida's arguments. In general, the *shukan* is the cognitive, epistemological, phenomenological subject, the subject that is taken to exist prior to cognition, knowing, and experience and which aspires to transcend its finitude. The *shutai*, however, is constituted in poiesis and production, in the contradictory coimplication, the transduction (or "metabolism") of singularities. The *shutai* is the subject of praxis qua poiesis. The *shutai* comes into being in the activity of making, in productive activity. The *shutai* does not exist prior to nor outside of that activity; neither does it survive its constitutive poiesis. It is critical to Nishida's thought to acknowledge that cognitive, epistemological, phenomenological subjectivity is not a prerequisite for the active, productive subject. On the contrary, cognition and knowing would be impossible without the active subject's prior (active) intuition.

INDEX

NISHIDA KITARŌ (1870–1945) was a professor of philosophy at Kyoto University and was credited with the founding of the Kyoto school of Japanese philosophy. He was the author of numerous books, including *An Inquiry into the Good*, *Intuition and Reflection in Self-Consciousness*, and *Fundamental Problems of Philosophy: The World of Action and the Dialectical World*.

WILLIAM HAVER is an associate professor of comparative literature at Binghamton University. He is the author of *The Body of This Death: Historicity and Sociality in the Time of AIDS*.

Library of Congress Cataloging-in-Publication Data
Nishida, Kitaro, 1870–1945.
Ontology of production : three essays / Nishida Kitaro ; translated and with an introduction by William Haver.
p. cm. — (Asia-Pacific)
Includes bibliographical references and index.
ISBN 978-0-8223-5164-1 (cloth : alk. paper)
ISBN 978-0-8223-5180-1 (pbk. : alk. paper)
1. Nishida, Kitaro, 1870–1945. 2. Philosophers—Japan. I. Haver, William Wendell, 1947– II. Title. III. Series: Asia-Pacific.
B5244.N553058 2012
181'.12—dc23
2011027534